Thackray's 2011 Investor's Guide

THACKRAY'S

2011

INVESTOR'S
GUIDE

Brooke Thackray MBA, CIM, CFP

Published in 2010 by: MountAlpha Media:

alphamountain.com

ISBN13: 978-0-9782200-4-4

Printed and Bound by Webcom
10 9 8 7 6 5 4 3 2 1

To my wife Jane

Acknowledgements

This book is the product of many years of research and could not have been written without the help of many people. I would like to thank my wife, Jane Steer-Thackray, and my children Justin, Megan, Carly and Madeleine, for the help they have given me and their patience during the many hours that I have devoted to writing this book. I would also like to thank the proofreaders and editors, Amanda ODonnell and Jane Stiegler. Special mention goes to Jane for the countless hours she spent helping with writing, formatting and editing. This book could not have been written without her help. In addition, I would like to thank Muhammed Faizan for all of his work in writing computer programs that have made much of the analysis in this book possible.

INTRODUCTION

WHAT'S NEW — 2011 INVESTOR'S GUIDE

Every year I try and add new features and strategies to the latest edition of the Investor's Guide. Many of the new features are based upon reader feedback – thank you.

Chart and Commentary on Last Year's Seasonal Performance

In addition to the weekly strategy page for each sector, a chart of its last year's performance and commentary has been added. Approximate buy and sell dates are illustrated to show the success of the strategy compared with other times of the year.

New Strategies

I am always looking to add value by researching and presenting new seasonal strategies that will help investors generate greater profits and reduce risk. Investors do not have to use every strategy in this book and may feel more comfortable with certain sector strategies. In the end, the more strategies to choose from the better.

New Short Selling Strategies

In the past I have avoided writing about short selling strategies as most investors are more comfortable with long only strategies (buying low and selling high). Pairing up a short position with a long position (pair trade) can help reduce risk in a portfolio and more and more investors are becoming interested in using "pair trades." For investors that favor long only strategies, knowing when a sector performs poorly will at least provide information on when it might be best to avoid a sector.

Definition – Short selling. The sale of borrowed securities. In a short sale, one borrows securities, usually from a brokerage, and sells them. One then buys the same securities in order to repay the brokerage. Selling short is practiced if one believes that the price of a security will soon fall. That is, one expects to sell the borrowed securities at a higher price than the price at which one will buy in order to return the securities. Selling short is one of the most common practices of hedge funds (Farlex Financial Dictionary).

Having an arsenal of short selling strategies that are applicable throughout the year, gives investors an option to adjust their portfolio for macro market expectations. If less optimistic expectations develop, an investor has the choice to hedge a portfolio using short selling strategies.

New Divided Strategies

There are some seasonal strategies that have their period of strength divided by a period of weakness. In other words, the sector tends to outperform for a certain period of time, then decline and then once again resume its outperformance. Depending on the type of investor and even different market conditions, there are different techniques that can be used to take advantage of the strong-weak-strong trend.

A lot of long-term investors will decide that they would prefer not to exit a sector for a short-term and then reenter in case the sector has appreciated while they were divested. This is particularly true if the weak period of time tends to be short and/or the sector is in a strong bull run with lots of momentum.

Other investors that are more nimble, may decide to exit the trade and get back in for the second part of the seasonal trade, even if the sector has appreciated when they were divested. These investors are willing to take the risk of a loss, based upon long-term positive historical data.

More aggresive investors may decide to "short" the sector during its weak period, particularly if there is other evidence that the sector might have a pull back.

Other investors will rely on the use technical and fundamental analysis to help them make a decision of whether to exit a sector temporarily or remain invested.

All of these techniques are viable, and their use should be based upon investor expertise, risk tolerance and individual circumstance.

Canadian Strategies

A large percentage of the readers of the Investor's Guide series are Canadian investors. I frequently get asked why I do not write more about Canadian strategies. Last year I introduced a *Canadians Give 3 Cheers for American Holidays* strategy. This year I have introduced a seasonal strategy for *Canadian Banks*. Despite the Canadian market not being very robust, I am planning on introducing more Canadian strategies in the future.

THACKRAY'S 2011 INVESTOR'S GUIDE

You can choose great companies to invest in and still underperform the market. Unless you are in the market at the right time and in the best sectors, your investment expertise can be all for naught.

Successful investors know when they should be in the market. Very successful investors know when they should be in the market, and the best sectors in which to invest. *Thackray's 2011 Investor's Guide* is designed to provide investors with the knowledge of when and what to buy, and when to sell.

The goal of this book is to help investors capture extra profits by taking advantage of the seasonal trends in the markets. This book is straightforward. There are no complicated rules and there are no complex algorithms. The strategies put forward are intuitive and easy to understand.

It does not matter if you are a short-term or long-term investor, this book can be used to help establish entry and exit points. For the short-term investor, specific periods are identified that can provide profitable opportunities. For the long-term investor best buy dates are identified to launch new investments on a sound footing.

The stock market has its seasonal rhythms. Historically, the broad markets, such as the S&P 500, have a seasonal trend of outperforming during certain times of the year. Likewise, different sectors of the market have their own seasonal trends of outperformance. When oil stocks tend to do well in the springtime before "driving season," health care stocks tend to underperform the market. When utilities do well in the summertime, industrials do not. With different markets and different sectors having a tendency to outperform at different times of the year, there is always a place to invest.

Until recently, investors did not have access to the information necessary to analyze and create sector strategies. In recent years there have been a great number of sector Exchange Traded Funds (ETFs) and sector indexes introduced into the market. For the first time, investors are now able to easily implement a sector rotation strategy. This book provides a seasonal road map of what sectors tend to do well at different times of the year. It is a first of its kind, revealing new sector-based strategies that have never before been published.

In terms of market timing there are ample strategies in this book to help determine the times when equities should be over or underweight. During a favorable time for the market, investments can be purchased to overweight equities relative to their target weight in a portfolio (staying within risk tolerances). During an unfavorable time, investments can be sold to underweight equities relative to their target.

A large part of the book is devoted to sector seasonality – the underpinnings for a sector rotation strategy. The most practical rotation strategy is to create a core part of a portfolio that represents the broad market and then set aside an allocation to be rotated between favored sectors from one time period to the next.

It does not makes sense to apply any investment strategy only once with a large investment. Seasonal strategies are no exception. The best way to apply an investment strategy is to use a disciplined methodology that allows for diversification and a large enough number of investments to help remove the anomalies of the market. This reduces risk and increases the probability of a long term gain.

Following the specific buy and sell dates put forth in this book would have netted an investor large, above market returns. To "turbo-charge" gains, an investor can combine seasonality with technical analysis. As the seasonal periods are never exactly the same, technical analysis can help investors capture the extra gains when a sector turns up early, or momentum extends the trend.

IMPORTANT: Strategy Buy and Sell Dates

The beginning date of every strategy period in this book represents a full day in the market; therefore, investors should buy at the end of the preceding market day. For example the *Biotech Summer Solstice* seasonal period of strength is from June 23rd to September 13th. To be in the sector for the full seasonal period, an investor would enter the market before the closing bell on June 22nd. If the buy date landed on a weekend or holiday, then the buy would occur at the end of the preceding trading day.

The last day of a trading strategy is the sell date. For example, the Biotech sector investment would be sold at the end of the day on September 13th. If the sell date is a holiday or weekend, then the investment would be sold at the close on the preceding trading day.

What is Seasonal Investing?

In order to properly understand seasonal investing in the stock market, it is important to look briefly at its evolution. It may surprise investors to know that seasonal investing at the broad market level, i.e. Dow Jones or S&P 500, has been around for a long time. The initial seasonal strategies were written by Fields (1931, 1934) and Watchel (1942), who focused on the *January Effect*. Coincidentally, this strategy is still bantered about in the press every year.

Yale Yirsch Senior has been largely responsible for the next stage in the evolution, producing the Stock Trader's Almanac over the last forty years. This publication focuses on broad market trends such as the best six months of the year and tendencies of the market to do well depending on the political party in power and holiday trades.

In 1999, Brooke Thackray and Bruce Lindsay wrote, Time In Time Out: Outsmart the Market Using Calendar Investment Strategies. This work focused on a comprehensive analysis of the six month seasonal cycle and other shorter seasonal cycles in the broad markets such as the S&P 500.

Don Vialoux, considered the patriarch of seasonal investing in Canada, has written many articles on seasonal investing. His writings on this topic have developed a large following, via his free newsletter available at www.timingthemarket.ca.

Seasonal investing has changed over time. The focus has shifted from broad market strategies to taking advantage of sector rotation opportunities – investing in different sectors at different times of the year, depending on their seasonal strength. This has created a whole new set of investment opportunities. Rather than just being "in or out" of the market, investors can now always be invested by shifting between different sectors and asset classes, taking advantage of both up and down markets.

Definition – Seasonal investing is a method of investing in the market at the time of the year when it typically does well, or investing in a sector of the market when it typically outperforms the broad market such as the S&P 500.

The term seasonal investing is somewhat of a misnomer, and it is easy to see why some investors might believe that the discipline relates to investing based upon the seasons of the year – winter, spring, summer and autumn. Other than with agricultural commodities, generally, seasonal investment strategies only use the calendar as a reference for buy and sell dates. It is usually a specific event, i.e. Christmas sales, that occurs on a recurring annual basis that creates the opportunity.

The discipline of seasonal investing is not restricted to the stock market. It has been used successfully for a number of years in the commodities market. The opportunities in this market tend to be based upon changes in supply and/or demand that occur on a yearly basis. Most commodities, especially the agricultural commodities, tend to have cyclical supply cycles, i.e., crops are harvested only at certain times of the year. The supply bulge that occurs at the same time every year provides seasonal investors with profit opportunities. Recurring increased seasonal demand for commodities also plays a major part in providing opportunities for seasonal investors. This applies to most metals and many other commodities, whether the end-product is industrial or consumer based.

Seasonal investment strategies can be used with a lot of different types of investments. The premise is the same, outperformance during a certain period of the year based upon a repeating event in the markets or economy. In my past writings I have developed seasonal strategies that have been used successfully in the stock, commodity, bond and foreign exchange markets. Seasonal investing is still relatively new for most markets with a lot of new opportunities waiting to be discovered.

How Does Seasonal Investing Work?

Most stock market sector seasonal trends are the result of a recurring annual catalyst: an event that affects the sector positively. These events can range from a seasonal spike in demand, seasonal inventory lows, weather effects, conferences and other events. Mainstream investors very often anticipate a move in a sector and incorrectly try to take a position just before an event takes place that is supposed to drive a sector higher. A good example of this would be investors buying oil just before the cold weather sets in. Unfortunately, their efforts are usually unsuccessful as they are too late to the party and the opportunity has already passed.

By the time the anticipated event occurs, a substantial amount of investors have bought into the sector – fully pricing in the expected benefit. At this time there is little potential left in the short-term. Unless there is a strong positive surprise, the sector's outperformance tends to slowly roll over. If the event produces less than its desired result, the sector can be severely punished.

So how does the seasonal investor take advantage of this opportunity? "Be there" before the mainstream investors, and get out before they do. Seasonal investors usually enter a sector two or three months before an event is anticipated to have a positive effect on a sector and get out before the actual event takes place. In essence, seasonal investors are benefiting from the mainstream investor's tendency to "buy in" too late.

Seasonality in the markets occurs because of three major reasons: money flow, changing market analyst expectations and the *Anticipation-Realization Cycle*. First, money flows vary throughout the year and at different times of the month. Generally, money flows increase at the end of the year and into the start of the next year. This is a result of year end bonuses and tax related investments. In addition, money flows increase at month end from money managers "window dressing" their portfolios. As a result of these money flows, the months around the end of the year and the days around the end of the month, tend to have a stronger performance than the other times of the year.

Second, the analyst expectations cycle tends to push markets up at the end of the year and the beginning of the next year. Stock market analysts tend to be a positive bunch – the large investment houses pay them to be positive. They start the year with aggressive earnings for all of their favorite companies. As the year progresses, they generally back off their earnings forecast, which decreases their support for the market. After a lull in the summer and early autumn months, they start to focus on the next year with another rosy forecast. As a result, the stock market tends to rise once again at the end of the year.

Third, at the sector level, sectors of the market tend to be greatly influenced by the *Anticipation-Realization Cycle*. Although some investors may not be familiar with the term "anticipation-realization," they probably are familiar with the concept of "buy the rumor – sell the fact," or in the famous words of Lord Rothschild "Buy on the sound of the war-cannons; sell on the sound of the victory trumpets."

The *Anticipation-Realization Cycle* as it applies to human behavior has been much studied in psychology journals. In the investment world, the premise of this cycle rests on investors anticipating a positive event in the market to drive prices higher and buying in ahead of the event. When the event takes place, or is realized, upward pressure on prices decreases as there is very little impetus for further outperformance.

A good example of the *Anticipation-Realization Cycle* takes place with the "conference effect." Very often large industries have major conferences that occur at approximately the same time every year. Major companies in the industry often hold back positive announcements and product introductions to be released during the conference.

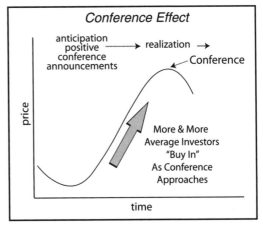

Two to three months prior to the conference, seasonal investors tend to buy into the sector. Shortly afterwards, the mainstream investors anticipate "good news" from the conference and start to buy in. As a result, prices are pushed up. Just before the conference starts, seasonal investors capture their profits by exiting their positions. As the conference unfolds, company announcements are made (realized), but as the potential good news has already been priced into the sector, there is little to push prices higher and the sector typically starts to rolls over.

The same *Anticipation-Realization Cycle* takes place with increased demand for oil to meet the "summer driving season", increased sales of goods at Christmas time, increased demand for gold jewellery to meet the autumn and winter demand, and many other events that tend to drive the outperformance of different sectors.

Does Seasonal Investing ALWAYS Work?

The simple answer to the above question is "No." There is not any investment system in the world that works all of the time. When following any investment system, it is probability of success that counts. It has often been said that "being correct in the markets 60% of the time will make you rich." Investors tend to forget this and become too emotionally attached to their losses. Just about every investment trading book states that investors typically fail to let their profits run and cut their losses quickly. I concur. In my many years in the investment industry, the biggest mistake that I have found with investors is not being able to cut their losses. Everyone wants to be right, that is how we have been raised. Investors feel that if they sell at a loss they have failed, and as a result, often suffer bigger losses by waiting for their position to trade at profit.

With any investment system, investors should let probability work for them. This means that investors should be able to enter and exit positions capturing both gains and losses without becoming emotionally attached to any positions. Emotional attachment clouds judgement, which leads to errors. When all of the trades are put together, the goal is for profits to be larger than losses in a way that minimizes risks and beats the market.

If we examine the winter oil stock trade, my favorite seasonal trade, we can see how probability has worked in an investor's favor. This trade is based upon the premise that at the tail end of winter, the refineries drive up demand for oil in order to produce enough gas for the approaching "driving season" that starts in the spring. As a result, oil stocks tend to increase and outperform the market (from February 25th to May 9th).

The oil stock sector, represented by the Amex Oil Index (XOI), has been very successful at this time of year, producing an average return of 8.5% and beating the S&P 500 by 5.3%, from 1984 to 2010. In addition it has been positive 24 out of 27 times. Not all seasonal trades are created equal:

XOI / S&P 500 1984 to 2010

Feb 25 to May 9	XOI	positive S&P 500	Diff
1984	5.6 %	1.7 %	3.9 %
1985	4.9	1.4	3.5
1986	7.7	6.0	1.7
1987	25.5	3.7	21.8
1988	5.6	-3.0	8.6
1989	8.1	6.3	1.8
1990	-0.6	5.8	-6.3
1991	6.8	4.8	2.0
1992	5.8	0.9	4.9
1993	6.3	0.3	6.0
1994	3.2	-4.7	7.9
1995	10.3	7.3	3.1
1996	2.2	-2.1	4.3
1997	4.7	1.8	2.9
1998	9.8	7.5	2.3
1999	35.4	7.3	28.1
2000	22.2	4.3	17.9
2001	10.2	0.8	9.4
2002	5.3	-1.5	6.9
2003	5.7	12.1	-6.4
2004	4.0	-3.5	7.5
2005	-1.0	-1.8	0.8
2006	9.4	2.8	6.6
2007	10.1	4.2	5.8
2008	7.6	2.6	5.0
2009	15.8	20.2	-4.4
2010	-2.3	0.5	-2.8
Avg	8.5 %	3.2 %	5.3 %

this strategic sector trade is at the top of the list. Investors should always evaluate the strength of seasonal trades before applying them to their own portfolios. Above is a table of the results.

If an investor started using the seasonal investment discipline in 1984 and chose to invest in the winter-oil trade, they would have been very happy with the results. If they had chosen almost any other year in the last 25 years, they would have also been very pleased with the results. The exception to this occurs in the years 1990, 2005 and 2010. These years produced nominal losses of 0.6%, 1.0% and 2.3% respectively.

Does this mean the system does not work? No. An investor can start any methodology of trading at the "wrong time," and be unsuccessful for a particular trade. In fact, if the investor started in 1990 and had given up in the same year, they would have missed the following successful twelve years. They would have also missed all of the other successful seasonal trades that took place in the year. Investors have to remember that it is the final score that counts, after all of the gains have been weighed against the losses.

In practical terms, investors should not put all of their investment strategies in one basket. If one or two large investments were made based upon seasonal strategies, it is possible that the seasonal methodology might be inappropriately evaluated and its use discontinued. A much more prudent strategy is to use a larger number of strategic seasonal investments with smaller investments. The end result will be to put the seasonal probability to work with a much greater chance of success.

Measuring Seasonal Performance

How do you determine if a seasonal strategy has been successful? Many people feel that ten years of data is a good sample size, others feel that fifteen years is better, and yet others feel that the more data the better. I tend to fall into the camp that, if possible, it is best to use fifteen or twenty years of data for sectors and more data for the broad markets, such as the S&P 500. Although the most recent data in almost any analytical framework is the most relevant, it is important to get enough data to reflect a sector's performance across different economic conditions. Given that historically the economy has performed on an eight year cycle, four years of expansion and then four years of contraction, using a short data set does not provide for enough exposure to different economic conditions.

A data set that is too long can run into the problem of older data having too much of an influence on the numbers when fundamental factors affecting a sector have changed. It is important to look at trends over time and assess if there has been a change that should be considered in determining the dates for a seasonal cycle. Each sector should be judged on its own merit. The analysis tables in this book illustrate the performance level for each year in order to provide the opportunity for readers to determine any relevant changes.

In order to determine if a seasonal strategy is effective there are two possible benchmarks, absolute and relative performance. Absolute performance measures if a profit is made and relative performance measures the performance of a sector in relationship to a major market. Both measurements have their merits and depending on your investment style, one measurement may be more valuable than another. This book provides both sets of measurement in tables and graphs.

It is not just the average percent gain of a sector over a certain time period that determines success. It is possible that one or two spectacular years of performance skew the results substantially (particularly with a small data set). The frequency of success is also very important: the higher the percentage of success the better. Also, the fewer large drawdowns the better. There is no magic number (percent success rate) per se of what constitutes a successful strategy. The success rate should be above fifty percent, otherwise it would be better to just invest in the broad market. Ideally speaking a strategy should have a high percentage success rate on both an absolute and relative basis. Some strategies are stronger than others, but that does not mean that the weaker strategies should not be used. Prudence should be used in determining the ideal portfolio allocation.

Illustrating the strength of a sector's seasonal performance can be accomplished through either an absolute yearly average performance graph, or a relative yearly average performance graph. The absolute graph shows the average yearly cumulative gain for a set number of years. It lets a reader visually identify the strong periods during the year. The relative graph shows the average yearly cumulative gain for the sector relative to the benchmark index.

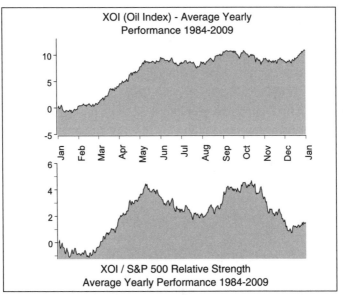

Both graphs are useful in determining the strength of a particular seasonal strategy. In the above diagram, the top graph illustrates the average year for the XOI (Oil Index) from 1984 to 2009. Essentially it illustrates the cumulative average gain if an investment were made in the index. The steep rising line starting in January/February shows the overall price rise that typically occurs in this sector at this time of year. In May the line flattens out and then rises very modestly starting in July.

The bottom graph is a ratio graph, illustrating the strength of the XOI Index relative to the S&P 500. It is derived by dividing the average year of the XOI by the average year of the S&P 500. When the line in the graph is rising, the XOI is outperforming the S&P 500, and vise versa when it is declining. This is an important graph and should be used in considering seasonal investments because the S&P 500 is a viable alternative to the energy sector. If both markets are increasing, but the S&P 500 is increasing at a faster rate, the S&P 500 represents a more attractive opportunity. This is particularly true when measuring the risk of a volatile sector relative to the broad market. If both investments were expected to produce the same rate of return, generally the broad market is a better investment because of its diversification.

Who Can Use Seasonal Investing?

Any investor from novice to expert, from short-term trader to long-term investor can benefit from using seasonal analysis. Seasonal investing is unique because it is an easy to understand system that can be used by itself or as a complement to another investment discipline. For the novice it provides an easy to follow strategy that makes intuitive sense. For the expert it can be used as a stand-alone system or as a complement to an existing system.

Behind the scenes money managers use seasonal analysis a lot more than they let on. I have talked to money managers who have extolled the virtues of making investments based upon seasonal trends. Because of its simplicity, they tend not to emphasize the methodology in public. They fear that the investing public will question why they are getting paid the "big bucks" if they are using such a simple system.

Seasonal investing is easily understood by all levels of investors, which allows investors to make rational decisions. This may seem obvious, but it is very common for investors to listen to a "guru of the market", be impressed and blindly follow his advice. When the advice works there is no problem. When the advice does not work investors wonder why they made the investment in the first place. When investors do not understand their investments it causes stress, bad decisions and a lack of "stick-to-it ness" with any investment discipline. Even expert investors realize the importance of understanding your investments. Michael Lynch of Fidelity Investments used to say "Never invest in any idea that you can't illustrate with a crayon." Investors do not need to go that far, but they should understand their investments.

Novice investors find seasonal strategies very easy to understand because they are intuitive. They do not have to be investing for years to understand why seasonal strategies work. They understand that an increase in demand for gold every year at the same time causes a ripple effect in the stock market pushing up gold stocks at the same time every year.

Most expert investors use information from a variety of sources in making their decisions. Even experts that primarily use fundamental analysis can benefit from using seasonal trends to get an edge in the market. Fundamental analysis is a very crude tool and provides very little in the way of timing an investment. Using seasonal trends can help with the timing of the buy and sell decisions and produce extra profit.

Seasonal investing can be used by both short-term and long-term investors, but in different ways. For short-term investors it provides a complete trade – buy and sell dates. For long-term investors it can provide a buy date for a sector of interest.

Combining Seasonal Analysis with other Investment Disciplines

Seasonal investing used by itself has historically produced above average market returns. Depending on an investor's particular style, it can be combined with one of the other three investment disciplines: fundamental, quantitative and technical analysis. There are two basic ways to combine seasonal analysis with other investment methodologies – as the primary or secondary method. If it is used as a primary method, seasonally strong time periods are established for a number of sectors and then appropriate sectors are chosen based upon fundamental, quantitative or technical screens. If it is used as a secondary method, sector selections are first made based upon one of three methods and then final sectors are chosen based upon which ones are in their seasonally strong period.

Technical analysis is an ideal mate for seasonal analysis. Unlike fundamental and quantitative analysis, which are very blunt timing tools at best, seasonal and technical analysis can provide specific trigger points to buy and sell. The combination can turbo-charge investment strategies, adding extra profits by fine-tuning entry and exit dates.

Seasonal analysis provides both buy and sell dates. Although a sector in the market can sometimes bottom on the exact seasonal buy date, it more often bottoms a bit early or a bit late. After all, the seasonal buy date is based upon an average of historical performance. Depending on the sector, buying opportunities start to develop approximately one month before and after the seasonal buy date. Using technical analysis gives an investor the advantage of buying into a sector when it turns up early or waiting when it turns up late. Likewise, technical analysis can be used to trigger a sell signal when the market turns down before or after the sell date.

The sell decision can be extended with the help of a trailing stop-loss order. If a sector has strong momentum and the technical tools do not provide a sell signal, it is possible to let the sector "run." When a trailing stop-loss is used, a profitable sell point is established. If the price continues to run, then the selling point is raised. If, on the other hand, the price falls through the stop-loss point, the position is sold.

Sectors of the Market

Standard & Poor's has done an excellent job in categorizing the U.S. stock market into its different parts. Although the demand for this service initially came from institutional investors, many individual investors now seek the same information. Knowing the sector breakdown in the market allows investors to see how different their portfolio is relative to the market. As a result, they are able to make conscious decisions on what parts of the stock market to overweight based upon their beliefs of which sectors will outperform. It also helps control the amount of desired risk.

Standard & Poor's uses four levels of detail in its Global Industry Classification Standard (GICS$^{©}$) to categorize stock markets around the world. From the most specific, it classifies companies into sub-industries, industries, industry groups and finally economic sectors. All companies in the Standard & Poor's global family of indices are classified according to the GICS structure.

This book focuses on the U.S. market, analyzing the trends of the venerable S&P 500 index and its economic sectors and industry groups. The following diagram illustrates the index classified according to its economic sectors.

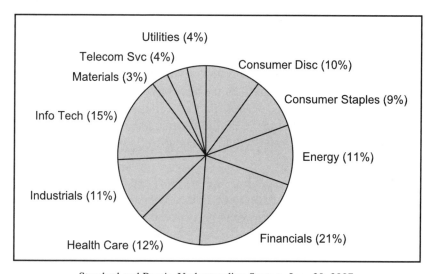

Standard and Poor's, Understanding Sectors, June 30, 2007

For more information on Standard and Poor's Global Industry Classification Standard (GICS$^{©}$), refer to www.standardandpoors.com

Investment Products – Which One Is The Right One?

There are many ways to take advantage of the seasonal trends at the broad stock market and sector levels. Regardless of the investment products that you currently use, whether exchange traded funds, mutual funds, stocks or options, all can be used with the strategies in this book. Different investments offer different risk-reward relationships and return potential.

Exchange Traded Funds (ETFs)

Exchange Traded Funds (ETFs) offer the purest method of seasonal investment. The broad market ETFs are designed to track the major indices and the sector ETFs are designed to track specific sectors without using active management. Relatively new, ETFs are a great way to capture both market and sector trends. They were originally introduced into the Canadian market in 1993 to represent the Toronto stock market index. Shortly afterward they were introduced to the U.S. market and there are now hundreds of ETFs to represent almost every market, sector, style of investing and company capitalization. Originally ETFs were mainly of interest to institutional investors, but individual investors have fast realized the merits of ETF investing and have made some of the broad market ETFs the most heavily traded securities in the world.

An ETF is a single security that represents a market, such as the S&P 500; a sector of the market, such as the financial sector; or a commodity, such as gold. In the case of the S&P 500, an investor buying one security is buying all 500 stocks in the index. By investing into a financial ETF, an investor is buying the companies that make up the financial sector of the market. By investing into a gold commodity ETF, an investor is buying a security that represents the price of gold.

ETFs trade on the open market just like stocks. They have a bid and an ask, can be shorted and many are option eligible. They are a very low cost, tax efficient method of targeting specific parts of the market.

Mutual Funds

Mutual funds are a good way to combine market or sector investing with active management. In recent years, many mutual fund companies have added sector funds to accommodate an increasing appetite in this area.

As the seasonal strategies put forward in this book have a short-term nature, it is important to make sure that there are no fees (or a nominal charge) for getting into and out of a position in the market.

Stocks

Stocks provide an opportunity to make better returns than the market or sector. If the market increases during its seasonal period, some stocks will increase dramatically more than the index. Choosing one of the outperforming stocks will greatly enhance returns; choosing one of the underperforming stocks can create substantial loses. Using stocks requires increased attention to diversification and security selection.

Options

Disclaimer: Options involve risk and are not suitable for every investor. Because they are cash-settled, investors should be aware of the special risks associated with index options and should consult a tax advisor. Prior to buying or selling options, a person must receive a copy of Characteristics and Risks of Standardized Options and should thoroughly understand the risks involved in any use of options. Copies may be obtained from The Options Clearing Corporation, 440 S. LaSalle Street, Chicago, IL 60605.

Options, for more sophisticated investors, are a good tool to take advantage of both market and sector opportunities. An option position can be established with either stocks or ETFs. There are many different ways to use options for seasonal trends: establish a long position on the market during its seasonally strong period, establish a short position during its seasonally weak period, or create a spread trade to capture the superior gains of a sector over the market.

THACKRAY'S 2011 INVESTOR'S GUIDE

CONTENTS

JANUARY

MONDAY	TUESDAY	WEDNESDAY
27	28	29
3 28 CAN Market Closed- New Year's Day	**4** 27	**5** 26
10 21	**11** 20	**12** 19
17 14 USA Market Closed- Martin Luther King Jr. Day	**18** 13	**19** 12
24 7	**25** 6	**26** 5

WEEK 01   WEEK 02   WEEK 03   WEEK 04

THURSDAY		FRIDAY	
30		31	
6	25	7	24
13	18	14	17
20	11	21	10
27	4	28	3

FEBRUARY

M	T	W	T	F	S	S
	1	2	3	4	5	6
7	8	9	10	11	12	13
14	15	16	17	18	19	20
21	22	23	24	25	26	27
28						

MARCH

M	T	W	T	F	S	S
	1	2	3	4	5	6
7	8	9	10	11	12	13
14	15	16	17	18	19	20
21	22	23	24	25	26	27
28	29	30	31			

APRIL

M	T	W	T	F	S	S
				1	2	3
4	5	6	7	8	9	10
11	12	13	14	15	16	17
18	19	20	21	22	23	24
25	26	27	28	29	30	

MAY

M	T	W	T	F	S	S
						1
2	3	4	5	6	7	8
9	10	11	12	13	14	15
16	17	18	19	20	21	22
23	24	25	26	27	28	29
30	31					

JANUARY
S U M M A R Y

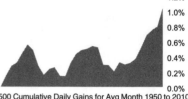
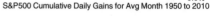

S&P500 Cumulative Daily Gains for Avg Month 1950 to 2010

BEST / WORST JANUARY BROAD MKTS. 2001-2010

BEST JANUARY MARKETS
- Nasdaq (2001) 12.2%
- Russell 2000 (2006) 8.9%
- Russell 3000 Gr (2001) 7.0%

WORST JANUARY MARKETS
- Russell 3000 Value (2009) -11.9%
- Russell 2000 (2009) -11.2%
- Nasdaq (2008) -9.9%

Index Values End of Month

	2001	2002	2003	2004	2005	2006	2007	2008	2009	2010
Dow	10,887	9,920	8,054	10,488	10,490	10,865	12,622	12,650	8,001	10,067
S&P 500	1,366	1,130	856	1,131	1,181	1,280	1,438	1,379	826	1,074
Nasdaq	2,773	1,934	1,321	2,066	2,062	2,306	2,464	2,390	1,476	2,147
TSX	9,322	7,648	6,569	8,521	9,204	11,946	13,034	13,155	8,695	11,094
Russell 1000	1,389	1,147	873	1,163	1,219	1,341	1,507	1,444	860	1,133
Russell 2000	1,263	1,201	925	1,443	1,551	1,822	1,989	1,773	1,102	1,496
Russell 3000 Growth	2,654	1,944	1,378	1,872	1,871	2,066	2,238	2,214	1,386	1,879
Russell 3000 Value	2,213	2,051	1,668	2,229	2,450	2,717	3,151	2,883	1,638	2,100

Percent Gain for January

	2001	2002	2003	2004	2005	2006	2007	2008	2009	2010
Dow	0.9	-1.0	-3.5	0.3	-2.7	1.4	1.3	-4.6	-8.8	-3.5
S&P 500	3.5	-1.6	-2.7	1.7	-2.5	2.5	1.4	-6.1	-8.6	-3.7
Nasdaq	12.2	-0.8	-1.1	3.1	-5.2	4.6	2.0	-9.9	-6.4	-5.4
TSX	4.3	-0.5	-0.7	3.7	-0.5	6.0	1.0	-4.9	-3.3	-5.5
Russell 1000	3.2	-1.4	-2.5	1.8	-2.6	2.7	1.8	-6.1	-8.3	-3.7
Russell 2000	5.1	-1.1	-2.9	4.3	-4.2	8.9	1.6	-6.9	-11.2	-3.7
Russell 3000 Growth	7.0	-1.9	-2.5	2.2	-3.5	2.4	2.5	-8.0	-5.1	-4.4
Russell 3000 Value	0.4	-0.8	-2.6	1.7	-2.1	4.1	1.1	-4.2	-11.9	-3.0

January Market Avg. Performance 2001 to 2010 [1]

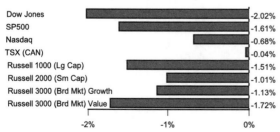

Dow Jones	-2.02%
SP500	-1.61%
Nasdaq	-0.68%
TSX (CAN)	-0.04%
Russell 1000 (Lg Cap)	-1.51%
Russell 2000 (Sm Cap)	-1.01%
Russell 3000 (Brd Mkt) Growth	-1.13%
Russell 3000 (Brd Mkt) Value	-1.72%

Interest Corner Jan[2]

	Fed Funds %[3]	3 Mo. T-Bill %[4]	10 Yr %[5]	20 Yr %[6]
2010	0.25	0.08	3.63	4.38
2009	0.25	0.24	2.87	3.86
2008	3.00	1.96	3.67	4.35
2007	5.25	5.12	4.83	5.02
2006	4.50	4.47	4.53	4.74

(1) Russell Data provided by Russell (2) Federal Reserve Bank of St. Louis- end of month values (3) Target rate set by FOMC (4)(5)(6) Constant yield maturities.

THACKRAY SECTOR THERMOMETER

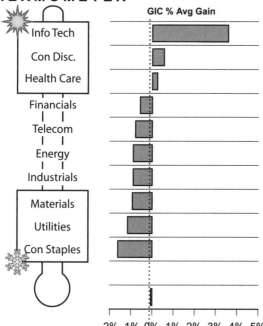

GIC(2) % Avg Gain	Fq % Gain >S&P 500	
SP GIC SECTOR 1990-2009(1)		
3.6 %	80 %	Information Technology
0.6	50	Consumer Discretionary
0.2	60	Health Care
-0.6	60	Financials
-0.8	50	Telecom
-0.9	40	Energy
-0.9	25	Industrials
-0.9	45	Materials
-1.2	35	Utilities
-1.6 %	25 %	Consumer Staples
-0.1 %	N/A %	S&P 500

Sector Commentary

♦ On average from 1990 to 2009, January has been the month for Information Technology, returning an average 3.6% and beating the S&P 500, 80% of the time. ♦ Information Technology has been the best sector in November, the worst in December and then the best in January. Overall this has presented a good strategy for short-term investors willing to trade the volatility of the market ♦ The Consumer Discretionary has also done well in January. The sector is in its seasonal sweet spot and is bolstered towards the end of the month when one of its sub-sectors, Retail, starts its period of seasonal performance. In 2010 the Technology sector performed poorly producing a loss of 8.5%. The only positive sector was Health Care, with a return of 0.4%.

Sub-Sector Commentary

♦ The Semiconductor sector is a turbo charged version of Information Technology. It has produced an average return of 4.8% since 1990 and beaten the S&P 500 53% of the time. Although the frequency outperformance over the S&P 500 is not stellar, the average gain is substantially better. ♦ In 2010 the SOX index was down over 12%, showing the sector's volatility. ♦ When January is expected to perform poorly, it is best not to favor the Semiconductor sector.

		SELECTED SUB-SECTORS 1990-2009(3)
4.8 %	53 %	Semiconductor (SOX) 95-2009
2.8	70	Software & Services
1.5	47	Biotech (93-2009)
1.3	55	Auto & Components
-0.1	45	Transportation
-0.1	55	Pharmaceuticals
-0.1	50	Retail
-0.2	45	Gold (XAU)
-0.2	44	Agriculture Products (94-2009)
-0.3	50	Metals & Mining
-0.6	50	Banks
-1.1	45	Integrated Oil & Gas
-2.1	40	Insurance
-2.4	35	Airlines

(1) Sector data provided by Standard and Poors (2) GIC is short form for Global Industry Classification (3) Sub Sector data provided by Standard and Poors, except where marked by symbol.

THACKRAY SECTOR THERMOMETER PORTFOLIO (TSTP) BEATS MARKET BY 14% per year (avg.) (1990-2009)

Investing in the three sectors (S&P GIC) that have averaged the best monthly performance over the long-term, has significantly rewarded investors.

From a portfolio perspective, funds are divided up evenly amongst the three top sectors at the beginning of the starting month. At the end of the month the three sectors are sold and the proceeds are invested in the top three sectors for the next month. The process repeats itself with the accumulated funds being invested at the start of each month. Funds are accumulated month by month until the end of the time period.

For each month the same sectors are used from year to year, over the study period. For example the same three sectors would be used every January.

TSTP Avg. Gain of 22% vs. 8% for S&P 500

Following the Thackray Sector Thermometer Portfolio (TSTP) from 1990 to 2009 has produced an average return of 22%, compared with the S&P 500 which produced an average return of 8% over the same period. To illustrate how much of an impact investing in different sectors of the market can have on a portfolio, I used the same sector selection process, for the three worst performing sectors. Investing in

the three worst sectors from 1990 to 2009 has produced an average loss of 3% per year.

Most investors get caught up investing in a certain stock or company. There is a lot of research proving that it is much more important to pick the appropriate asset class or sector of the market compared to picking stocks.

Hot and Cold Box Sector Portfolios

The *Hot Box* refers to the top three sectors on the Thackray Sector Thermometer tagged with an image of the sun.

The *Cold Box* refers to the bottom three sectors tagged with an image of a snowflake.

Monthly results for each sector in the Hot and Cold Boxes are posted on the Monthly Sector Performance pages beside the Thackray Sector Thermometer (TST).

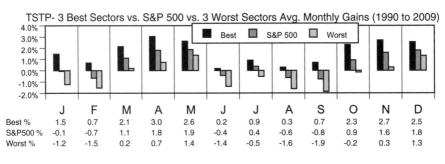

TSTP- 3 Best Sectors vs. S&P 500 vs. 3 Worst Sectors Avg. Monthly Gains (1990 to 2009)

	J	F	M	A	M	J	J	A	S	O	N	D	Avg. Year Gain
Best %	1.5	0.7	2.1	3.0	2.6	0.2	0.9	0.3	0.7	2.3	2.7	2.5	21.9%
S&P500 %	-0.1	-0.7	1.1	1.8	1.9	-0.4	0.4	-0.6	-0.8	0.9	1.6	1.8	7.8%
Worst %	-1.2	-1.5	0.2	0.7	1.4	-1.4	-0.5	-1.6	-1.9	-0.2	0.3	1.3	-3.5%

TSTP- 3 Best Sectors vs. S&P 500 vs. 3 Worst Sectors By Year (1990 to 2009)

	90	91	92	93	94	95	96	97	98	99	00	01	02	03	04	05	06	07	08	09	Total Period Gain
Best %	8.8	30.5	8.7	21.5	8.1	45.5	25.4	42.4	46.2	57.6	31.6	23.0	-8.1	36.7	17.7	7.1	17.1	11.8	-37.0	43.9	3588%
S&P500 %	-6.6	26.3	4.5	7.1	-1.5	34.1	20.3	31.0	26.7	19.5	-10.1	-13.0	-23.4	26.4	9.0	3.0	13.6	3.5	-38.5	23.5	216%
Worst %	-16.7	11.8	-5.1	0.2	-7.8	19.4	3.4	11.9	5.3	-4.0	-24.4	-32.0	-33.6	9.4	11.0	-1.8	17.1	8.1	-47.7	6.2	-67%

3 MONDAY	028 / 362	**4** TUESDAY	027 / 361

5 WEDNESDAY	026 / 360	**6** THURSDAY	025 / 359

7 FRIDAY	024 / 358

WEEK 01

Market Indices & Rates
Weekly Values**

Stock Markets	2009	2010
Dow	8,741	10,591
S&P500	899	1,139
Nasdaq	1,568	2,307
TSX	8,922	11,908
FTSE	4,427	5,523
DAX	4,829	6,034
Nikkei	8,803	10,710
Hang Seng	14,499	22,217

Commodities	2009	2010
Oil	42.5	82.4
Gold	874.8	1126.4

Bond Yields	2009	2010
USA 5 Yr Treasury	1.55	2.60
USA 10 Yr T	2.24	3.83
USA 20 Yr T	3.02	4.60
Moody's Aaa	4.73	5.30
Moody's Baa	8.07	6.34
CAN 5 Yr T	1.72	2.74
CAN 10 Yr T	2.70	3.61

Money Market	2009	2010
USA Fed Funds	0.25	0.25
USA 3 Mo T-B	0.09	0.06
CAN tgt overnight rate	1.50	0.25
CAN 3 Mo T-B	0.84	0.18

Foreign Exchange	2009	2010
USD/EUR	1.41	1.44
USD/GBP	1.46	1.60
CAN/USD	1.22	1.04
JPY/USD	90.17	92.56

JANUARY

M	T	W	T	F	S	S
					1	2
3	4	5	6	7	8	9
10	11	12	13	14	15	16
17	18	19	20	21	22	23
24	25	26	27	28	29	30
31						

FEBRUARY

M	T	W	T	F	S	S
	1	2	3	4	5	6
7	8	9	10	11	12	13
14	15	16	17	18	19	20
21	22	23	24	25	26	27
28						

MARCH

M	T	W	T	F	S	S
	1	2	3	4	5	6
7	8	9	10	11	12	13
14	15	16	17	18	19	20
21	22	23	24	25	26	27
28	29	30	31			

2009 Strategy Performance*

TSTP 2009 Best 3 Sectors vs. S&P 500 vs. Worst 3 Sectors

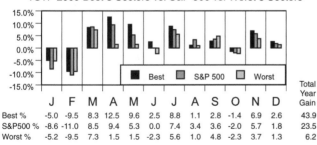

	J	F	M	A	M	J	J	A	S	O	N	D	Total Year Gain
Best %	-5.0	-9.5	8.3	12.5	9.6	2.5	8.8	1.1	2.8	-1.4	6.9	2.6	43.9
S&P500 %	-8.6	-11.0	8.5	9.4	5.3	0.0	7.4	3.4	3.6	-2.0	5.7	1.8	23.5
Worst %	-5.2	-9.5	7.3	1.5	1.5	-2.3	5.6	1.0	4.8	-2.3	3.7	1.3	6.2

The year 2009 ended up being a very good year for the market with the S&P 500 producing a final gain of 23.5%. More amazingly, the TSTP best three sectors (see previous page for details), almost doubled the S&P 500 gain, producing a return of 43.9%. The TSTP managed to outperform the broad market 10 out of the 12 months. To reference the monthly statistics for the TSTP and to see the sectors that were used each month, refer to the Thackray Sector Thermometer on the Monthly Sector Performance page, found at the beginning of each month.

* TSTP uses S&P GIC sectors
** Weekly avg closing values- except Fed Funds & CAN overnight tgt rate weekly closing values.

PLATINUM RECORDS SOLID RESULTS
January 1st to May 31st

Most investors focus on gold in the precious metals sector, some look at silver, but few notice platinum. Platinum outperforms gold starting at the beginning of the year until the end of May.

A large portion of the platinum produced each year is consumed by catalytic converters, mainly used in the automotive sector to control exhaust emissions. Approximately 40% of platinum is used for jewellery, 37% for catalytic converters and the rest used for other industrial purposes.

7.4% extra and 79% of the time better than Gold

Platinum vs. Gold 1987 to 2010*

Jan 1 to May 31	Platinum	Positive Gold	Diff
1987 %	22.1 %	16.0 %	6.1 %
1988	13.8	-5.9	19.7
1989	-2.6	-11.8	9.2
1990	-0.9	-8.9	8.0
1991	-4.9	-6.7	1.8
1992	4.5	-4.4	9.0
1993	9.0	12.6	-3.6
1994	2.0	-1.1	3.1
1995	3.5	0.3	3.2
1996	-0.2	0.9	-1.2
1997	10.5	-6.4	16.9
1998	0.1	1.2	-1.0
1999	0.4	-6.7	7.1
2000	23.4	-6.2	29.6
2001	-0.6	-2.5	2.0
2002	14.8	18.1	-3.4
2003	7.6	4.1	3.5
2004	2.9	-5.5	8.4
2005	0.5	-4.9	5.3
2006	32.6	27.3	5.3
2007	13.7	4.3	9.4
2008	31.2	6.2	24.9
2009	29.4	12.2	17.3
2010	6.9	11.0	-4.1
Avg.	9.2 %	1.8 %	7.4 %

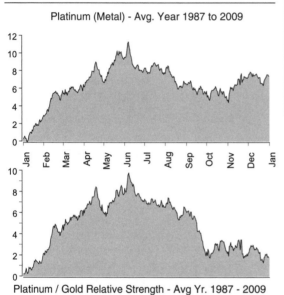

Platinum (Metal) - Avg. Year 1987 to 2009

Platinum / Gold Relative Strength - Avg Yr. 1987 - 2009

Platinum does well at the beginning of the year as it benefits from positive worldwide economic forecasts that dominate the market at the time. Strong economic forecasts translates into healthy worldwide auto production, which in turn translates into healthy platinum demand. Later in the year as economic forecasts are curtailed, platinum tends to lose its upwards momentum. In recent years, platinum has been in a strong bull market because of increasing inflation expectations, increasing jewellery usage, more stringent automotive emission requirements and supply problems in the South African mines.

Although palladium, a cheaper metal in the Platinum Group of Metals (PGM) can be substituted for plati-num in auto catalyst usage, platinum is a more effective agent with diesel emissions. Currently, approximately 50% of Europe's automobiles are diesel powered. As higher fuel prices change North American driving patterns (a small fraction of autos are powered by diesel), it is expected that the automotive industry will respond by offering a greater selection of diesel powered autos. This should help increase overall platinum demand.

In addition, China is adding more and more demand for cars. It was not too long ago that rush hour in Beijing was crowded with bikes, now it is cars. China has recently started to outpace America in auto sales. In August of 2010 the Chinese purchased more cars than Americans (*Gartman 2010, September*). Increasing demand for cars translates into an increase in the demand for platinum.

* *Platinum data based upon Bloomberg closing prices & Gold data based upon London PM price.*

10 MONDAY	021 / 355	**11** TUESDAY	020 / 354

Market Indices & Rates
Weekly Values**

Stock Markets	2009	2010
Dow	8,816	10,658
S&P500	914	1,143
Nasdaq	1,614	2,301
TSX	9,237	11,822
FTSE	4,536	5,493
DAX	4,922	5,962
Nikkei	9,015	10,876
Hang Seng	14,971	21,972

Commodities	2009	2010
Oil	44.5	80.1
Gold	850.7	1139.6

Bond Yields	2009	2010
USA 5 Yr Treasury	1.62	2.51
USA 10 Yr T	2.48	3.77
USA 20 Yr T	3.40	4.55
Moody's Aaa	5.04	5.24
Moody's Baa	8.23	6.25
CAN 5 Yr T	1.83	2.69
CAN 10 Yr T	2.88	3.56

Money Market	2009	2010
USA Fed Funds	0.25	0.25
USA 3 Mo T-B	0.11	0.05
CAN tgt overnight rate	1.50	0.25
CAN 3 Mo T-B	0.84	0.18

Foreign Exchange	2009	2010
USD/EUR	1.35	1.45
USD/GBP	1.49	1.62
CAN/USD	1.20	1.03
JPY/USD	92.48	91.65

12 WEDNESDAY	019 / 353	**13** THURSDAY	018 / 352

14 FRIDAY		017 / 351

JANUARY

M	T	W	T	F	S	S
					1	2
3	4	5	6	7	8	9
10	11	12	13	14	15	16
17	18	19	20	21	22	23
24	25	26	27	28	29	30
31						

FEBRUARY

M	T	W	T	F	S	S
	1	2	3	4	5	6
7	8	9	10	11	12	13
14	15	16	17	18	19	20
21	22	23	24	25	26	27
28						

MARCH

M	T	W	T	F	S	S
	1	2	3	4	5	6
7	8	9	10	11	12	13
14	15	16	17	18	19	20
21	22	23	24	25	26	27
28	29	30	31			

2010 Strategy Performance*

Platinum % Gain 2010

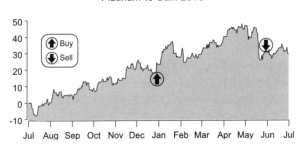

At the beginning of 2009, platinum was set up for a strong rally at the start of its seasonal cycle. It shone, producing a return of almost 30% in its seasonal period and it continued to soar for the rest of the year, producing over a 50% gain.

In 2010 platinum continued to rally in its next seasonal period, but corrected substantially at the beginning of May when global economic concerns brought the stock markets around the world tumbling down. In the end, the sector still managed to produce a positive gain during its seasonal period.

* Buy and Sell dates are approximate representations of strategy dates.
** Weekly avg closing values- except Fed Funds & CAN overnight tgt rate weekly closing values.

RETAIL – POST HOLIDAY BARGAIN
1st of II Retail Strategies for the Year
SHOP Jan 21st and RETURN Your Investment Apr 12th

A few weeks after the Christmas holidays retail stocks go on sale, representing a good buying opportunity in mid to late January. The opportunity coincides with the earnings season.

Historically, the retail sector has outperformed the S&P 500 from January 21st until April 12th - the start of the next earnings season. From 1990 to 2010, during its seasonally strong period, the retail sector has averaged 8.8%, compared with the S&P 500 which has averaged 2.0%. Not only has the retail sector had greater gains than the broad market, but it has also outperformed it on a fairly regular basis: 81% of the time.

> ### 6.8% extra & 81% of the time
> ### better than the S&P 500

Jan 21 to Apr 12	Retail	Positive S&P 500	Diff
1990	9.7 %	1.5 %	8.1 %
1991	29.9	14.5	15.4
1992	-2.7	-2.9	0.2
1993	-0.6	3.5	-4.0
1994	2.0	-5.8	7.8
1995	7.4	9.1	-1.8
1996	19.7	4.1	15.7
1997	6.0	-5.0	11.0
1998	20.1	13.5	6.6
1999	23.4	8.1	15.2
2000	5.8	1.5	4.3
2001	-0.5	-11.8	11.3
2002	6.7	-1.5	8.2
2003	6.5	-3.7	10.3
2004	6.7	0.6	6.1
2005	-1.6	1.1	-2.7
2006	3.4	2.1	1.3
2007	-0.7	1.2	-1.9
2008	3.5	0.6	3.0
2009	25.1	6.4	18.7
2010	15.5	5.1	10.4
Avg.	8.8 %	2.0 %	6.8 %

Retail Sector vs. S&P 500 1990 to 2010

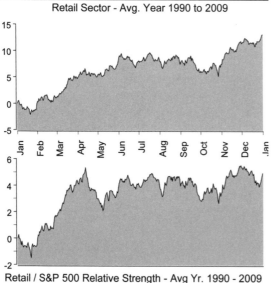

Retail Sector - Avg. Year 1990 to 2009

Retail / S&P 500 Relative Strength - Avg Yr. 1990 - 2009

Most investors think the best time to invest in retail stocks is before Black Friday in November. Yes, there is a positive seasonal cycle at this time, but it is not nearly as strong as the cycle from January to April.

The January retail bounce coincides with the "rosy" stock market analysts' forecasts that tend to occur at the beginning of the year. These forecasts generally rely on healthy consumer spending as it makes up approximately 2/3 of the GDP. The retail sector benefits from the optimistic forecasts and tends to outperform.

Surprisingly, there have only been minimal drawdowns over the last twenty years during the retail seasonal period. The worst loss was 2.7% in 1992, and even in this year the retail sector beat the S&P 500.

In 2010 the retail sector performed extremely well, more than tripling the performance of the S&P 500 during its seasonal strong period. Very shortly after the sector finished its seasonal run, the market peaked and lost ground over the next two months.

> (i) *Retail SP GIC Sector # 2550:*
> *An index designed to represent a cross section of retail companies*
> *For more information on the retail sector, see www.standardandpoors.com.*

17 MONDAY	014 / 348

18 TUESDAY	013 / 347

19 WEDNESDAY	012 / 346

20 THURSDAY	011 / 345

21 FRIDAY	010 / 344

WEEK 03

Market Indices & Rates
Weekly Values**

Stock Markets	2009	2010
Dow	8,323	10,473
S&P500	856	1,124
Nasdaq	1,523	2,271
TSX	8,849	11,601
FTSE	4,255	5,413
DAX	4,496	5,838
Nikkei	8,276	10,763
Hang Seng	13,568	21,203

Commodities	2009	2010
Oil	36.9	76.7
Gold	823.8	1116.0

Bond Yields	2009	2010
USA 5 Yr Treasury	1.42	2.42
USA 10 Yr T	2.30	3.66
USA 20 Yr T	3.23	4.42
Moody's Aaa	4.89	5.22
Moody's Baa	7.97	6.16
CAN 5 Yr T	1.62	2.55
CAN 10 Yr T	2.65	3.43

Money Market	2009	2010
USA Fed Funds	0.25	0.25
USA 3 Mo T-B	0.12	0.06
CAN tgt overnight rate	1.50	0.25
CAN 3 Mo T-B	0.73	0.16

Foreign Exchange	2009	2010
USD/EUR	1.33	1.42
USD/GBP	1.47	1.63
CAN/USD	1.22	1.04
JPY/USD	89.67	90.81

JANUARY

M	T	W	T	F	S	S
					1	2
3	4	5	6	7	8	9
10	11	12	13	14	15	16
17	18	19	20	21	22	23
24	25	26	27	28	29	30
31						

FEBRUARY

M	T	W	T	F	S	S
	1	2	3	4	5	6
7	8	9	10	11	12	13
14	15	16	17	18	19	20
21	22	23	24	25	26	27
28						

MARCH

M	T	W	T	F	S	S
	1	2	3	4	5	6
7	8	9	10	11	12	13
14	15	16	17	18	19	20
21	22	23	24	25	26	27
28	29	30	31			

2010 Strategy Performance*

Retail % Gain 2009-2010

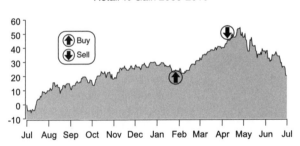

At times the strength of the consumer can be mind boggling. Despite a high unemployment rate at the beginning of 2010 and a weak housing market, consumers continued to spend money. Although the average American increased their savings rate, they still managed to spend more money than most analysts expected. With the market in rally mode earlier in 2010, the retail sector outperformed, more than tripling the S&P 500 gain during Retail's seasonal time period, ending up with a gain of over 15%.

The moral of the story – do not be too quick to discount the American consumer.

* Buy and Sell dates are approximate representations of strategy dates.
** Weekly avg closing values- except Fed Funds & CAN overnight tgt rate weekly closing values.

🛒 CONSUMER STAPLES — Not Needed In January
SHORT SELL – January 1st to January 22

January has the reputation of being a strong month. Since 1950 the S&P 500 has produced an average gain of 1.1% and been positive 62% of the time. In the last ten years January has only been positive 40% of the time and has suffered some big drops.

-1.9% & negative 71% of the time

One of the weaker sectors in the market in January has been consumer staples. From 1990 to 2010 the sector has produced a loss of 1.6% and has been negative 57% of the time for the full month of January.

The worst performance for the sector is focused on the time period from January 1st to January 22nd. In this time period the consumer staples sector has produced an average loss of 1.9% and has been negative 71% of the time.

Con. Staples vs. S&P 500 1990 to 2010

Jan 1 to Jan 22	Staples	Negative S&P 500	Diff
1990 %	-8.3 %	-6.5 %	-1.8 %
1991	-1.1	-0.6	-0.5
1992	-3.2	0.3	-3.4
1993	-3.5	0.1	-3.6
1994	-0.6	1.8	-2.4
1995	-1.1	1.2	-2.3
1996	1.4	-0.4	1.8
1997	6.2	6.1	0.0
1998	-0.9	-0.8	-0.1
1999	-6.8	-0.3	-6.4
2000	-2.0	-1.9	-0.1
2001	-8.4	1.7	-10.1
2002	0.5	-2.5	3.0
2003	1.0	-0.2	1.1
2004	-1.0	2.9	-3.9
2005	0.4	-3.6	4.1
2006	-0.8	1.1	-1.8
2007	1.7	0.3	1.4
2008	-6.7	-10.8	4.1
2009	-4.9	-8.4	3.5
2010	-1.1	-2.1	1.0
Avg.	-1.9 %	-1.1 %	-0.8 %

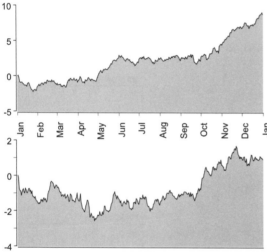

Consumer Staples Sector - Avg. Year 1990 to 2009

Staples / S&P 500 Relative Strength - Avg. Yr. 1990 - 2009

The Consumer Staples vs. S&P 500 table illustrates the relationship between the two sectors. In general when the S&P 500 is positive or slightly negative the consumer staples sector tends to under perform. On the other hand, when the S&P 500 suffers large losses the consumer staples sector tends to outperform the S&P 500.

The direction of the US dollar has an impact on the performance of the consumer staples sector. When the US dollar is rising, the sector tends to fall and when the dollar is falling, the sector tends to increase.

The reason that this relationship exists is that consumer staples companies receive a higher percentage of their revenues from offshore companies compared with the S&P 500.

This means that if the US dollar is falling, then consumer staples companies will benefit from increased revenues because of the lower exchange rate and vice versa. This relationship is important because the US dollar tends to rise in January (see *U.S. Dollar – Short and Long* strategy) and therefore put downward pressure on the consumer staples sector.

ⓘ *The SP GICS Consumer Staples Sector encompasses a wide range consumer staples based companies. For more information on the information technology sector, see www.standardandpoors.com*

24 MONDAY	007 / 341	**25** TUESDAY	006 / 340

26 WEDNESDAY	005 / 339	**27** THURSDAY	004 / 338

28 FRIDAY   003 / 337

WEEK 04

Market Indices & Rates
Weekly Values**

Stock Markets	2009	2010
Dow	8,094	10,163
S&P500	826	1,089
Nasdaq	1,473	2,192
TSX	8,644	11,286
FTSE	4,073	5,218
DAX	4,243	5,619
Nikkei	8,004	10,340
Hang Seng	12,824	20,244

Commodities	2009	2010
Oil	42.2	74.0
Gold	854.3	1090.0

Bond Yields	2009	2010
USA 5 Yr Treasury	1.58	2.39
USA 10 Yr T	2.56	3.66
USA 20 Yr T	3.52	4.42
Moody's Aaa	5.10	5.28
Moody's Baa	8.15	6.23
CAN 5 Yr T	1.71	2.46
CAN 10 Yr T	2.74	3.36

Money Market	2009	2010
USA Fed Funds	0.25	0.25
USA 3 Mo T-B	0.11	0.07
CAN tgt overnight rate	1.00	0.25
CAN 3 Mo T-B	0.80	0.16

Foreign Exchange	2009	2010
USD/EUR	1.30	1.40
USD/GBP	1.40	1.61
CAN/USD	1.25	1.06
JPY/USD	89.72	89.96

2010 Strategy Performance*

Consumer Staples % Gain Nov. 2009 to Jun 2010

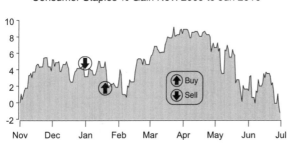

In January 2010 the consumer staples sector fell along with the market. It also bottomed in February along with the rest of the market. It is important to note that although it rose with the rest of the market, it under performed the market into April.

After the bottom of the market in February, it was much better to be invested in the consumer discretionary sector compared to the consumer staples sector. From February to April the discretionary sector strongly outperformed the staples sector.

JANUARY

M	T	W	T	F	S	S
					1	2
3	4	5	6	7	8	9
10	11	12	13	14	15	16
17	18	19	20	21	22	23
24	25	26	27	28	29	30
31						

FEBRUARY

M	T	W	T	F	S	S
1	2	3	4	5	6	
7	8	9	10	11	12	13
14	15	16	17	18	19	20
21	22	23	24	25	26	27
28						

MARCH

M	T	W	T	F	S	S
1	2	3	4	5	6	
7	8	9	10	11	12	13
14	15	16	17	18	19	20
21	22	23	24	25	26	27
28	29	30	31			

* Buy and Sell dates are approximate representations of strategy dates.
** Weekly avg closing values- except Fed Funds & CAN overnight tgt rate weekly closing values.

- 12 -

JANUARY PREDICTOR
Predicting the Rest of the Year

January has an uncanny trait of predicting the rest of the year. "As January goes, the rest of the year goes." In other words, if January is positive, the rest of the year tends to be positive, and if January is negative, the rest of the year tends to be negative.

> *73% accuracy predicting S&P 500 direction 1950 to 2009*

There have been quite a few different theories as to why January is a good predictor for the rest of the year. Generally speaking, the explanation that makes the most sense is that investors and money managers are setting up their expectations for the rest of the year.

If money managers are expecting a good year, they are more inclined to move more money into the market in January, boosting the performance of January and the rest of the year. If money managers are expecting a sub-performance year, they are more inclined to hold back on funds in January, producing a negative January and rest of the year.

It is important to note, however, that January is much better at predicting a positive remainder of the year, as compared to a negative remainder.

Since 1950 it has correctly predicted positive "rest of the years," 33 out of 37 years or 89% of the time. This compares to predicting negative "rest of the years," 11 out of 23 times, or 48% of the time.

In other words, it is really a flip of the coin when January is negative. Investors should pay more attention to positive January performances, rather than negative performances in considering the future direction of the markets during the year.

> ⚠ *Basing a yearly investment decision on one month's returns is not considered to be a reasonable portfolio investment strategy and large returns can be missed. For example, in 2003 the January Predictor forecasted a negative rest of year return. The market returned an astonishing 30%.*

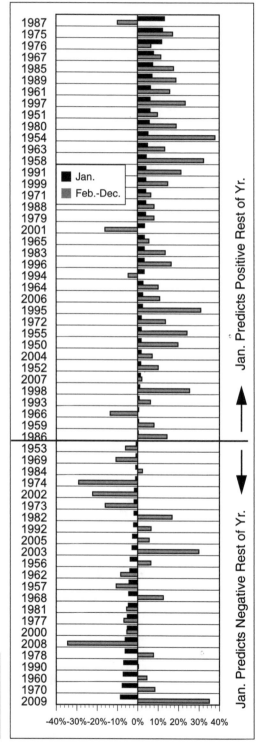

- 13 -

31 MONDAY	000 / 334	**1** TUESDAY	027 / 333

2 WEDNESDAY	026 / 332	**3** THURSDAY	025 / 331

4 FRIDAY 024 / 330

WEEK 05

Market Indices & Rates
Weekly Values**

Stock Markets	2009	2010
Dow	8,163	10,153
S&P500	845	1,084
Nasdaq	1,507	2,164
TSX	8,756	11,294
FTSE	4,208	5,197
DAX	4,387	5,601
Nikkei	8,019	10,279
Hang Seng	13,216	20,249

Commodities	2009	2010
Oil	42.5	74.6
Gold	903.0	1090.8

Bond Yields	2009	2010
USA 5 Yr Treasury	1.74	2.33
USA 10 Yr T	2.75	3.66
USA 20 Yr T	3.74	4.42
Moody's Aaa	5.23	5.29
Moody's Baa	8.22	6.25
CAN 5 Yr T	2.02	2.46
CAN 10 Yr T	2.98	3.38

Money Market	2009	2010
USA Fed Funds	0.25	0.25
USA 3 Mo T-B	0.19	0.10
CAN tgt overnight rate	1.00	0.25
CAN 3 Mo T-B	0.82	0.17

Foreign Exchange	2009	2010
USD/EUR	1.31	1.39
USD/GBP	1.42	1.59
CAN/USD	1.22	1.06
JPY/USD	89.52	90.29

2009-2010 Strategy Performance

January Predictor S&P 500 (2009 & 2010)

FEBRUARY

M	T	W	T	F	S	S
	1	2	3	4	5	6
7	8	9	10	11	12	13
14	15	16	17	18	19	20
21	22	23	24	25	26	27
28						

MARCH

M	T	W	T	F	S	S
	1	2	3	4	5	6
7	8	9	10	11	12	13
14	15	16	17	18	19	20
21	22	23	24	25	26	27
28	29	30	31			

APRIL

M	T	W	T	F	S	S
				1	2	3
4	5	6	7	8	9	10
11	12	13	14	15	16	17
18	19	20	21	22	23	24
25	26	27	28	29	30	

The January Predictor is mainly added to this book because its "cousin" the January Barometer (Yale Hirsch, Stock Trader's Almanac) is often cited in the press. The press loves to publish yearly forecasts at the beginning of the year. The year 2009 showed why it is not a good investment practice to base almost an entire year's portfolio decision on one indicator. January was an abysmal month (one of the worst on record), but it was just over one month later that the market bottomed and then rallied almost 80% (S&P 500). Investors should remember that negative Januaries have historically had no predictive results.

** Weekly avg closing values- except Fed Funds & CAN overnight tgt rate weekly closing values.

FEBRUARY

	MONDAY	TUESDAY	WEDNESDAY
WEEK 05	31	1 27	2 26
WEEK 06	7 21	8 20	9 19
WEEK 07	14 14	15 13	16 12
WEEK 08	21 7 CAN Market Closed - Family Day USA Market Closed - Presidents' Day	22 6	23 5
WEEK 09	28	1	2

THURSDAY		FRIDAY	
3	25	**4**	24
10	18	**11**	17
17	11	**18**	10
24	4	**25**	3
3		4	

MARCH

M	T	W	T	F	S	S
	1	2	3	4	5	6
7	8	9	10	11	12	13
14	15	16	17	18	19	20
21	22	23	24	25	26	27
28	29	30	31			

APRIL

M	T	W	T	F	S	S
				1	2	3
4	5	6	7	8	9	10
11	12	13	14	15	16	17
18	19	20	21	22	23	24
25	26	27	28	29	30	

MAY

M	T	W	T	F	S	S
						1
2	3	4	5	6	7	8
9	10	11	12	13	14	15
16	17	18	19	20	21	22
23	24	25	26	27	28	29
30	31					

JUNE

M	T	W	T	F	S	S
		1	2	3	4	5
6	7	8	9	10	11	12
13	14	15	16	17	18	19
20	21	22	23	24	25	26
27	28	29	30			

FEBRUARY
S U M M A R Y

S&P500 Cumulative Daily Gains for Avg Month 1950 to 2010

Prob. of Daily Gain

♦ In 2009 the market was hit hard in February, down almost 12%. In 2010, February was looking bad once again, but managed to bottom early in the month and set up a rally that lasted into April. ♦ On average since 1950, February has been the second worst month for the S&P 500, producing a loss of 0.3% and positive only 52% of the time. ♦ Typically the favored sectors are Materials, Energy and Consumer Staples (see February TST) ♦ Oil stocks tend to either do well in February or bottom towards the end of the month with a strong move into May.

BEST / WORST FEBRUARY BROAD MKTS. 2001-2010

BEST FEBRUARY MARKETS
♦ TSX (2005) 5.0%
♦ TSX (2010) 4.8%
♦ Russell 2000 (2010) 4.4%

WORST FEBRUARY MARKETS
♦ Nasdaq (2001) -22.4%
♦ Russell 3000 Gr (2001) -16.8%
♦ Russell 3000 Value (2009) -13.8%

Index Values End of Month

	2001	2002	2003	2004	2005	2006	2007	2008	2009	2010
Dow	10,495	10,106	7,891	10,584	10,766	10,993	12,269	12,266	7,063	10,325
S&P 500	1,240	1,107	841	1,145	1,204	1,281	1,407	1,331	735	1,104
Nasdaq	2,152	1,731	1,338	2,030	2,052	2,281	2,416	2,271	1,378	2,238
TSX	8,079	7,638	6,555	8,788	9,668	11,688	13,045	13,583	8,123	11,630
Russell 1000	1,258	1,122	858	1,178	1,244	1,341	1,478	1,396	768	1,168
Russell 2000	1,179	1,166	896	1,455	1,576	1,816	1,972	1,705	967	1,562
Russell 3000 Growth	2,208	1,858	1,367	1,880	1,889	2,059	2,195	2,165	1,276	1,942
Russell 3000 Value	2,152	2,051	1,619	2,272	2,522	2,725	3,094	2,755	1,412	2,164

Percent Gain for February

	2001	2002	2003	2004	2005	2006	2007	2008	2009	2010
Dow	-3.6	1.9	-2.0	0.9	2.6	1.2	-2.8	-3.0	-11.7	2.6
S&P 500	-9.2	-2.1	-1.7	1.2	1.9	0.0	-2.2	-3.5	-11.0	2.9
Nasdaq	-22.4	-10.5	1.3	-1.8	-0.5	-1.1	-1.9	-5.0	-6.7	4.2
TSX	-13.3	-0.1	-0.2	3.1	5.0	-2.2	0.1	3.3	-6.6	4.8
Russell 1000	-9.4	-2.1	-1.7	1.2	2.0	0.0	-1.9	-3.3	-10.7	3.1
Russell 2000	-6.7	-2.8	-3.1	0.8	1.6	-0.3	-0.9	-3.8	-12.3	4.4
Russell 3000 Growth	-16.8	-4.4	-0.7	0.5	1.0	-0.3	-1.9	-2.2	-7.9	3.3
Russell 3000 Value	-2.8	0.0	-3.0	1.9	2.9	0.3	-1.8	-4.5	-13.8	3.0

February Market Avg. Performance 2001 to 2010[1]

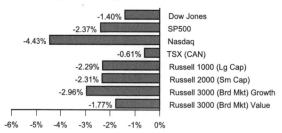

	-1.40%	Dow Jones
	-2.37%	SP500
-4.43%		Nasdaq
	-0.61%	TSX (CAN)
	-2.29%	Russell 1000 (Lg Cap)
	-2.31%	Russell 2000 (Sm Cap)
	-2.96%	Russell 3000 (Brd Mkt) Growth
	-1.77%	Russell 3000 (Brd Mkt) Value

-6% -5% -4% -3% -2% -1% 0%

Interest Corner Feb[2]

	Fed Funds % [3]	3 Mo. T-Bill % [4]	10 Yr % [5]	20 Yr % [6]
2010	0.25	0.13	3.61	4.40
2009	0.25	0.26	3.02	3.98
2008	3.00	1.85	3.53	4.37
2007	5.25	5.16	4.56	4.78
2006	4.50	4.62	4.55	4.70

(1) Russell Data provided by Russell (2) Federal Reserve Bank of St. Louis- end of month values (3) Target rate set by FOMC (4)(5)(6) Constant yield maturities.

THACKRAY SECTOR THERMOMETER

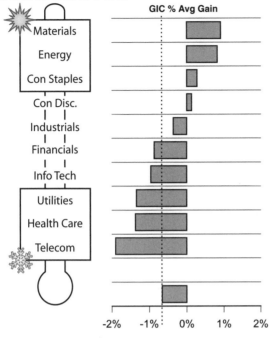

GIC[2] % Avg Gain	Fq % Gain >S&P 500	
SP GIC SECTOR 1990-2009[1]		
0.9 %	65 %	Materials
0.8	50	Energy
0.3	55	Consumer Staples
0.1	70	Consumer Discretionary
-0.4	55	Industrials
-0.9	65	Financials
-1.0	50	Information Technology
-1.3	25	Utilities
-1.4	40	Health Care
-1.9 %	40 %	Telecom
-0.7 %	N/A %	S&P 500

Sector Commentary

♦ Although typically February is a mediocre month, there are four sectors that have produced positive results from 1990 to 2009: Materials, Energy, Consumer Discretionary and Consumer Staples. ♦ In 2010 (not included in results of TST) the Consumer Discretionary sector was the strongest sector producing a 5.3% gain. ♦ In 2010 the only two sectors that produced a negative return were the Telecom and Utilities sectors, which are typically at the bottom of the TST.

Sub-Sector Commentary

♦ From 1990 to 2009 the SOX index led the Sub-Sectors with a 1.9% gain, but it must be noted that the index has only beaten the S&P 500, 53% of the time, illustrating the volatility of the index. ♦ The frequency rate of beating the S&P 500 jumps up to 75% with the Retail sector which has produced an average gain of 1.1%. ♦ Of the sub-sectors listed, it is the Health Care sub-sectors (Biotech and Pharmaceuticals) that are at the bottom of the barrel with poor results. In 2010, both the Health Care subsectors (Pharmaceuticals and Biotech) were in the bottom four of the list. Biotech was slightly positive and Pharmaceuticals was slightly negative.

SELECTED SUB-SECTORS 1990-2009[3]		
1.9 %	53 %	Semiconductor (SOX) 95-2009
1.2	60	Metals & Mining
1.2	70	Gold (XAU)
1.1	75	Retail
0.5	50	Integrated Oil & Gas
0.3	55	Airlines
-0.1	60	Transportation
-0.3	65	Banks
-0.5	45	Auto & Components
-0.9	50	Software & Services
-1.2	55	Insurance
-1.3	50	Agriculture Products (94-2009)
-1.4	40	Pharmaceuticals
-1.9	59	Biotech (93-2009)

(1) Sector data provided by Standard and Poors (2) GIC is short form for Global Industry Classification (3) Sub Sector data provided by Standard and Poors, except where marked by symbol.

CHANGE YOUR OIL SECTOR
Exploration & Production (E&P) Jan 30 to Apr 13
Equipment and Services (E&S) Apr 14 to May 17

Periodically, drivers change their oil to extend the life of their car. Investors that have changed their oil sectors at the right time have extended their profits.

The energy seasonal cycle takes place from February 25th to May 9th (see *Oil- Winter/Spring Effect* strategy).

This cycle can be extended on both sides by investing in exploration and production stocks at the end of January, and then switching to equipment and services stocks in mid-April and holding until mid-May.

14% extra & 18 out of 21 times better than the S&P 500

Very often when a sector seasonally outperforms, such as energy, it is the more speculative sub-sector, such as exploration and production, that starts the outperformance. At the end of the cycle the more conservative sub-sector, such as equipment and services often outperforms.

Investors developing a seasonal energy strategy have the option of combining the *Oil Winter/Spring Strategy* with the *Change Your Oil strategy*.

(i) *Exploration and Production - S&P GIC sector Equipment and Services 10102020 & S&P GIC Oil Integrated sector 10102010. For more information please see www.standardandpoors.com*

(Y) *Alternate Strategy - The cumulative gain graph for the three major sub-sectors of the energy market has been included to illustrate a possible strategy for money managers to maintain an equity position in the energy sector throughout the year. The Oil Integrated companies (major oil companies involved in all aspects of oil production and sales), provide a good alternative to the Oil E&P sector during less favorable times for oil stocks.*

Oil E&P and E&S Sector Switch 1990 to 2010*				Positive	
	E&P Jan 30 to Apr 13	E&S Apr 14 to May 17	E&P & E&S Jan 30 to May 17**	S&P 500 Jan 30 to May 17	Diff
1990	12.7%	10.8%	24.9%	9.0%	15.9%
1991	11.2	2.0	13.5	10.9	2.6
1992	4.8	10.4	15.8	-0.1	15.8
1993	27.0	3.7	31.7	0.4	31.4
1994	-11.4	8.3	-4.1	-6.1	2.0
1995	14.3	9.7	25.3	12.0	13.2
1996	7.7	-0.7	7.0	7.2	-0.2
1997	-16.3	13.9	-4.6	7.4	-12.1
1998	9.0	7.9	17.5	12.5	5.0
1999	35.7	9.7	48.8	4.7	44.1
2000	17.9	22.2	44.0	6.4	37.6
2001	5.4	17.8	24.2	-5.5	29.8
2002	14.3	4.1	19.0	0.5	18.5
2003	1.2	15.3	16.7	9.2	7.4
2004	8.9	-5.1	3.3	-4.4	7.7
2005	14.6	-3.8	10.3	0.2	10.1
2006	-4.0	4.0	-0.2	-1.0	0.9
2007	12.4	7.3	20.6	6.5	14.1
2008	29.9	16.8	51.7	4.6	47.1
2009	-3.3	15.4	11.6	4.5	7.1
2010	8.4	-5.8	2.1	5.9	-3.7
Avg.	9.5%	7.8%	18.1%	4.0%	14.0%

* Buy date uses close value from day before
** Cumulative Gain - E&P Jan 30 to Apr 13 and E&S Apr 14 to May 17

Oil E&P / Oil E&S - Relative Strength
Avg. Jan 30 to Jun 1 - 1990 - 2010

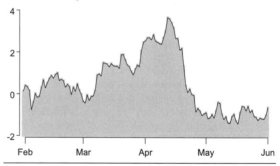

Oil E&P & Oil E&S & Oil Integrated
Avg. Cumulative Gain 1990 - 2009

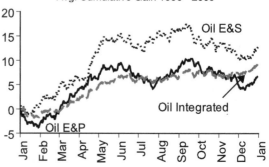

7 MONDAY	021 / 327

8 TUESDAY	020 / 326

9 WEDNESDAY	019 / 325

10 THURSDAY	018 / 324

11 FRIDAY	017 / 323

WEEK 06

Market Indices & Rates
Weekly Values**

Stock Markets	2009	2010
Dow	8,063	10,050
S&P500	842	1,070
Nasdaq	1,533	2,157
TSX	8,763	11,316
FTSE	4,198	5,128
DAX	4,459	5,505
Nikkei	7,953	9,985
Hang Seng	13,107	19,965

Commodities	2009	2010
Oil	40.5	73.9
Gold	912.2	1072.6

Bond Yields	2009	2010
USA 5 Yr Treasury	1.88	2.34
USA 10 Yr T	2.92	3.69
USA 20 Yr T	3.86	4.48
Moody's Aaa	5.29	5.36
Moody's Baa	8.18	6.36
CAN 5 Yr T	2.03	2.49
CAN 10 Yr T	3.05	3.42

Money Market	2009	2010
USA Fed Funds	0.25	0.25
USA 3 Mo T-B	0.29	0.11
CAN tgt overnight rate	1.00	0.25
CAN 3 Mo T-B	0.83	0.17

Foreign Exchange	2009	2010
USD/EUR	1.29	1.37
USD/GBP	1.44	1.56
CAN/USD	1.23	1.06
JPY/USD	89.81	89.69

2010 Strategy Performance*

Oil E&P & Oil E&S 2010

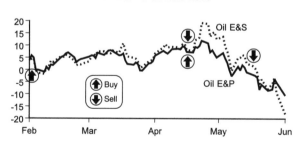

In 2010 this seasonal strategy started off on solid footing, with the exploration and production sector outperforming the S&P 500.

Unfortunately, the BP oil rig exploded in the Gulf of Mexico on April 20th. Despite the large negative impact on the Oil Equipment and Services sector, the overall strategy still managed to produce a positive return of just over 2%. Even though the strategy had a positive return, it under performed the S&P 500 by 3.7%.

FEBRUARY
M	T	W	T	F	S	S
	1	2	3	4	5	6
7	8	9	10	11	12	13
14	15	16	17	18	19	20
21	22	23	24	25	26	27
28						

MARCH
M	T	W	T	F	S	S
	1	2	3	4	5	6
7	8	9	10	11	12	13
14	15	16	17	18	19	20
21	22	23	24	25	26	27
28	29	30	31			

APRIL
M	T	W	T	F	S	S
			1	2	3	
4	5	6	7	8	9	10
11	12	13	14	15	16	17
18	19	20	21	22	23	24
25	26	27	28	29	30	

* Buy and Sell dates are approximate representations of strategy dates.
** Weekly avg closing values- except Fed Funds & CAN overnight tgt rate weekly closing values.

OIL – WINTER/SPRING STRATEGY
1st of II Oil Stock Strategies for the Year
February 25th to May 9th

(Stocks)

The *Oil- Winter/Spring Strategy* is one of the strongest seasonal outperformance trends. From 1984 to 2010, for the two and half months starting on February 25th and ending May 9th, the energy sector (XOI) has outperformed the S&P 500 by an average 5.3%.

What is even more impressive are the positive returns 24 out of 27 times, and the outperformance of the S&P 500, 23 out of 27 times.

5.3% extra and 24 out of 27 times positive, in just over two months

XOI / S&P 500 1984 to 2010			
Feb 25 to May 9	positive		
	XOI	S&P 500	Diff
1984	5.6 %	1.7 %	3.9 %
1985	4.9	1.4	3.5
1986	7.7	6.0	1.7
1987	25.5	3.7	21.8
1988	5.6	-3.0	8.6
1989	8.1	6.3	1.8
1990	-0.6	5.8	-6.3
1991	6.8	4.8	2.0
1992	5.8	0.9	4.9
1993	6.3	0.3	6.0
1994	3.2	-4.7	7.9
1995	10.3	7.3	3.1
1996	2.2	-2.1	4.3
1997	4.7	1.8	2.9
1998	9.8	7.5	2.3
1999	35.4	7.3	28.1
2000	22.2	4.3	17.9
2001	10.2	0.8	9.4
2002	5.3	-1.5	6.9
2003	5.7	12.1	-6.4
2004	4.0	-3.5	7.5
2005	-1.0	-1.8	0.8
2006	9.4	2.8	6.6
2007	10.1	4.2	5.8
2008	7.6	2.6	5.0
2009	15.8	20.2	-4.4
2010	-2.3	0.5	-2.8
Avg	8.5 %	3.2 %	5.3 %

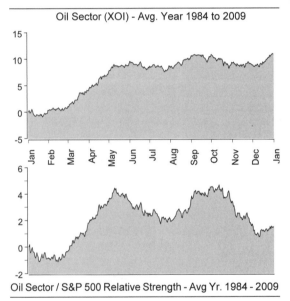

Oil Sector (XOI) - Avg. Year 1984 to 2009

Oil Sector / S&P 500 Relative Strength - Avg Yr. 1984 - 2009

A lot of investors assume that the time to buy oil stocks is just before the winter cold sets in. The rationale is that oil will climb in price as the temperature drops.

The results in the market have not supported this assumption. The dynamic of the price for a barrel of oil has more to do with oil inventory. Refineries have a choice: they can produce either gasoline or heating oil. As the winter progresses, refineries start to convert their operations from heating oil to gasoline.

During this switch-over time, low inventory levels of both heating oil and gasoline can drive up the price of a barrel of oil and oil stocks. In early May, before the kick-off of the driving season (Memorial Day in May), the refineries have finished their conversion to gasoline. The price of oil and oil stocks tend to decline.

Investors are given another chance for above average gains in the energy sector, when the second seasonal for oil stocks takes place in late July (*see Oil – Summer Autumn Strategy*). Although this seasonal cycle is not as strong as the February to May cycle, it is definitely worth while for seasonal investors to investigate.

> (i) *Amex Oil Index (XOI):*
> *An index designed to represent a cross section of widely held oil corporations involved in various phases of the oil industry.*
> *For more information on the XOI index, see www.cboe.com*

14 MONDAY	014 / 320	**15** TUESDAY	013 / 319

16 WEDNESDAY	012 / 318	**17** THURSDAY	011 / 317

18 FRIDAY	010 / 316

WEEK 07

Market Indices & Rates
Weekly Values**

Stock Markets	2009	2010
Dow	7,976	10,343
S&P500	839	1,103
Nasdaq	1,545	2,232
TSX	8,812	11,656
FTSE	4,229	5,274
DAX	4,505	5,631
Nikkei	7,850	10,163
Hang Seng	13,594	20,283

Commodities	2009	2010
Oil	36.9	78.3
Gold	924.3	1112.7

Bond Yields	2009	2010
USA 5 Yr Treasury	1.83	2.42
USA 10 Yr T	2.88	3.74
USA 20 Yr T	3.80	4.56
Moody's Aaa	5.21	5.44
Moody's Baa	8.01	6.45
CAN 5 Yr T	2.09	2.54
CAN 10 Yr T	2.97	3.48

Money Market	2009	2010
USA Fed Funds	0.25	0.25
USA 3 Mo T-B	0.30	0.10
CAN tgt overnight rate	1.00	0.25
CAN 3 Mo T-B	0.72	0.16

Foreign Exchange	2009	2010
USD/EUR	1.29	1.36
USD/GBP	1.45	1.56
CAN/USD	1.24	1.04
JPY/USD	90.92	90.58

FEBRUARY

M	T	W	T	F	S	S
	1	2	3	4	5	6
7	8	9	10	11	12	13
14	15	16	17	18	19	20
21	22	23	24	25	26	27
28						

MARCH

M	T	W	T	F	S	S
	1	2	3	4	5	6
7	8	9	10	11	12	13
14	15	16	17	18	19	20
21	22	23	24	25	26	27
28	29	30	31			

APRIL

M	T	W	T	F	S	S
				1	2	3
4	5	6	7	8	9	10
11	12	13	14	15	16	17
18	19	20	21	22	23	24
25	26	27	28	29	30	

2010 Strategy Performance*

XOI % Gain July 2009 to June 2010

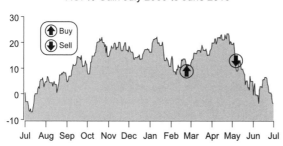

Although the stock market started to rally in February, investors were not totally convinced that a global economic recovery was in place and as a result, the oil sector under performed the broad stock market.

The S&P 500 peaked on April 26th, 2010 and then corrected into May. As a result, the oil sector suffered a minor decline during its seasonally strong period.

* Buy and Sell dates are approximate representations of strategy dates.
** Weekly avg closing values- except Fed Funds & CAN overnight tgt rate weekly closing values.

PRESIDENTS' DAY NEGATIVE TRIO

Markets Not Very Patriotic
2 Days Before and 1 Day After

You may like the current President, but that does not mean that you have to invest on either side of Presidents' Day. Two days before and one day after Presidents' Day, have produced results that are less than stellar and have often been back to back negative days. These three days are aptly called the Presidents' Day Negative Trio.

The day before Presidents' Day is typically the worst day of the Trio - Trio has an average negative return and down 58% of the time

From 1971 to 2010, all three days of the trio have produced an average negative return. The two market days before have been negative most of the time. The market day after has just scraped by with an even chance at being positive or negative.

Presidents' Day S&P 500 1971 to 2010

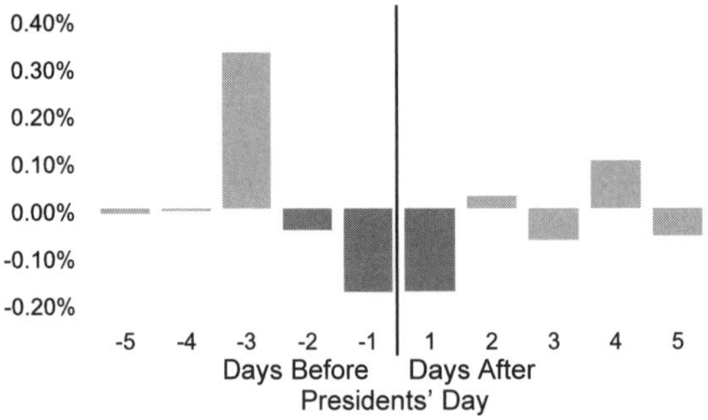

The average negative returns may have more to do with the part of the month the holiday falls on rather than the holiday itself.

Presidents' Day often occurs right after the third Friday, which tends to be the most negative day of the month. This Friday is the day that the options and futures contracts expire and is commonly referred to as Witching Day.

The third Friday and the day after, tend to be volatile and produce negative returns (see *Witches' Hangover* strategy). If Presidents' Day occurs after the third Friday, then it tends to be surrounded by days with poor performance. Investors would be wise to pay attention to the years in which Presidents' Day occurs at this time.

Negative (shaded)

S&P500	2 Days Before	1 Day Before	PRESIDENTS' DAY	1 Day After
1971	0.53	0.53%		0.23%
1972	-0.03	-0.29		0.01
1973	-0.56	0.46		0.37
1974	-0.03	1.45		-0.16
1975	1.36	0.60		-0.70
1976	-0.52	-0.58		-0.62
1977	-0.57	-0.43		0.00
1978	-0.84	-0.14		-0.42
1979	-0.14	-0.06		0.76
1980	-1.45	-1.12		-0.70
1981	-0.59	-0.39		0.65
1982	-0.20	-0.04		-0.28
1983	0.01	0.38		-1.70
1984	-0.08	-0.25		-0.71
1985	-0.51	-0.44		-0.15
1986	0.66	1.09		1.22
1987	-0.69	1.48		2.07
1988	-0.28	0.66		0.85
1989	0.19	0.66		-0.26
1990	0.87	-0.65		-1.42
1991	-1.30	1.33		0.09
1992	-0.82	-0.29		-1.24
1993	0.32	-0.69		-2.40
1994	-0.52	-0.56		0.81
1995	0.14	-0.67		0.16
1996	-0.65	-0.51		-1.13
1997	1.13	-0.41		0.97
1998	0.40	-0.40		0.26
1999	2.49	-1.91		0.95
2000	0.04	-3.04		0.45
2001	0.81	-1.89		-1.74
2002	-0.18	-1.10		-1.89
2003	-0.16	2.14		1.95
2004	-0.49	-0.55		0.98
2005	-0.79	0.07		-1.45
2006	0.73	-0.17		-0.33
2007	0.10	-0.09		0.28
2008	-1.34	0.08		-0.09
2009	0.17	-1.00		-4.56
2010	0.97	-0.27		1.80
Avg	-0.05%	-0.17%		-0.18%
Fq > 0	42.5%	32.5%		47.5%

ⓘ *Presidents' Day was originally set aside to honor George Washington's birthday, and later incorporated Abraham Lincoln's birthday which also fell in February. To stem the confusion about which day to celebrate, legislation was enacted in 1971, setting the date to the third Monday in February. The day is now commonly used to celebrate all past American Presidents.*

FEBRUARY

21 MONDAY	007 / 313	**22** TUESDAY	006 / 312

23 WEDNESDAY	005 / 311	**24** THURSDAY	004 / 310

25 FRIDAY   003 / 309

WEEK 08

Market Indices & Rates
Weekly Values**

Stock Markets	2009	2010
Dow	7,485	10,337
S&P500	782	1,103
Nasdaq	1,456	2,233
TSX	8,172	11,589
FTSE	4,017	5,329
DAX	4,204	5,608
Nikkei	7,581	10,236
Hang Seng	13,028	20,495

Commodities	2009	2010
Oil	37.1	79.2
Gold	968.8	1105.6

Bond Yields	2009	2010
USA 5 Yr Treasury	1.79	2.37
USA 10 Yr T	2.75	3.69
USA 20 Yr T	3.80	4.48
Moody's Aaa	5.25	5.31
Moody's Baa	8.01	6.33
CAN 5 Yr T	2.07	2.53
CAN 10 Yr T	2.88	3.44

Money Market	2009	2010
USA Fed Funds	0.25	0.25
USA 3 Mo T-B	0.30	0.12
CAN tgt overnight rate	1.00	0.25
CAN 3 Mo T-B	0.69	0.16

Foreign Exchange	2009	2010
USD/EUR	1.27	1.36
USD/GBP	1.43	1.54
CAN/USD	1.25	1.05
JPY/USD	92.61	90.13

2010 Strategy Performance

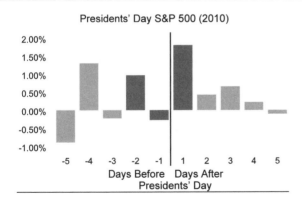

Presidents' Day S&P 500 (2010)

FEBRUARY

M	T	W	T	F	S	S
	1	2	3	4	5	6
7	8	9	10	11	12	13
14	15	16	17	18	19	20
21	22	23	24	25	26	27
28						

MARCH

M	T	W	T	F	S	S
	1	2	3	4	5	6
7	8	9	10	11	12	13
14	15	16	17	18	19	20
21	22	23	24	25	26	27
28	29	30	31			

APRIL

M	T	W	T	F	S	S
				1	2	3
4	5	6	7	8	9	10
11	12	13	14	15	16	17
18	19	20	21	22	23	24
25	26	27	28	29	30	

In 2010 the stock market bottomed on February 8th, only a few days before President's Day and rallied into April.

This year's holiday occurred as early in the month as possible (Monday February 15th) bringing it very close to the bottom of the market. The power of a strong rally will often overcome other negative influences. The end result for the strategy in 2010 was a return of 2.5% (S&P 500).

** Weekly avg closing values- except Fed Funds & CAN overnight tgt rate weekly closing values.

- 24 -

PRESIDENTIAL ELECTION CYCLE
3rd Year — Best Year

As 2011 is the third year of the Presidential election cycle, it is important to note that it is the strongest year of the four year cycle.

Historically, the first two years of the cycle tend to be weak and the last two years tend to be strong. This pattern tends to repeat as the President makes tough decisions to bring the economy back on track in the first and second years of his term and in the third and fourth years, he creates policies that help get him re-elected.

Best year of Presidential Cycle

The third year has been the best year of the Presidential Cycle, having produced an average annual return of 12.6% and has been positive 82% of the time from 1901 to 2008. In fact, the last loss

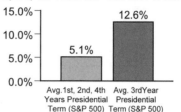

Avg. 3rd Year Presidential Term vs. 1st, 3rd, 4th Years S&P 500 1901 to 2008

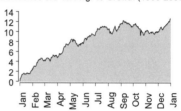

DowJones 3rd Yr. Avg. % Growth (1903-2007)

occurred in 1937. Since 1901 the third year of the cycle has only been negative five times.

This is in comparison to the average of the other years of the election cycle where the S&P 500 has returned 5.0% in the first year, 2.8% in the second year and 7.5% in the fourth year.

Given the persistent weak state of the economy, large government deficits and the economic crisis, the current President will have his work cut out for him. Obama has endeavored to spend his way out of the recession and if history of the Presidential Cycle is any guide, the spending trend will continue. In the past, the government spending has helped to stimulate the economy and the stock market. The difference this time is that the government has record high deficits and investors are starting to worry about the long-term economic impact. Nevertheless, the third year of the cycle points to a higher finish.

4 Year President Cycle- Dow Jones

	President	1st Year	2nd Year	3rd Year	4th Year
1901	McKinley (R)	-8.7 %	-0.4 %	-23.6 %	41.7 %
1905	T. Roosevelt (R)	38.2	-1.9	-37.7	46.6
1909	Taft (R)	15.0	-17.9	0.4	7.6
1913	Wilson (D)	-10.3	-30.7	81.7	-4.2
1917	Wilson (D)	-21.7	10.5	30.5	-32.9
1921	Harding (R)	12.7	21.7	-3.3	26.2
1925	Coolidge (R)	30.0	0.3	28.8	48.2
1929	Hoover (R)	-17.2	-33.8	-52.7	-23.1
1933	Roosevelt (R)	66.8	4.1	38.6	24.8
1937	Roosevelt (R)	-32.8	28.0	-3.0	-12.7
1941	Roosevelt (R)	-15.3	7.6	13.8	12.1
1945	Roosevelt (R)	26.7	-8.1	2.3	-2.2
1949	Truman (D)	12.9	17.6	14.4	8.4
1953	Eisenhower (R)	-3.8	44.0	20.8	2.3
1957	Eisenhower (R)	-12.8	34.0	16.4	-9.3
1961	Kennedy (D)	18.7	-10.8	17.0	14.6
1965	Johnson (D)	10.9	-18.9	15.2	4.3
1969	Nixon (R)	-15.2	4.8	6.1	14.6
1973	Nixon (R)	-16.6	-27.6	38.3	17.9
1977	Carter (D)	-17.3	-3.2	4.2	14.9
1981	Reagan (R)	-9.2	19.6	20.3	-3.7
1985	Reagan (R)	27.7	22.6	2.3	11.9
1989	G. H. Bush (R)	27.0	-4.3	20.3	4.2
1993	Clinton (D)	13.7	2.1	33.5	26.0
1997	Clinton (D)	22.6	16.1	25.2	-6.2
2001	G.W. Bush (R)	-7.1	-16.8	25.3	3.1
2005	G.W. Bush (R)	-0.6	16.3	6.4	-33.8
	Average Return	5.0	2.8	12.6	7.5
	% of Years Positive	48 %	56 %	82 %	67 %

(i) *The Presidential Cycle is closely aligned with the well known and closely followed 4 Year Cycle. In this cycle the market tends to bottom approximately every four years. The bottom is typically predicted to occur towards the end of the 2nd year in the Presidential Cycle at the time of mid-term elections.*

28 MONDAY	000 / 306	**1** TUESDAY	030 / 305

2 WEDNESDAY	029 / 304	**3** THURSDAY	028 / 303

4 FRIDAY			027/ 302

WEEK 09

Market Indices & Rates
Weekly Values**

Stock Markets	2009	2010
Dow	7,196	10,443
S&P500	754	1,123
Nasdaq	1,405	2,291
TSX	7,950	11,842
FTSE	3,852	5,510
DAX	3,893	5,796
Nikkei	7,426	10,232
Hang Seng	12,937	20,841

Commodities	2009	2010
Oil	41.7	80.2
Gold	967.4	1129.3

Bond Yields	2009	2010
USA 5 Yr Treasury	1.97	2.29
USA 10 Yr T	2.91	3.63
USA 20 Yr T	3.87	4.43
Moody's Aaa	5.31	5.24
Moody's Baa	8.13	6.26
CAN 5 Yr T	2.07	2.61
CAN 10 Yr T	2.99	3.42

Money Market	2009	2010
USA Fed Funds	0.25	0.25
USA 3 Mo T-B	0.29	0.14
CAN tgt overnight rate	1.00	0.25
CAN 3 Mo T-B	0.65	0.18

Foreign Exchange	2009	2010
USD/EUR	1.28	1.36
USD/GBP	1.44	1.50
CAN/USD	1.25	1.04
JPY/USD	96.57	89.18

2nd Year Presidential Cycle Strategy Performance

Avg. 2nd Year Election Cycle S&P 500 (1901-2008)

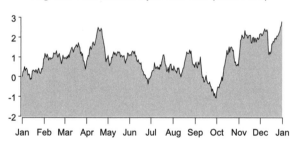

The second year of the Presidential Cycle has typically been the worst year of the four year cycle. So far 2010 has had a similar pattern as the average second year of the cycle.

The second year of the Presidential Cycle has averaged a peak in April, and 2010 has followed the same pattern. The good news is that on average in the second year, the market has bottomed at the end of September or beginning of October and started a rally that followed through to the next year.

MARCH

M	T	W	T	F	S	S
	1	2	3	4	5	6
7	8	9	10	11	12	13
14	15	16	17	18	19	20
21	22	23	24	25	26	27
28	29	30	31			

APRIL

M	T	W	T	F	S	S
				1	2	3
4	5	6	7	8	9	10
11	12	13	14	15	16	17
18	19	20	21	22	23	24
25	26	27	28	29	30	

MAY

M	T	W	T	F	S	S
						1
2	3	4	5	6	7	8
9	10	11	12	13	14	15
16	17	18	19	20	21	22
23	24	25	26	27	28	29
30	31					

** Weekly avg closing values- except Fed Funds & CAN overnight tgt rate weekly closing values.

MARCH

	MONDAY	TUESDAY	WEDNESDAY
WEEK 09	28	1 30	2 29
WEEK 10	7 24	8 23	9 22
WEEK 11	14 17	15 16	16 15
WEEK 12	21 10	22 9	23 8
WEEK 13	28 3	29 2	30 1

THURSDAY		FRIDAY	
3	28	**4**	27
10	21	**11**	20
17	14	**18**	13
24	7	**25**	6
31		1	

APRIL

M	T	W	T	F	S	S
				1	2	3
4	5	6	7	8	9	10
11	12	13	14	15	16	17
18	19	20	21	22	23	24
25	26	27	28	29	30	

MAY

M	T	W	T	F	S	S
						1
2	3	4	5	6	7	8
9	10	11	12	13	14	15
16	17	18	19	20	21	22
23	24	25	26	27	28	29
30	31					

JUNE

M	T	W	T	F	S	S
		1	2	3	4	5
6	7	8	9	10	11	12
13	14	15	16	17	18	19
20	21	22	23	24	25	26
27	28	29	30			

JULY

M	T	W	T	F	S	S
				1	2	3
4	5	6	7	8	9	10
11	12	13	14	15	16	17
18	19	20	21	22	23	24
25	26	27	28	29	30	31

MARCH
S U M M A R Y

STRATEGIES	PAGE

STRATEGIES STARTING

None

STRATEGIES FINISHING

Small Cap (Small Company) Effect — 149

S&P500 Cumulative Daily Gains for Avg Month 1950 to 2010

Prob. of Daily Gain

♦ In 2010 March was a very strong month for the S&P 500 as it returned 5.9% ♦ According to the Thackray Sector Thermometer the top sectors for March 2010 should have been Energy, Consumer Discretionary and Industrials. The top sectors ended up being Industrials, Consumer Discretionary and Financials, with all three sectors each returning more than 7%. ♦ Investors should note that although information technology has on average been positive since 1990 in the month of March, it can peak early in the month.

BEST / WORST MARCH BROAD MKTS. 2001-2010

BEST MARCH MARKETS
- ♦ Nasdaq (2009) 10.9%
- ♦ Russell 3000 Gr (2009) 8.7%
- ♦ Russell 2000 (2009) 8.7%

WORST MARCH MARKETS
- ♦ Nasdaq (2001) -14.5%
- ♦ Russell 3000 Gr (2001) -10.8%
- ♦ Russell 1000 (2001) -6.7%

Index Values End of Month

	2001	2002	2003	2004	2005	2006	2007	2008	2009	2010
Dow	9,879	10,404	7,992	10,358	10,504	11,109	12,354	12,263	7,609	10,857
S&P 500	1,160	1,147	848	1,126	1,181	1,295	1,421	1,323	798	1,169
Nasdaq	1,840	1,845	1,341	1,994	1,999	2,340	2,422	2,279	1,529	2,398
TSX	7,608	7,851	6,343	8,586	9,612	12,111	13,166	13,350	8,720	12,038
Russell 1000	1,173	1,167	866	1,160	1,222	1,359	1,492	1,385	834	1,238
Russell 2000	1,120	1,259	906	1,467	1,529	1,902	1,990	1,710	1,051	1,687
Russell 3000 Growth	1,970	1,928	1,391	1,847	1,850	2,094	2,206	2,149	1,387	2,054
Russell 3000 Value	2,076	2,150	1,620	2,252	2,481	2,765	3,137	2,733	1,529	2,304

Percent Gain for March

	2001	2002	2003	2004	2005	2006	2007	2008	2009	2010
Dow	-5.9	2.9	1.3	-2.1	-2.4	1.1	0.7	0.0	7.7	5.1
S&P 500	-6.4	3.7	0.8	-1.6	-1.9	1.1	1.0	-0.6	8.5	5.9
Nasdaq	-14.5	6.6	0.3	-1.8	-2.6	2.6	0.2	0.3	10.9	7.1
TSX	-5.8	2.8	-3.2	-2.3	-0.6	3.6	0.9	-1.7	7.4	3.5
Russell 1000	-6.7	4.0	0.9	-1.5	-1.7	1.3	0.9	-0.8	8.5	6.0
Russell 2000	-5.0	7.9	1.1	0.8	-3.0	4.7	0.9	0.3	8.7	8.0
Russell 3000 Growth	-10.8	3.7	1.7	-1.8	-2.1	1.7	0.5	-0.7	8.7	5.8
Russell 3000 Value	-3.5	4.8	0.0	-0.9	-1.6	1.5	1.4	-0.8	8.3	6.5

March Market Avg. Performance 2001 to 2010 [(1)]

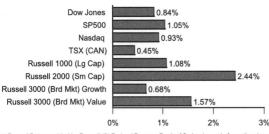

Dow Jones	0.84%	
SP500	1.05%	
Nasdaq	0.93%	
TSX (CAN)	0.45%	
Russell 1000 (Lg Cap)	1.08%	
Russell 2000 (Sm Cap)	2.44%	
Russell 3000 (Brd Mkt) Growth	0.68%	
Russell 3000 (Brd Mkt) Value	1.57%	

Interest Corner Mar[(2)]

	Fed Funds % [(3)]	3 Mo. T-Bill % [(4)]	10 Yr % [(5)]	20 Yr % [(6)]
2010	0.25	0.16	3.84	4.55
2009	0.25	0.21	2.71	3.61
2008	2.25	1.38	3.45	4.30
2007	5.25	5.04	4.65	4.92
2006	4.75	4.63	4.86	5.07

(1) Russell Data provided by Russell (2) Federal Reserve Bank of St. Louis- end of month values (3) Target rate set by FOMC (4)(5)(6) Constant yield maturities.

THACKRAY SECTOR THERMOMETER

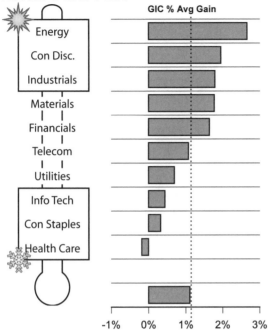

GIC[2] % Avg Gain	Fq % Gain >S&P 500	SP GIC SECTOR 1990-2009[1]
2.7 %	65 %	Energy
1.9	75	Consumer Discretionary
1.8	70	Industrials
1.8	50	Materials
1.6	55	Financials
1.1	60	Telecom
0.7	50	Utilities
0.4	40	Information Technology
0.3	50	Consumer Staples
-0.2 %	25 %	Health Care
1.1 %	N/A %	S&P 500

Sector Commentary

♦ In March it is the Energy sector that is on top again. This is the seasonal sweet spot for the sector (see *Oil-Winter/Spring Effect*). ♦ Consumer Discretionary is once again close to the top, as the positive beginning of the year forecasts for consumer spending still have an uplifting affect. ♦ Industrials which usually track the market closely, are for the second month in a row a solid performing sector. ♦ Although both Materials and Financials have fallen down the list, their performance is still solid. As a result they are still on the favored list. ♦ The defensive Consumer Staples sector falls from the favored list and turns in a slightly positive performance and beats the market half of the time. ♦ In 2010 the Industrials sector was the best performing sector, producing a gain of 8.8%.

Sub-Sector Commentary

♦ Retail is usually strong in March and Biotech weak. ♦ In March 2010 Retail turned in a reasonably good performance producing a gain of 6.7%, placing it above the S&P 500 return for the month of 5.9% ♦ Biotech, as expected, turned in a very weak performance, producing a gain of 0.8%.

SELECTED SUB-SECTORS 1990-2009[3]		
3.7 %	75 %	Retail
3.5	65	Airlines
2.5	60	Integrated Oil & Gas
2.0	70	Transportation
1.5	65	Software & Services
1.4	35	Insurance
1.2	40	Semiconductor (SOX) 95-2009
1.1	50	Auto & Components
0.9	40	Metals & Mining
0.9	45	Banks
0.3	31	Agriculture Products (94-2009)
0.1	40	Gold (XAU)
0.0	25	Pharmaceuticals
-1.2	29	Biotech (93-2009)

(1) Sector data provided by Standard and Poors (2) GIC is short form for Global Industry Classification (3) Sub Sector data provided by Standard and Poors, except where marked by symbol.

There are many ways to invest in the markets. A lot of money managers define their investment approach as either "growth" or "value."

> Value stocks generally have low prices relative to their book values and/or low price to earnings ratios.
>
> Growth stocks generally have high prices relative to their book values and/or high price to earnings ratios.

There have been many studies over time about which style of investing, value or growth, produces better returns with less risk, and in which type of economic environment. The scope of this book is concerned with the annual cycle of outperformance.

On an annual basis, growth tends to outperform value during the last three months of the year and value stocks tend to outperform for the first four months.

In the summer months there is not a clear trend between growth and value investment styles, except for the month of June when growth stocks outperform.

Compared with value stocks, growth stocks tend to be better known companies with greater earnings stability. As a result, investors are willing to pay a higher premium for growth stocks.

At the beginning of the year, almost every analyst on Wall Street calls for a market return between 8% and 12%. In this positive environment value stocks tend to outperform.

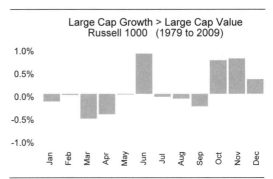

Large Cap Growth > Large Cap Value
Russell 1000 (1979 to 2009)

Large Cap Growth (Russell 1000 Growth) vs.
Large Cap Value (Russell 1000 Value)

	Jan. to Apr. (Value > Growth)		
	Oct. to Dec. (Growth > Value)		

	Jan to Apr % Gain			Oct to Dec % Gain		
Year	Value	- Growth	= Diff	Growth	- Value	= Diff
1979	7.9	6.0	1.9	3.7	-4.2	7.9
1980	-2.8	-2.2	-0.7	10.6	4.7	5.9
1981	2.9	-6.6	9.5	8.0	4.1	4.0
1982	-5.1	-7.0	2.0	20.3	14.2	6.1
1983	17.7	15.6	2.1	-3.3	0.1	-3.4
1984	-1.7	-8.2	6.6	0.4	1.1	-0.7
1985	8.8	7.6	1.2	18.4	13.3	5.1
1986	9.6	15.0	-5.4	4.4	2.6	1.8
1987	13.6	20.9	-7.3	-23.9	-22.5	-1.4
1988	10.0	2.5	7.5	2.2	1.1	1.1
1989	10.3	12.6	-2.3	2.1	-1.4	3.4
1990	-7.9	-5.6	-2.3	10.2	6.7	3.4
1991	12.4	16.6	-4.2	12.3	3.4	8.9
1992	4.3	-4.9	9.1	6.4	4.9	1.5
1993	7.2	-5.4	12.6	3.4	-1.1	4.4
1994	-2.7	-4.5	1.8	0.3	-2.6	2.9
1995	11.6	11.4	0.3	4.2	5.8	-1.6
1996	5.1	7.7	-2.6	5.7	9.2	-3.5
1997	6.0	6.8	-0.8	1.3	3.9	-2.6
1998	11.6	16.4	-4.8	26.5	16.0	10.5
1999	10.2	6.2	4.0	25.0	4.9	20.1
2000	-1.4	1.9	-3.2	-21.4	3.1	-24.5
2001	-1.8	-11.0	9.2	14.9	6.8	8.1
2002	-0.1	-10.7	10.6	6.8	8.4	-1.6
2003	2.6	5.9	-3.2	10.1	13.4	-3.4
2004	-0.2	-0.7	0.4	8.9	9.7	0.8
2005	-2.5	-6.2	3.8	2.7	0.6	2.1
2006	7.8	2.6	5.2	5.6	7.3	-1.7
2007	4.2	5.6	-1.4	-1.1	-6.5	5.4
2008	-5.1	-5.8	0.7	-23.2	-23.0	-0.2
2009	-8.9	4.5	-13.4	7.5	3.6	3.9
Avg.	4.0	2.8	1.2	4.8	2.8	2.0

(i) *Russell 1000 Growth: Growth companies from the Russell 1000 index. Russell 1000 Value: Value companies from the Russell 1000 index.*
For more information on the Russell indexes, see www.russell.com.

7 MONDAY	024 / 299

8 TUESDAY	023 / 298

9 WEDNESDAY	022 / 297

10 THURSDAY	021 / 296

11 FRIDAY	020 / 295

WEEK 10

Market Indices & Rates
Weekly Values**

Stock Markets	2009	2010
Dow	6,717	10,584
S&P500	695	1,145
Nasdaq	1,318	2,354
TSX	7,671	11,967
FTSE	3,569	5,619
DAX	3,731	5,914
Nikkei	7,281	10,627
Hang Seng	12,163	21,210

Commodities	2009	2010
Oil	43.3	81.8
Gold	921.7	1114.5

Bond Yields	2009	2010
USA 5 Yr Treasury	1.87	2.39
USA 10 Yr T	2.90	3.72
USA 20 Yr T	3.85	4.51
Moody's Aaa	5.40	5.28
Moody's Baa	8.23	6.30
CAN 5 Yr T	1.87	2.81
CAN 10 Yr T	2.98	3.52

Money Market	2009	2010
USA Fed Funds	0.25	0.25
USA 3 Mo T-B	0.24	0.16
CAN tgt overnight rate	0.50	0.25
CAN 3 Mo T-B	0.45	0.20

Foreign Exchange	2009	2010
USD/EUR	1.26	1.36
USD/GBP	1.41	1.50
CAN/USD	1.29	1.03
JPY/USD	98.37	90.33

MARCH

M	T	W	T	F	S	S
	1	2	3	4	5	6
7	8	9	10	11	12	13
14	15	16	17	18	19	20
21	22	23	24	25	26	27
28	29	30	31			

APRIL

M	T	W	T	F	S	S
				1	2	3
4	5	6	7	8	9	10
11	12	13	14	15	16	17
18	19	20	21	22	23	24
25	26	27	28	29	30	

MAY

M	T	W	T	F	S	S
						1
2	3	4	5	6	7	8
9	10	11	12	13	14	15
16	17	18	19	20	21	22
23	24	25	26	27	28	29
30	31					

2009 Strategy Performance

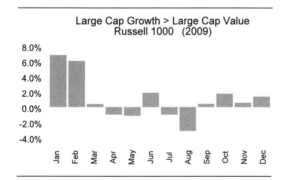

Large Cap Growth > Large Cap Value
Russell 1000 (2009)

As the market fell apart at the beginning of 2009, investors favored stocks with stability and earnings potential, and as a result favored the growth part of the market and shunned the value part. With the market putting in a bottom at the beginning of March, the damage had already been done and the value sector under performed the growth sector. In the last few months of the year the growth sector outperformed the value sector, as predicted by the strategy, but the performance was not enough to bring the total strategy gain into positive territory.

** Weekly avg closing values- except Fed Funds & CAN overnight tgt rate weekly closing values.

WITCHES' HANGOVER
Day After Witching Day – Worst Day of the Month

Double, double toil and trouble;
Fire burn and cauldron bubble.
(Shakespeare, *Macbeth*, Act IV, Scene 1)

Looking for a negative day to establish a long position, or even short the market? In our book <u>Time In Time Out, Outsmart the Market Using Calendar Investment Strategies</u>, Bruce Lindsay and I coined the term "Witches' Hangover" (WH) to describe the most negative day of the month. It is aptly coined because it is the trading day after Witching Day (WD).

WH avg. gain -0.1% & negative 61% of the time

Witches' Hangover (WH) S&P 500
Days Before & After Avg. 1974 to 2009

Witching Day (WD), the third Friday of every month, has a track record of volatility and negative performance. This is the day that stock options and futures expire.

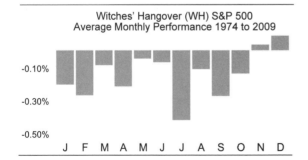

Witches' Hangover (WH) S&P 500
Average Monthly Performance 1974 to 2009

Although investors have been led to believe that Witching Day is the worst day of the month, Witches' Hangover has produced a bigger negative performance. This may be a result of investors, after a Friday of volatility and poor performance, suffering a stock market hango-

Daily Avg. Gains for WD & WH S&P 500 1974 to 2009 Negative		
	WD	WH
1974	-0.54 %	-0.64 %
1975	-0.13	-0.23
1976	-0.01	0.03
1977	-0.07	-0.26
1978	-0.35	-0.04
1979	-0.16	0.03
1980	-0.14	-0.13
1981	0.16	-0.19
1982	0.32	0.24
1983	-0.09	-0.07
1984	-0.33	-0.20
1985	0.04	0.27
1986	0.23	0.07
1987	-0.02	-1.81
1988	0.62	-0.27
1989	0.22	-0.56
1990	0.02	-0.69
1991	-0.11	-0.33
1992	0.15	-0.24
1993	-0.13	-0.12
1994	-0.19	-0.34
1995	-0.02	0.08
1996	0.27	0.09
1997	-0.46	0.10
1998	0.37	0.55
1999	0.06	0.07
2000	-0.81	-0.44
2001	-0.72	0.45
2002	-0.26	-0.55
2003	0.30	-0.86
2004	-0.03	-0.12
2005	-0.05	-0.08
2006	-0.13	-0.02
2007	0.28	0.00
2008	1.03	0.36
2009	0.77	0.68
Avg.	0.00 %	-0.14 %

ver and selling into the market on the Monday. In the graph "Witches' Hangover (WH) - Days Before & After Avg" the average daily performance of Witches' Hangover is marked WH and is the darker column. Witching Day (WD) is the previous day. WH is clearly the worst day. Together they make a wicked pair.

Witches' Hangover is a one day strategy and the average investor should not make investment portfolio decisions on one day performances.

14 MONDAY	017 / 292	**15** TUESDAY	016 / 291

16 WEDNESDAY	015 / 290	**17** THURSDAY	014 / 289

18 FRIDAY 013 / 288

WEEK 11

Market Indices & Rates
Weekly Values**

Stock Markets	2009	2010
Dow	6,960	10,717
S&P500	725	1,160
Nasdaq	1,371	2,379
TSX	8,009	12,037
FTSE	3,683	5,630
DAX	3,881	5,979
Nikkei	7,257	10,778
Hang Seng	11,899	21,238

Commodities	2009	2010
Oil	45.7	81.5
Gold	915.6	1115.8

Bond Yields	2009	2010
USA 5 Yr Treasury	1.93	2.42
USA 10 Yr T	2.92	3.68
USA 20 Yr T	3.86	4.43
Moody's Aaa	5.49	5.21
Moody's Baa	8.40	6.21
CAN 5 Yr T	1.89	2.79
CAN 10 Yr T	2.93	3.47

Money Market	2009	2010
USA Fed Funds	0.25	0.25
USA 3 Mo T-B	0.22	0.16
CAN tgt overnight rate	0.50	0.25
CAN 3 Mo T-B	0.42	0.22

Foreign Exchange	2009	2010
USD/EUR	1.27	1.37
USD/GBP	1.39	1.52
CAN/USD	1.29	1.02
JPY/USD	98.02	90.52

2009 Strategy Performance

Witches' Hangover Performance by Month S&P 500 (2009)

Although the day after Witching day had a positive average performance for 2009, buried in the average number is some large moves up and down. January and February produced two large negative results and then March produced an extremely large positive result. The March result was just a mere two weeks after the March bottom of the market.

Although the day after Witching day is the most negative day of the month, it is important for investors to remember that large macro trends can overwhelm the strength of the strategy.

MARCH

M	T	W	T	F	S	S
	1	2	3	4	5	6
7	8	9	10	11	12	13
14	15	16	17	18	19	20
21	22	23	24	25	26	27
28	29	30	31			

APRIL

M	T	W	T	F	S	S
				1	2	3
4	5	6	7	8	9	10
11	12	13	14	15	16	17
18	19	20	21	22	23	24
25	26	27	28	29	30	

MAY

M	T	W	T	F	S	S
						1
2	3	4	5	6	7	8
9	10	11	12	13	14	15
16	17	18	19	20	21	22
23	24	25	26	27	28	29
30	31					

** Weekly avg closing values- except Fed Funds & CAN overnight tgt rate weekly closing values.

SUPER SEVEN DAYS
7 Best Days of the Month

The end of the month tends to be an excellent time to invest: portfolio managers "window dress" (adjust their portfolios to look good for month end reports), investors stop procrastinating and invest their extra cash, and brokers try to increase their commissions by investing their client's extra cash.

From 1950 to 2009
All 7 days better
than market average

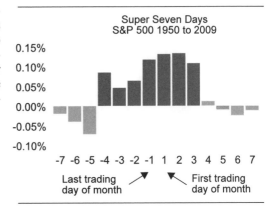

Super Seven Days
S&P 500 1950 to 2009

Last trading day of month → ↖ First trading day of month

All of these factors tend to produce above average returns for the market.

The above graph illustrates the strength of the Super Seven days. The Super Seven days are the last four trading days of the month and the first three of the next month represented by the dark columns from day -4 to day 3. All of the Super Seven days have daily average gains above the daily market average gain of 0.03% (since 1950).

% Gain Super Seven Day Period From 2000 to 2009

	2000	2001	2002	2003	2004	2005	2006	2007	2008	2009	Avg.
Jan	1.1 %	-0.2%	-3.8 %	-1.1 %	-2.5 %	1.8 %	-0.1 %	1.6 %	-4.5	-0.5	-0.8 %
Feb	3.6	-0.9	5.2	-0.3	0.9	2.2	-0.4	-5.6	-2.8	4.1	-0.2
Mar	-2.4	-4.3	-2.0	0.2	3.7	0.9	0.8	0.1	1.2	3.5	0.2
Apr	-1.0	3.2	-1.8	1.7	-1.2	1.2	0.0	1.5	1.3	4.3	0.9
May	4.9	-0.7	-3.1	5.7	1.9	0.2	0.5	1.6	0.1	5.0	1.6
Jun	0.1	0.1	-3.6	0.2	-2.1	0.3	1.9	1.8	-3.9	-0.2	-0.5
Jul	-1.5	2.0	-0.5	-3.3	1.3	1.3	0.9	-5.6	2.2	2.1	-0.1
Aug	-0.9	-6.2	-7.3	3.4	0.8	1.7	0.4	0.8	-2.4	-2.4	-1.2
Sep	-0.3	6.9	0.0	2.0	2.9	-1.6	1.8	1.4	-7.3	-1.0	0.5
Oct	4.5	0.2	2.0	2.0	4.4	2.0	-1.3	-0.8	12.2	-1.9	2.3
Nov	2.6	1.1	-2.6	2.8	1.2	-0.3	1.0	5.5	8.8	-0.6	2.0
Dec	2.1	2.4	4.1	2.7	-1.8	0.4	-0.1	-5.7	7.7	0.9	1.3
Avg.	1.1	0.3	-1.1	1.3	0.8	0.8	0.0	0.0	1.1	0.4	0.5

Although the Super Seven has done extremely well, there have been two trouble spots of negative performance. First, in 1998 when the *Asian Financial Flu* currency crisis struck the market, the market had three separate declines of more than 10%, which in turn resulted in three negative performances of the Super Seven greater than 5% at month ends.

⚠ *Historically it has been best not to use the Super Seven for July and August. Both of these months have negative average performances and have been negative more often than positive over the last ten years.*

The months affected were July, August and September. Second, 2002 was a disastrous year for the market. The first major decline started on March 12 and pushed the market down more than 30%. The second major decline started on August 22 and pushed the market down more than 15%. Both of these declines had a large effect on the results of the Super Seven for the year. Despite these negative periods, the Super Seven has outperformed the broad market over the last ten years.

21 MONDAY 010 / 285

22 TUESDAY 009 / 284

23 WEDNESDAY 008 / 283

24 THURSDAY 007 / 282

25 FRIDAY 006 / 281

WEEK 12

Market Indices & Rates
Weekly Values**

Stock Markets	2009	2010
Dow	7,356	10,840
S&P500	776	1,168
Nasdaq	1,460	2,400
TSX	8,554	11,978
FTSE	3,837	5,685
DAX	4,028	6,059
Nikkei	7,893	10,854
Hang Seng	12,987	20,952

Commodities	2009	2010
Oil	49.5	80.7
Gold	927.8	1095.8

Bond Yields	2009	2010
USA 5 Yr Treasury	1.75	2.55
USA 10 Yr T	2.75	3.79
USA 20 Yr T	3.78	4.53
Moody's Aaa	5.62	5.30
Moody's Baa	8.50	6.28
CAN 5 Yr T	1.79	2.84
CAN 10 Yr T	2.79	3.51

Money Market	2009	2010
USA Fed Funds	0.25	0.25
USA 3 Mo T-B	0.22	0.14
CAN tgt overnight rate	0.50	0.25
CAN 3 Mo T-B	0.40	0.24

Foreign Exchange	2009	2010
USD/EUR	1.32	1.34
USD/GBP	1.42	1.50
CAN/USD	1.26	1.02
JPY/USD	97.40	91.31

MARCH

M	T	W	T	F	S	S
	1	2	3	4	5	6
7	8	9	10	11	12	13
14	15	16	17	18	19	20
21	22	23	24	25	26	27
28	29	30	31			

APRIL

M	T	W	T	F	S	S
			1	2	3	
4	5	6	7	8	9	10
11	12	13	14	15	16	17
18	19	20	21	22	23	24
25	26	27	28	29	30	

MAY

M	T	W	T	F	S	S
						1
2	3	4	5	6	7	8
9	10	11	12	13	14	15
16	17	18	19	20	21	22
23	24	25	26	27	28	29
30	31					

2009 Strategy Performance

Super Seven Days By Month S&P 500 (2009)

The Super Seven strategy was positive in 2009 mainly as a result of the gains in March, April and May. Most of the gains for the strategy were made in the first few days of the month, rather than the last few days.

In the past ten years, seven years were positive, two years returned zero percent and one year produced a loss. The 2009 Super Seven days were slightly below the average of Super Seven gains over the last ten years.

** Weekly avg closing values- except Fed Funds & CAN overnight tgt rate weekly closing values.

CANADIANS GIVE 3 CHEERS FOR AMERICAN HOLIDAYS

When I used to work on the retail side of the investment business I was always amazed at how often the Canadian market increased on American holidays, when the Canadian stock market was open and the American market was closed.

The holiday always had light volume, tended not to have large increases or decreases, but nevertheless usually ended the day with a gain.

1% average gain from 1977 to 2009 and 94% of the time positive

How the trade works

For the three big holidays in the United States that do not exist in Canada (Memorial, Independence and Thanksgiving Days), buy at the end of the market day before the holiday (TSX Composite) and sell at the end of the U.S. holiday when the U.S markets are closed.

For U.S. investors to take advantage of this trade they must have access to the TSX Composite. Unfortunately, as of the current time SEC regulations do not allow Americans to purchase foreign ETFs.

Generally, markets perform well around most major American holidays, hence the trading strategies for American holidays included in this book.

The main reason for the strong performance around these holidays is a lack of institutional involvement in the markets, allowing bullish retail investors to push up the markets.

On the actual holidays, there are no economic news releases in America and very seldom is there anything released in Canada of significance. During market hours, without any influences the market tends to float, preferring to wait until the next day before making any significant moves.

Despite this laxidasical action during the day, the TSX Comp tends to end the day on a gain. This is true for the three major holidays that are covered in this book: Memorial, Independence and Thanksgiving Day.

From a theoretical perspective a lot of the gain that is captured on the U.S. holiday is realized on the next day that the markets are open in the United States. This does not invalidate the *Canadians Give 3 Cheers* trade – it presents more alternatives for the astute investor.

For example, an investor can allocate a portion of money to a standard American holiday trade and another portion to the Canadian version. By spreading out the exit days the overall risk in the trade is reduced.

TSX Comp
Gain 1977-2009   Positive

	Memorial	Independence	Thanksgiving	Compound Growth
1977	0.10 %	-0.08 %	0.61 %	0.63 %
1978	-0.05	-0.16	0.57	0.36
1979	1.11	0.23	0.58	1.93
1980	1.64	0.76	0.89	3.32
1981	0.51	-0.15	1.03	1.40
1982	-0.18	-0.01	0.35	0.17
1983	0.29	0.53	0.15	0.97
1984	0.86	-0.11	0.73	1.48
1985	0.61	0.31	0.31	1.24
1986	0.23	-0.02	0.22	0.44
1987	-0.11	1.08	1.57	2.55
1988	0.44	0.08	0.58	1.11
1989	0.10	-0.12	-0.11	-0.13
1990	0.11	0.43	0.02	0.57
1991	0.02	0.18	-0.09	0.11
1992	-0.06	0.35	0.36	0.65
1993	0.42	-0.18	0.14	0.38
1994	-0.19	0.70	0.91	1.43
1995	0.14	0.25	0.29	0.68
1996	0.11	0.25	0.54	0.90
1997	1.08	-0.04	-0.85	0.18
1998	0.56	0.18	0.51	1.25
1999	0.57	1.63	1.14	3.39
2000	0.43	1.04	0.91	2.40
2001	-0.02	-0.23	0.70	0.45
2002	-0.01	0.08	0.38	0.45
2003	0.03	0.03	0.26	0.31
2004	0.84	-0.02	0.55	1.39
2005	0.56	0.39	1.48	2.45
2006	0.70	1.04	0.70	2.46
2007	0.35	-0.03	0.76	1.08
2008	0.24	-0.94	1.28	0.56
2009	0.76	0.36	-1.29	-0.18
Avg	0.37 %	0.24 %	0.49 %	1.10 %
Fq > 0	79 %	61 %	88 %	94 %

28 MONDAY   003 / 278   **29** TUESDAY   002 / 277

30 WEDNESDAY   001 / 276   **31** THURSDAY   000 / 275

1 FRIDAY   029 / 274

WEEK 13

Market Indices & Rates
Weekly Values**

Stock Markets	2009	2010
Dow	7,777	10,897
S&P500	818	1,174
Nasdaq	1,547	2,404
TSX	8,884	12,066
FTSE	3,918	5,702
DAX	4,210	6,172
Nikkei	8,489	11,141
Hang Seng	13,842	21,347

Commodities	2009	2010
Oil	53.1	83.3
Gold	932.9	1113.4

Bond Yields	2009	2010
USA 5 Yr Treasury	1.76	2.60
USA 10 Yr T	2.74	3.89
USA 20 Yr T	3.69	4.60
Moody's Aaa	5.51	5.36
Moody's Baa	8.53	6.35
CAN 5 Yr T	1.88	2.90
CAN 10 Yr T	2.89	3.57

Money Market	2009	2010
USA Fed Funds	0.25	0.25
USA 3 Mo T-B	0.18	0.16
CAN tgt overnight rate	0.50	0.25
CAN 3 Mo T-B	0.38	0.28

Foreign Exchange	2009	2010
USD/EUR	1.35	1.35
USD/GBP	1.45	1.51
CAN/USD	1.23	1.02
JPY/USD	97.72	93.30

APRIL

M	T	W	T	F	S	S
				1	2	3
4	5	6	7	8	9	10
11	12	13	14	15	16	17
18	19	20	21	22	23	24
25	26	27	28	29	30	

MAY

M	T	W	T	F	S	S
						1
2	3	4	5	6	7	8
9	10	11	12	13	14	15
16	17	18	19	20	21	22
23	24	25	26	27	28	29
30	31					

JUNE

M	T	W	T	F	S	S
	1	2	3	4	5	
6	7	8	9	10	11	12
13	14	15	16	17	18	19
20	21	22	23	24	25	26
27	28	29	30			

2009 Strategy Performance

Holiday Strategy S&P/TSX Comp (2009)

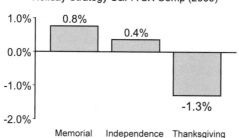

In 2009, for both Memorial Day and Independence Day the *Canadians Give 3 Cheers* strategy produced positive results. Thanksgiving was uncharacteristically negative.

The Thanksgiving loss was greater than the gains of the other two holidays, producing a loss for the overall strategy. Despite the loss in 2009 the strategy has historically had a good success rate.

** Weekly avg closing values- except Fed Funds & CAN overnight tgt rate weekly closing values.

APRIL

WEEK 13	28	29	30
WEEK 14	**4** 26	**5** 25	**6** 24
WEEK 15	**11** 19	**12** 18	**13** 17
WEEK 16	**18** 12	**19** 11	**20** 10
WEEK 17	**25** 5	**26** 4	**27** 3

THURSDAY	FRIDAY
31	**1** 29
7 23	**8** 22
14 16	**15** 15
21 9	**22** 8
	USA Market Closed- Good Friday
	CAN Market Closed- Good Friday
28 2	**29** 1

MAY

M	T	W	T	F	S	S
						1
2	3	4	5	6	7	8
9	10	11	12	13	14	15
16	17	18	19	20	21	22
23	24	25	26	27	28	29
30	31					

JUNE

M	T	W	T	F	S	S
		1	2	3	4	5
6	7	8	9	10	11	12
13	14	15	16	17	18	19
20	21	22	23	24	25	26
27	28	29	30			

JULY

M	T	W	T	F	S	S
				1	2	3
4	5	6	7	8	9	10
11	12	13	14	15	16	17
18	19	20	21	22	23	24
25	26	27	28	29	30	31

AUGUST

M	T	W	T	F	S	S
1	2	3	4	5	6	7
8	9	10	11	12	13	14
15	16	17	18	19	20	21
22	23	24	25	26	27	28
29	30	31				

APRIL
S U M M A R Y

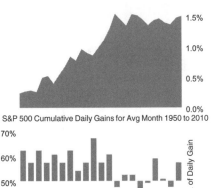

S&P 500 Cumulative Daily Gains for Avg Month 1950 to 2010

STRATEGIES	PAGE
STRATEGIES STARTING	
Oil – Equipment and Services	19
18 Day Earnings Month Effect	43
Consumer Switch - Sell Con. Disc. - Buy Con Staples	45
1/2 and 1/2	47
Canadian Dollar Strong April	49
STRATEGIES FINISHING	
Retail – Post Holiday Bargain	9
Oil – Exploration and Production	19
18 Day Earnings Month Effect	43
1/2 and 1/2	47
Canadian Dollar Strong April	49
Canadian Banks – In - Out - In Again	115
Consumer Switch - Sell Con. Staples. - Buy Con. Disc.	125
Financial Year End Clean Up	155

BEST / WORST APRIL BROAD MKTS. 2001-2010

BEST APRIL MARKETS
- Russell 2000 (2009) 15.3%
- Nasdaq (2001) 15.0%
- Russell 3000 Gr (2001) 12.6%

WORST APRIL MARKETS
- Nasdaq (2002) -8.5%
- Russell 3000 Gr (2002) -7.8%
- S&P500 (2002) -6.1%

♦ April is always an interesting time in the markets, as the dynamics within the month present interesting opportunities. ♦ Historically, mid-month (last date to file taxes) tends to be an inflection point with a lot of sectors of the market reversing their trends. ♦ First, the broad market tends to peak. ♦ Second, short-term T-Bill rates tend to bottom. ♦ Third, technology stocks tend to bottom before a short-term up-trend.

Index Values End of Month

	2001	2002	2003	2004	2005	2006	2007	2008	2009	2010
Dow	10,735	9,946	8,480	10,226	10,193	11,367	13,063	12,820	8,168	11,009
S&P 500	1,249	1,077	917	1,107	1,157	1,311	1,482	1,386	873	1,187
Nasdaq	2,116	1,688	1,464	1,920	1,922	2,323	2,525	2,413	1,717	2,461
TSX	7,947	7,663	6,586	8,244	9,369	12,204	13,417	13,937	9,325	12,211
Russell 1000	1,266	1,100	934	1,138	1,198	1,373	1,553	1,453	917	1,259
Russell 2000	1,206	1,269	991	1,391	1,440	1,900	2,024	1,780	1,212	1,781
Russell 3000 Growth	2,218	1,778	1,495	1,820	1,807	2,090	2,305	2,261	1,524	2,081
Russell 3000 Value	2,174	2,084	1,759	2,188	2,426	2,825	3,241	2,858	1,696	2,369

Percent Gain for April

	2001	2002	2003	2004	2005	2006	2007	2008	2009	2010
Dow	8.7	-4.4	6.1	-1.3	-3.0	2.3	5.7	4.5	7.3	1.4
S&P 500	7.7	-6.1	8.1	-1.7	-2.0	1.2	4.3	4.8	9.4	1.5
Nasdaq	15.0	-8.5	9.2	-3.7	-3.9	-0.7	4.3	5.9	12.3	2.6
TSX	4.5	-2.4	3.8	-4.0	-2.5	0.8	1.9	4.4	6.9	1.4
Russell 1000	7.9	-5.8	7.9	-1.9	-2.0	1.1	4.1	5.0	10.0	1.8
Russell 2000	7.7	0.8	9.4	-5.2	-5.8	-0.1	1.7	4.1	15.3	5.6
Russell 3000 Growth	12.6	-7.8	7.5	-1.5	-2.3	-0.2	4.5	5.2	9.9	1.3
Russell 3000 Value	4.7	-3.0	8.6	-2.8	-2.2	2.1	3.3	4.6	10.9	2.8

April Market Avg. Performance 2001 to 2010[1]

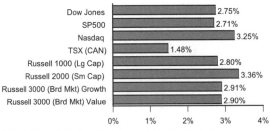

	Dow Jones	2.75%
	SP500	2.71%
	Nasdaq	3.25%
	TSX (CAN)	1.48%
	Russell 1000 (Lg Cap)	2.80%
	Russell 2000 (Sm Cap)	3.36%
	Russell 3000 (Brd Mkt) Growth	2.91%
	Russell 3000 (Brd Mkt) Value	2.90%

Interest Corner Apr[2]

	Fed Funds % [3]	3 Mo. T-Bill % [4]	10 Yr % [5]	20 Yr % [6]
2010	0.25	0.16	3.69	4.36
2009	0.25	0.14	3.16	4.10
2008	2.00	1.43	3.77	4.49
2007	5.25	4.91	4.63	4.88
2006	4.75	4.77	5.07	5.31

(1) Russell Data provided by Russell (2) Federal Reserve Bank of St. Louis- end of month values (3) Target rate set by FOMC (4)(5)(6) Constant yield maturities.

THACKRAY SECTOR THERMOMETER

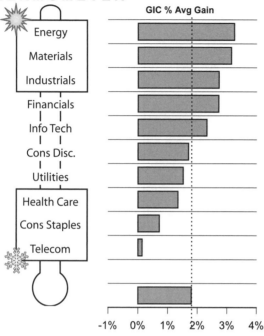

	GIC[2] % Avg Gain	Fq % Gain >S&P 500	
	SP GIC SECTOR 1990-2009[1]		
Energy	3.2 %	70 %	Energy
Materials	3.1	55	Materials
Industrials	2.7	65	Industrials
Financials	2.7	60	Financials
Info Tech	2.3	50	Information Technology
Cons Disc.	1.7	50	Consumer Discretionary
Utilities	1.5	40	Utilities
Health Care	1.3	45	Health Care
Cons Staples	0.7	40	Consumer Staples
Telecom	0.1 %	30 %	Telecom
	1.8 %	N/A %	S&P 500

Sector Commentary

♦ April is typically a strong month for the market and the cyclical sectors tend to be at the top of the market. As a result the defensive sectors tend to be at the bottom. ♦ The three bottom sectors in the TST - Telecom, Consumer Staples and Health Care were the three bottom sectors in 2010. They produced a loss of 1.4%, 1.6% and 3.9%, respectively. They were the only three losing sectors in April. The top three sectors for 2010 were Consumer Discretionary, Energy and Industrials, producing returns of gains of 6.0%, 4.4% and 4.1%, respectively.

Sub-Sector Commentary

♦ Typically Gold stocks, Agriculture and Biotech are at the bottom of the pack. In 2010, Gold was the leading sub-sector in the sub-sector thermometer, but Agriculture and Biotech remained close to the bottom. In April the S&P 500 gained 1.5%, Gold gained 8.3%, Agriculture lost 3.3% and Biotech lost 5.3%.

SELECTED SUB-SECTORS 1990-2009[3]		
7.8 %	55 %	Auto & Components
5.3	67	Semiconductor (SOX) 95-2009
3.2	55	Banks
2.8	70	Integrated Oil & Gas
2.6	55	Transportation
2.5	60	Airlines
2.1	45	Metals & Mining
1.8	50	Pharmaceuticals
1.7	45	Software & Services
1.7	50	Insurance
0.3	35	Retail
-0.1	63	Agriculture Products (94-2009)
-0.1	35	Biotech (93-2009)
-1.2	30	XAU Gold

(1) Sector data provided by Standard and Poors (2) GIC is short form for Global Industry Classification (3) Sub Sector data provided by Standard and Poors, except where marked by symbol.

18 DAY EARNINGS MONTH EFFECT
Markets Outperform 1st 18 Calendar Days of Earnings Months

Earnings season occurs the first month of every quarter. At this time, public companies report their financials for the previous quarter and often give guidance on future expectations. As a result investors tend to bid up stocks, anticipating good earnings.

Earnings are a major driver of stock market prices as investors generally like to get in the stock market early in anticipation of favorable results, which helps to run up stock prices in the first half of the month.

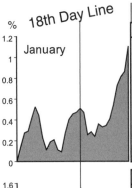

18th Day Line

%
1.2
1
0.8
0.6
0.4
0.2
0

January

1st to 18th Day 1950-2009

Avg Gain 0.5%	Fq Pos 62%

The first month of the year generally has a good start. Investors and money managers generally push the market upward as they try to lock in their new positions for the year. The result is that the market tends to increase for the first eighteen days, pause, and then accelerate through the end of the month.

1.6
1.4
1.2
1
0.8
0.6
0.4
0.2
0

April

Avg Gain 1.5%	Fq Pos 72%

This month has a reputation of being a strong month. If you look at the graph you can see that almost all of the gains have come in the first half of the month. It is interesting to note that the month returns tend to peak just after the last day to file tax returns.

1
0.9
0.8
0.7
0.6
0.5
0.4
0.3
0.2
0.1
0

July

Avg Gain 0.7%	Fq Pos 63%

This is the month in which the market can peak in strong bull markets. The returns in the first half of the month can be positive, but investors should be cautious, as the time period following in August and September has a tendency towards negative returns.

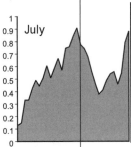

0.7
0.6
0.5
0.4
0.3
0.2
0.1
0

October

Avg Gain 0.7%	Fq Pos 63%

This is the month with a bad reputation. Once again, the first part of the month tends to do well. It is the middle segment, centered around the notorious Black Monday, that brings down the results. Toward the end of the month investors realize that the world has not ended and start to buy stocks again, providing a strong finish.

	1st to 18th Day Gain S&P500			
	Jan	Apr	Jul	Oct
1950	0.54 %	4.28 %	-3.56 %	2.88 %
1951	4.85	3.41	4.39	1.76
1952	2.02	-3.57	-0.44	-1.39
1953	-2.07	-2.65	0.87	3.38
1954	2.50	3.71	2.91	-1.49
1955	-3.28	4.62	3.24	-4.63
1956	-2.88	-1.53	4.96	2.18
1957	-4.35	2.95	2.45	-4.93
1958	2.78	1.45	1.17	2.80
1959	1.09	4.47	1.23	0.79
1960	-3.34	2.26	-2.14	1.55
1961	2.70	1.75	-0.36	2.22
1962	-4.42	-1.84	2.65	0.12
1963	3.30	3.49	-1.27	2.26
1964	2.05	1.99	2.84	0.77
1965	2.05	2.31	1.87	1.91
1966	1.64	2.63	2.66	2.77
1967	6.80	1.84	3.16	-1.51
1968	-0.94	7.63	1.87	2.09
1969	-1.76	-0.27	-2.82	3.37
1970	-1.24	-4.42	6.83	-0.02
1971	1.37	3.17	0.42	-1.01
1972	1.92	2.40	-1.22	-2.13
1973	0.68	0.02	2.00	1.46
1974	-2.04	0.85	-2.58	13.76
1975	3.50	3.53	-2.09	5.95
1976	7.55	-2.04	0.38	-3.58
1977	-3.85	2.15	0.47	-3.18
1978	-4.77	4.73	1.40	-2.00
1979	3.76	0.11	-1.19	-5.22
1980	2.90	-1.51	6.83	4.83
1981	-0.73	-0.96	-0.34	2.59
1982	-4.35	4.33	1.33	13.54
1983	4.10	4.43	-2.20	1.05
1984	1.59	-0.80	-1.16	1.20
1985	2.44	0.10	1.32	2.72
1986	-1.35	1.46	-5.77	3.25
1987	9.96	-1.64	3.48	-12.16
1988	1.94	0.12	-1.09	2.75
1989	3.17	3.78	4.20	-2.12
1990	-4.30	0.23	1.73	-0.10
1991	0.61	3.53	3.83	1.20
1992	0.42	3.06	1.83	-1.45
1993	0.26	-0.60	-1.06	2.07
1994	1.67	-0.74	2.46	1.07
1995	2.27	0.93	2.52	0.52
1996	-1.25	-0.29	-4.04	3.42
1997	4.78	1.22	3.41	-0.33
1998	-0.92	1.90	4.67	3.88
1999	1.14	2.54	3.36	-2.23
2000	-0.96	-3.80	2.69	-6.57
2001	2.10	6.71	-1.36	2.66
2002	-1.79	-2.00	-10.94	8.48
2003	2.50	5.35	1.93	4.35
2004	2.51	0.75	-3.46	-0.05
2005	-1.32	-2.93	2.50	-4.12
2006	2.55	1.22	0.51	3.15
2007	1.41	4.33	-3.20	1.48
2008	-9.75	5.11	-1.51	19.36
2009	-5.88	8.99	2.29	2.89
Avg	0.53 %	1.55 %	0.75 %	0.66 %

4 MONDAY	026 / 271

5 TUESDAY	025 / 270

6 WEDNESDAY	024 / 269

7 THURSDAY	023 / 268

8 FRIDAY	022 / 267

WEEK 14

Market Indices & Rates
Weekly Values**

Stock Markets	2009	2010
Dow	7,778	10,953
S&P500	815	1,188
Nasdaq	1,561	2,438
TSX	8,879	12,149
FTSE	3,960	5,757
DAX	4,194	6,224
Nikkei	8,433	11,257
Hang Seng	13,924	22,001

Commodities	2009	2010
Oil	50.3	85.9
Gold	914.4	1143.8

Bond Yields	2009	2010
USA 5 Yr Treasury	1.73	2.67
USA 10 Yr T	2.76	3.94
USA 20 Yr T	3.64	4.63
Moody's Aaa	5.41	5.38
Moody's Baa	8.47	6.38
CAN 5 Yr T	1.80	3.03
CAN 10 Yr T	2.83	3.66

Money Market	2009	2010
USA Fed Funds	0.25	0.25
USA 3 Mo T-B	0.21	0.17
CAN tgt overnight rate	0.50	0.25
CAN 3 Mo T-B	0.39	0.28

Foreign Exchange	2009	2010
USD/EUR	1.33	1.34
USD/GBP	1.45	1.52
CAN/USD	1.25	1.00
JPY/USD	98.77	93.79

2009 Strategy Performance

First 18 Days of Earnings Months S&P 500 (2009)

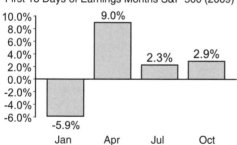

At the beginning of 2009 the market was expecting a major economic slowdown and less than stellar earnings. As a result the market performed negatively for the first eighteen days of January. The market started to rally in March with better economic conditions and better earnings.

The next earnings period took place in April and stocks climbed substantially in the first eighteen days. Earnings still kept coming in strong for the rest of the year and as a result the first eighteen days of both July and October produced positive results.

** Weekly avg closing values- except Fed Funds & CAN overnight tgt rate weekly closing values.

APRIL

M	T	W	T	F	S	S
				1	2	3
4	5	6	7	8	9	10
11	12	13	14	15	16	17
18	19	20	21	22	23	24
25	26	27	28	29	30	

MAY

M	T	W	T	F	S	S
						1
2	3	4	5	6	7	8
9	10	11	12	13	14	15
16	17	18	19	20	21	22
23	24	25	26	27	28	29
30	31					

JUNE

M	T	W	T	F	S	S
	1	2	3	4	5	
6	7	8	9	10	11	12
13	14	15	16	17	18	19
20	21	22	23	24	25	26
27	28	29	30			

CONSUMER SWITCH
SELL CONSUMER DISCRETIONARY
BUY CONSUMER STAPLES
Consumer Staples Outperform Apr 23 to Oct 27

The *Consumer Switch* strategy has allowed investors to use a set portion of their account to switch between the two related consumer sectors. To use this strategy, investors would invest in the Consumer Discretionary sector from October 28th to April 22nd, and then use the proceeds to invest in the Consumer Staples sector from April 23rd to October 27th, and then repeat the cycle.

The end result has been outperformance compared with buying and holding both consumer sectors, or buying and holding the broad market.

> *1,770% total aggregate gain compared with 268% for the S&P 500*

The basic premise of the strategy is that the Consumer Discretionary sector tends to outperform during the favorable six months when more money flows into the market, pushing up stock prices. On the other hand, the Consumer Staples sector tends to outperform when investors are looking for safety and stability of earnings in the six months when the market tends to move into a defensive mode.

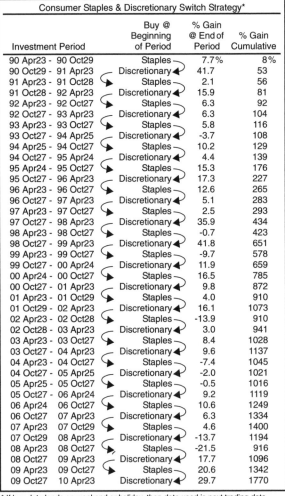

Consumer Staples & Discretionary Switch Strategy*			
Investment Period	Buy @ Beginning of Period	% Gain @ End of Period	% Gain Cumulative
90 Apr23 - 90 Oct29	Staples	7.7%	8%
90 Oct29 - 91 Apr23	Discretionary	41.7	53
91 Apr23 - 91 Oct28	Staples	2.1	56
91 Oct28 - 92 Apr23	Discretionary	15.9	81
92 Apr23 - 92 Oct27	Staples	6.3	92
92 Oct27 - 93 Apr23	Discretionary	6.3	104
93 Apr23 - 93 Oct27	Staples	5.8	116
93 Oct27 - 94 Apr25	Discretionary	-3.7	108
94 Apr25 - 94 Oct27	Staples	10.2	129
94 Oct27 - 95 Apr24	Discretionary	4.4	139
95 Apr24 - 95 Oct27	Staples	15.3	176
95 Oct27 - 96 Apr23	Discretionary	17.3	227
96 Apr23 - 96 Oct27	Staples	12.6	265
96 Oct27 - 97 Apr23	Discretionary	5.1	283
97 Apr23 - 97 Oct27	Staples	2.5	293
97 Oct27 - 98 Apr23	Discretionary	35.9	434
98 Apr23 - 98 Oct27	Staples	-0.7	423
98 Oct27 - 99 Apr23	Discretionary	41.8	651
99 Apr23 - 99 Oct27	Staples	-9.7	578
99 Oct27 - 00 Apr24	Discretionary	11.9	659
00 Apr24 - 00 Oct27	Staples	16.5	785
00 Oct27 - 01 Apr23	Discretionary	9.8	872
01 Apr23 - 01 Oct29	Staples	4.0	910
01 Oct29 - 02 Apr23	Discretionary	16.1	1073
02 Apr23 - 02 Oct28	Staples	-13.9	910
02 Oct28 - 03 Apr23	Discretionary	3.0	941
03 Apr23 - 03 Oct27	Staples	8.4	1028
03 Oct27 - 04 Apr23	Discretionary	9.6	1137
04 Apr23 - 04 Oct27	Staples	-7.4	1045
04 Oct27 - 05 Apr25	Discretionary	-2.0	1021
05 Apr25 - 05 Oct27	Staples	-0.5	1016
05 Oct27 - 06 Apr24	Discretionary	9.2	1119
06 Apr24 - 06 Oct27	Staples	10.6	1249
06 Oct27 - 07 Apr23	Discretionary	6.3	1334
07 Apr23 - 07 Oct29	Staples	4.6	1400
07 Oct29 - 08 Apr23	Discretionary	-13.7	1194
08 Apr23 - 08 Oct27	Staples	-21.5	916
08 Oct27 - 09 Apr23	Discretionary	17.7	1096
09 Apr23 - 09 Oct27	Staples	20.6	1342
09 Oct27 - 10 Apr23	Discretionary	29.7	1770

* If buy date lands on weekend or holiday, then date used is next trading date

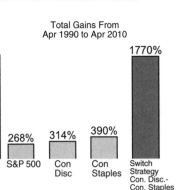

Total Gains From
Apr 1990 to Apr 2010

- S&P 500: 268%
- Con Disc: 314%
- Con Staples: 390%
- Switch Strategy Con. Disc.-Con. Staples: 1770%

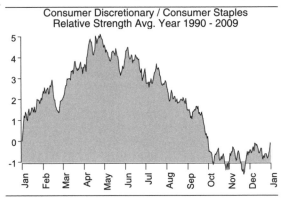

Consumer Discretionary / Consumer Staples
Relative Strength Avg. Year 1990 - 2009

11 MONDAY	019 / 264	**12** TUESDAY	018 / 263

13 WEDNESDAY	017 / 262	**14** THURSDAY	016 / 261

15 FRIDAY 015 / 260

WEEK 15

Market Indices & Rates
Weekly Values**

Stock Markets	2009	2010
Dow	7,921	11,062
S&P500	833	1,202
Nasdaq	1,603	2,485
TSX	8,999	12,147
FTSE	3,958	5,781
DAX	4,380	6,246
Nikkei	8,833	11,199
Hang Seng	14,826	22,077

Commodities	2009	2010
Oil	50.5	84.6
Gold	877.6	1153.4

Bond Yields	2009	2010
USA 5 Yr Treasury	1.88	2.57
USA 10 Yr T	2.93	3.85
USA 20 Yr T	3.80	4.54
Moody's Aaa	5.47	5.28
Moody's Baa	8.58	6.26
CAN 5 Yr T	1.87	3.11
CAN 10 Yr T	2.94	3.69

Money Market	2009	2010
USA Fed Funds	0.25	0.25
USA 3 Mo T-B	0.19	0.16
CAN tgt overnight rate	0.50	0.25
CAN 3 Mo T-B	0.39	0.27

Foreign Exchange	2009	2010
USD/EUR	1.33	1.36
USD/GBP	1.47	1.54
CAN/USD	1.23	1.00
JPY/USD	100.29	93.25

APRIL

M	T	W	T	F	S	S
				1	2	3
4	5	6	7	8	9	10
11	12	13	14	15	16	17
18	19	20	21	22	23	24
25	26	27	28	29	30	

MAY

M	T	W	T	F	S	S
						1
2	3	4	5	6	7	8
9	10	11	12	13	14	15
16	17	18	19	20	21	22
23	24	25	26	27	28	29
30	31					

JUNE

M	T	W	T	F	S	S
	1	2	3	4	5	
6	7	8	9	10	11	12
13	14	15	16	17	18	19
20	21	22	23	24	25	26
27	28	29	30			

2009 Strategy Performance*

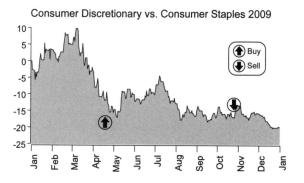

Consumer Discretionary vs. Consumer Staples 2009

The above graph is a relative strength graph between the consumer staples and discretionary sectors. When the line is rising, the staples sector is outperforming and when it is falling, the discretionary sector is outperforming.

In 2009 both the discretionary and staples sectors produced the same amount of gain. From April 23rd to October 27th, the consumers staples sector gained 20% and the consumer discretionary sector gained 21%.

* Buy and Sell dates are approximate representations of strategy dates.
** Weekly avg closing values- except Fed Funds & CAN overnight tgt rate weekly closing values.

1/2 and 1/2
First 1/2 of April – Financial Stocks
Second 1/2 of April – Information Technology Stocks

The half and half strategy is a short-term switch combination that takes advantage of the superior performance of financial stocks in the first part of April and information technology stocks in the second half.

The opportunity exists because technology stocks tend to increase at the same time financial stocks tend to decrease, creating an ideal switch opportunity.

3.4% extra & 16 times out of 21 better than the S&P 500

Why do financial stocks tend to start their decline relative to the broad market at mid-month? Is it a coincidence that the rate on the three month T-Bill tends to bottom out at the same time?

The common denominator that affects both of these markets is liquidity. Basically, investors sell-off their money market positions to cover their taxes, decreasing short-term money market rates.

Decreasing short-term yields are good for financial stocks, particularly banks. Banks tend to make more money with a steeper yield curve. They borrow short-term money (your savings account) and lend out long-term (mortgages). The steeper the curve, the more money banks make.

The end result is that financial stocks benefit from this trend in the first half of April.

On the flip side, investors stop selling their money market positions to cover taxes by mid-month. At this time, yields tend to increase and financial stocks decrease.

Fortunately, information technology stocks tend to present a good opportunity at this time. By mid-April, tech-

nology stocks tend to become oversold. as technology stocks typically start to correct after a strong December and January (see *Information Technology - Use It or Lose It* strategy).

The correction becomes exacerbated by investors selling off their holdings to pay their tax bill in mid-April. Investors typically sell off information technology stocks rather than the staid blue chip companies.

Financials & Info Tech & 1/2 & 1/2 > S&P 500

Year	April 1st to April 15th		April 16th to April 30		April Compound Growth	
	S&P 500	Finan cials	S&P 500	Info Tech	S&P 500	1/2 & 1/2
1990	1.3%	1.3%	-3.9%	-1.9%	-2.7%	-0.7%
1991	1.6	2.3	-1.5	-3.1	0.0	-0.9
1992	3.1	1.0	-0.3	-1.3	2.8	-0.3
1993	-0.7	3.5	-1.8	-2.2	-2.5	1.3
1994	0.1	4.9	1.1	3.5	1.2	8.6
1995	1.7	2.9	1.1	5.8	2.8	8.8
1996	-0.5	-2.3	1.8	8.2	1.3	5.8
1997	-0.3	0.3	6.2	11.3	5.8	11.6
1998	1.6	5.5	-0.7	4.3	0.9	10.0
1999	2.8	5.0	0.9	1.3	3.8	6.4
2000	-9.5	-7.0	7.1	14.8	-3.1	6.8
2001	2.0	0.2	5.6	8.3	7.7	8.5
2002	-3.9	-1.6	-2.3	-3.5	-6.1	-5.1
2003	5.0	9.3	2.9	5.3	8.1	15.1
2004	0.2	-3.0	-1.9	-5.0	-1.7	-7.8
2005	-3.2	-2.6	1.2	2.3	-2.0	-0.4
2006	-0.4	-0.3	1.7	-1.3	1.2	-1.6
2007	2.3	0.5	2.0	2.7	4.3	3.2
2008	0.9	-0.6	3.8	6.8	4.8	6.2
2009	6.8	23.0	2.4	5.8	9.4	30.1
2010	3.6	6.5	-2.1	-2.9	1.5	3.4
Avg.	0.7%	2.3%	1.1%	2.8%	1.8%	5.2%

Ⓨ *Alternate Strategy—*
The first few days in May tend to produce gains. An alternate strategy is to hold the information technology position for the first three trading days in May.

ⓘ *The SP GICS Financial Sector # 40 encompasses a wide range financial based companies.*
The SP GICS Information Technology Sector # 45 encompasses a wide range technology based companies.
For more information on the information technology sector, see www.standardandpoors.com

18 MONDAY	012 / 257

19 TUESDAY	011 / 256

20 WEDNESDAY	010 / 255

21 THURSDAY	009 / 254

22 FRIDAY	008 / 253

WEEK 16

Market Indices & Rates
Weekly Values**

Stock Markets	2009	2010
Dow	8,053	11,135
S&P500	857	1,207
Nasdaq	1,650	2,507
TSX	9,309	12,150
FTSE	4,026	5,725
DAX	4,598	6,217
Nikkei	8,835	10,953
Hang Seng	15,609	21,448

Commodities	2009	2010
Oil	49.8	83.1
Gold	882.4	1139.5

Bond Yields	2009	2010
USA 5 Yr Treasury	1.79	2.56
USA 10 Yr T	2.87	3.81
USA 20 Yr T	3.80	4.50
Moody's Aaa	5.32	5.25
Moody's Baa	8.40	6.20
CAN 5 Yr T	1.89	3.15
CAN 10 Yr T	2.95	3.70

Money Market	2009	2010
USA Fed Funds	0.25	0.25
USA 3 Mo T-B	0.15	0.16
CAN tgt overnight rate	0.50	0.25
CAN 3 Mo T-B	0.39	0.34

Foreign Exchange	2009	2010
USD/EUR	1.32	1.34
USD/GBP	1.49	1.54
CAN/USD	1.21	1.01
JPY/USD	99.50	93.01

APRIL

M	T	W	T	F	S	S
				1	2	3
4	5	6	7	8	9	10
11	12	13	14	15	16	17
18	19	20	21	22	23	24
25	26	27	28	29	30	

MAY

M	T	W	T	F	S	S
						1
2	3	4	5	6	7	8
9	10	11	12	13	14	15
16	17	18	19	20	21	22
23	24	25	26	27	28	29
30	31					

JUNE

M	T	W	T	F	S	S
	1	2	3	4	5	
6	7	8	9	10	11	12
13	14	15	16	17	18	19
20	21	22	23	24	25	26
27	28	29	30			

2010 Strategy Performance

1/2 and 1/2 Strategy April 2010

First Half April — Second Half April — Full Month Strategy

8.0%
6.0%
4.0%
2.0%
0.0%
-2.0%
-4.0%

S&P 500 — Financials — S&P 500 — Technology — S&P 500 — Financials & Technology

In 2010 the *1/2 and 1/2* strategy was extremely successful "on the back" of the financial sector. As the market rallied off the February low, investors anticipated strong second quarter earnings in the financial sector, leading the sector to outperform the S&P 500 in the first half of April.

The second half of the strategy, based upon the success of the technology sector, under performed mainly because the stock market corrected towards the end of April. Overall the *1/2 and 1/2* strategy was successful, producing a positive result and outperforming the S&P 500.

** Weekly avg closing values- except Fed Funds & CAN overnight tgt rate weekly closing values.

CANADIAN DOLLAR
STRONG APRIL

Since the year 2000 when oil started its ascent, the Canadian dollar has been labelled as a petro currency by foreign investors.

All other things being equal, if oil increases in price, investors favor the Canadian dollar over the U.S. dollar. They do so with good reason, as Canada is a net exporter of oil and benefits from its rising price.

Oil tends to do well in the month of April as this is the heart of one of the strongest seasonal strategies – oil and oil stocks outperform from February 25th to May 9th (see *Oil Winter/Spring Strategy*). With the rising price of oil in April the Canadian dollar gets a free ride upwards.

April has been a strong month for the Canadian dollar relative to the U.S. dollar. All of the largest losses occurred in years when the Fed Reserve was aggressively hiking their target rate.

At some point during the years 1987, 2000, 2004 and 2005, the Fed increased their target rate by a total of at least 1% in each year. Since 1971 these years were the four biggest losers for the Canadian dollar in the month of April.

The Canadian dollar has been strong in April regardless of the long-term trend

CAD vs USD Avg. % Gain 1971 to 2009

of the dollar either moving up or down. The Canadian dollar started at approximately par in 1971 and reached a low in 2002 of $0.62 and then it reached a recent high of $1.09 in 2007.

In both the ups and downs of the economy, the Canadian dollar has outperformed the U.S. dollar in April.

CAD vs USD Apr. % Gain 1971-2010   Positive ☐

	1980	0.44	%	1990	-1.89	%	2000	0.44	%	2010	0.44	%
1971	-0.10	%	1981	-0.74		1991	0.65		2001	2.76		
1972	0.53		1982	0.89		1992	-0.48		2002	1.77		
1973	-0.41		1983	0.64		1993	-1.02		2003	2.50		
1974	1.27		1984	-0.62		1994	0.14		2004	-4.46		
1975	-1.56		1985	0.04		1995	2.91		2005	-3.77		
1976	0.55		1986	1.69		1996	0.15		2006	4.17		
1977	0.91		1987	-2.38		1997	-0.97		2007	4.17		
1978	0.09		1988	0.41		1998	-0.85		2008	1.81		
1979	1.61		1989	0.60		1999	3.53		2009	5.59		
Avg.	0.32	%		0.08	%		0.45	%		1.27	%	0.44	%

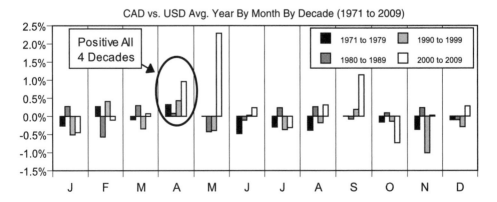

CAD vs. USD Avg. Year By Month By Decade (1971 to 2009)

Positive All 4 Decades

1971 to 1979   1990 to 1999
1980 to 1989   2000 to 2009

25 MONDAY	005/ 250	**26** TUESDAY	004 / 249

27 WEDNESDAY	003 / 248	**28** THURSDAY	002 / 247

29 FRIDAY   001 / 246

WEEK 17

Market Indices & Rates
Weekly Values**

Stock Markets	2009	2010
Dow	7,946	11,084
S&P500	849	1,196
Nasdaq	1,649	2,488
TSX	9,322	12,183
FTSE	4,037	5,623
DAX	4,559	6,171
Nikkei	8,784	11,090
Hang Seng	15,278	21,137

Commodities	2009	2010
Oil	47.9	84.2
Gold	891.4	1162.2

Bond Yields	2009	2010
USA 5 Yr Treasury	1.89	2.50
USA 10 Yr T	2.96	3.76
USA 20 Yr T	3.90	4.43
Moody's Aaa	5.33	5.20
Moody's Baa	8.26	6.14
CAN 5 Yr T	1.91	3.06
CAN 10 Yr T	2.95	3.65

Money Market	2009	2010
USA Fed Funds	0.25	0.25
USA 3 Mo T-B	0.13	0.16
CAN tgt overnight rate	0.25	0.25
CAN 3 Mo T-B	0.26	0.38

Foreign Exchange	2009	2010
USD/EUR	1.30	1.33
USD/GBP	1.46	1.53
CAN/USD	1.23	1.01
JPY/USD	98.03	93.90

APRIL

M	T	W	T	F	S	S
				1	2	3
4	5	6	7	8	9	10
11	12	13	14	15	16	17
18	19	20	21	22	23	24
25	26	27	28	29	30	

MAY

M	T	W	T	F	S	S
						1
2	3	4	5	6	7	8
9	10	11	12	13	14	15
16	17	18	19	20	21	22
23	24	25	26	27	28	29
30	31					

JUNE

M	T	W	T	F	S	S
	1	2	3	4	5	
6	7	8	9	10	11	12
13	14	15	16	17	18	19
20	21	22	23	24	25	26
27	28	29	30			

2009 Strategy Performance

CAD vs USD 2009

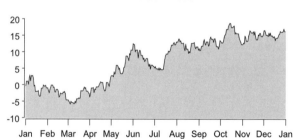

In 2009 the Canadian dollar was on a "tear," bottoming in March, rising to a peak in October and producing a gain of over 15% for the year. Typically the Canadian dollar does well against the U.S. dollar from mid-March to the beginning of June with the real sweet spot in April. The Canadian dollar rose over 5% against the U.S. dollar during the month of April, accounting for over one-third of the return for the year.

With the Canadian dollar being a "petro-currency", it is important to keep track of the strength of the price of oil. If the price of the oil is weak, it will put a damper on the value of the Canadian dollar and vice versa.

** Weekly avg closing values- except Fed Funds & CAN overnight tgt rate weekly closing values.

MAY

	MONDAY	TUESDAY	WEDNESDAY
WEEK 18	**2** 29	**3** 28	**4** 27
WEEK 19	**9** 22	**10** 21	**11** 20
WEEK 20	**16** 15	**17** 14	**18** 13
WEEK 21	**23** 8 CAN Market Closed- Victoria Day	**24** 7	**25** 6
WEEK 22	**30** 1 USA Market Closed- Memorial Day	**31**	1

THURSDAY	FRIDAY
5 26	**6** 25
12 19	**13** 18
19 12	**20** 11
26 5	**27** 4
2	3

JUNE

M	T	W	T	F	S	S
		1	2	3	4	5
6	7	8	9	10	11	12
13	14	15	16	17	18	19
20	21	22	23	24	25	26
27	28	29	30			

JULY

M	T	W	T	F	S	S
				1	2	3
4	5	6	7	8	9	10
11	12	13	14	15	16	17
18	19	20	21	22	23	24
25	26	27	28	29	30	31

AUGUST

M	T	W	T	F	S	S
1	2	3	4	5	6	7
8	9	10	11	12	13	14
15	16	17	18	19	20	21
22	23	24	25	26	27	28
29	30	31				

SEPTEMBER

M	T	W	T	F	S	S
			1	2	3	4
5	6	7	8	9	10	11
12	13	14	15	16	17	18
19	20	21	22	23	24	25
26	27	28	29	30		

MAY
S U M M A R Y

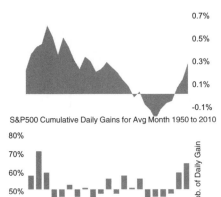

STRATEGIES	PAGE
STRATEGIES STARTING	
First 3 Days in May – 1/2% Difference	55
Six 'n' Six – Take a Break for Six Months	57
Canadian Six 'n' Six – Take a Break for Six Months	59
Bonds When You Need Them	61
Memorial Day – Be Early and Stay Late	63
STRATEGIES FINISHING	
Platinum Records Solid Results	7
Oil – Equipment and Services	19
Oil – Winter/Spring Strategy I of II	21
First 3 Days in May – 1/2% Difference	55
Material Stocks – Material Gains	135
Industrial Strength – In - Out - In Again	137
Metals & Mining – In - Out - In Again	139

S&P500 Cumulative Daily Gains for Avg Month 1950 to 2010

♦ The first three days in May tend to be positive (see *First 3 Market Days in May* strategy). ♦ The beginning of May is typically a good time to consider reducing equity exposure. ♦ In 2010 the correction in the stock market started on April 26th, bringing down the markets all the way until the end of June.

BEST / WORST MAY BROAD MKTS. 2001-2010

BEST MAY MARKETS
- TSX (2009) 11.2%
- Russell 2000 (2003) 10.6%
- Nasdaq (2003) 9.0%

WORST MAY MARKETS
- Russell 3000 Value (2010) -8.5%
- Nasdaq (2010) -8.3%
- S&P500 (2010) -8.2%

Index Values End of Month

	2001	2002	2003	2004	2005	2006	2007	2008	2009	2010
Dow	10,912	9,925	8,850	10,188	10,467	11,168	13,628	12,638	8,500	10,137
S&P 500	1,256	1,067	964	1,121	1,192	1,270	1,531	1,400	919	1,089
Nasdaq	2,110	1,616	1,596	1,987	2,068	2,179	2,605	2,523	1,774	2,257
TSX	8,162	7,656	6,860	8,417	9,607	11,745	14,057	14,715	10,370	11,763
Russell 1000	1,273	1,088	986	1,152	1,239	1,330	1,605	1,477	965	1,157
Russell 2000	1,234	1,211	1,096	1,412	1,533	1,792	2,105	1,860	1,247	1,644
Russell 3000 Growth	2,190	1,729	1,574	1,852	1,895	2,009	2,386	2,344	1,596	1,920
Russell 3000 Value	2,219	2,084	1,873	2,206	2,486	2,742	3,348	2,853	1,790	2,169

Percent Gain for May

	2001	2002	2003	2004	2005	2006	2007	2008	2009	2010
Dow	1.6	-0.2	4.4	-0.4	2.7	-1.7	4.3	-1.4	4.1	-7.9
S&P 500	0.5	-0.9	5.1	1.2	3.0	-3.1	3.3	1.1	5.3	-8.2
Nasdaq	-0.3	-4.3	9.0	3.5	7.6	-6.2	3.1	4.6	3.3	-8.3
TSX	2.7	-0.1	4.2	2.1	2.5	-3.8	4.8	5.6	11.2	-3.7
Russell 1000	0.5	-1.0	5.5	1.3	3.4	-3.2	3.4	1.6	5.3	-8.1
Russell 2000	2.3	-4.5	10.6	1.5	6.4	-5.7	4.0	4.5	2.9	-7.7
Russell 3000 Growth	-1.2	-2.7	5.3	1.8	4.9	-3.9	3.5	3.7	4.7	-7.7
Russell 3000 Value	2.1	0.0	6.4	0.8	2.5	-2.9	3.3	-0.2	5.5	-8.5

May Market Avg. Performance 2001 to 2010[1]

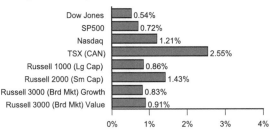

Dow Jones	0.54%
SP500	0.72%
Nasdaq	1.21%
TSX (CAN)	2.55%
Russell 1000 (Lg Cap)	0.86%
Russell 2000 (Sm Cap)	1.43%
Russell 3000 (Brd Mkt) Growth	0.83%
Russell 3000 (Brd Mkt) Value	0.91%

Interest Corner May[2]

	Fed Funds % [3]	3 Mo. T-Bill % [4]	10 Yr % [5]	20 Yr % [6]
2010	0.25	0.16	3.31	4.05
2009	0.25	0.14	3.47	4.34
2008	2.00	1.89	4.06	4.74
2007	5.25	4.73	4.90	5.10
2006	5.00	4.86	5.12	5.35

(1) Russell Data provided by Russell (2) Federal Reserve Bank of St. Louis- end of month values (3) Target rate set by FOMC (4)(5)(6) Constant yield maturities.

THACKRAY SECTOR THERMOMETER

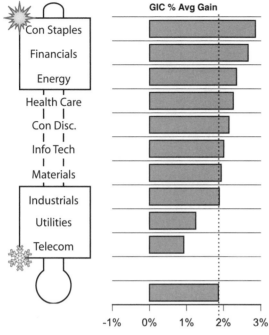

	GIC[2] % Avg Gain	Fq % Gain >S&P 500	
	SP GIC SECTOR 1990-2009[1]		
Con Staples	2.9 %	60 %	Consumer Staples
Financials	2.7	50	Financials
Energy	2.3	40	Energy
Health Care	2.3	45	Health Care
Con Disc.	2.1	50	Consumer Discretionary
Info Tech	2.0	60	Information Technology
Materials	1.9	40	Materials
Industrials	1.9	40	Industrials
Utilities	1.2	40	Utilities
Telecom	0.9 %	45 %	Telecom
	1.9 %	N/A %	S&P 500

GIC % Avg Gain: -1% 0% 1% 2% 3%

Sector Commentary

♦ In 2010 May was a disastrous month. It was down 8.2%. All major sectors of the market were down, it was a matter of how much ♦ Consumer Staples is at the top of the TST and in 2010 it was the second best sector with a loss of 4.7%. Ironically, the telecom sector is the worst performing sector, on average since 1990, but its defensive qualities made it the top sector.

Sub-Sector Commentary

♦ Gold stocks are at the top of the list producing a gain of 4.9% in the month of May from 1990 to 2009. In 2010 as the market was falling apart and global economic concerns brought back memories of the financial meltdown, investors were attracted to gold as an alternative currency, helping gold stocks do relatively well but nevertheless losing 2.8%. In 2010 the other sub-sectors of the market got "shuffled" in the mayhem and some sectors that are typically bottom performing, placed near the top and vice versa. All of the sub-sectors in May 2010 lost ground.

SELECTED SUB-SECTORS 1990-2009[3]		
4.9 %	65 %	Gold (XAU)
4.1	56	Agriculture Products (94-2009)
3.2	50	Banks
2.8	55	Metals & Mining
2.8	65	Biotech (93-2009)
2.6	60	Retail
2.6	55	Insurance
2.1	40	Pharmaceuticals
1.9	40	Integrated Oil & Gas
1.5	35	Software & Services
1.1	40	Transportation
0.9	30	Auto & Components
0.6	47	Semiconductor (SOX) 95-2009
-0.4	25	Airlines

(1) Sector data provided by Standard and Poors (2) GIC is short form for Global Industry Classification (3) Sub Sector data provided by Standard and Poors, except where marked by symbol.

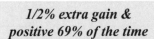

FIRST 3 MARKET DAYS IN MAY
The 1/2% Difference

A lot of investors have profited by investing in the stock markets for the six favorable months that run from the beginning of November to the end of April.

Although they have done well, they could have increased their profits by making two small adjustments: investing four trading days before the end of October and selling at the end of the first three trading days in May. Investing at the end of October is discussed later in the book.

1/2% extra gain & positive 69% of the time

For those investors that use the *6'N'6 Strategy*, selling just three trading days later has increased returns by an average of 1/2% from 1950 to 2010 (S&P 500). Using this strategy has produced positive returns 69% of the time.

The rationale for this is quite simple. The beginning of most months tends to be positive and May is no exception. The the first three trading days tend to be very strong.

On average, the first three days in May have had much better gains than the rest of the days in the month, and the average trading day for the entire year. Although the media likes to simplify strategies by using whole months for comparisons, seasonal investors who have stayed in the markets for a few extra days have earned extra profits.

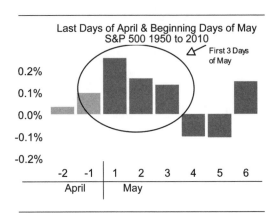

Last Days of April & Beginning Days of May
S&P 500 1950 to 2010

First 3 Days of May

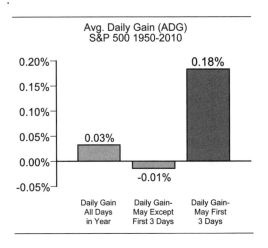

Avg. Daily Gain (ADG)
S&P 500 1950-2010

First 3 Days in May % Gain S&P 500 -1950 to 2010   Positive

1950	1.1 %	1960	1.2 %	1970	-3.6 %	1980	0.1 %	1990	1.4 %	2000	-2.6 %	2010	-1.8 %
1951	1.7	1961	1.3	1971	-0.2	1981	-1.9	1991	1.5	2001	-0.1		
1952	1.2	1962	2.0	1972	-1.6	1982	1.1	1992	0.5	2002	-0.3		
1953	1.7	1963	0.3	1973	3.0	1983	-0.7	1993	1.0	2003	1.1		
1954	0.1	1964	1.8	1974	1.1	1984	0.7	1994	0.2	2004	1.3		
1955	-0.8	1965	0.7	1975	3.2	1985	0.1	1995	1.1	2005	1.6		
1956	-0.1	1966	-1.8	1976	-0.7	1986	0.9	1996	-1.9	2006	-0.2		
1957	1.3	1967	-0.1	1977	1.5	1987	2.4	1997	3.6	2007	1.4		
1958	0.8	1968	1.2	1978	-0.6	1988	-0.4	1998	0.3	2008	1.6		
1959	0.3	1969	0.7	1979	0.0	1989	-0.5	1999	0.9	2009	0.6		
Avg.	0.7 %		0.7 %		0.2 %		0.2 %		0.9 %		0.4 %		-1.8 %

| **2** MONDAY | 029 / 243 |
| **3** TUESDAY | 028 / 242 |

| **4** WEDNESDAY | 027 / 241 |
| **5** THURSDAY | 026 / 240 |

| **6** FRIDAY | 025 / 239 |

Market Indices & Rates
Weekly Values**

Stock Markets	2009	2010
Dow	8,122	10,769
S&P500	867	1,156
Nasdaq	1,700	2,382
TSX	9,396	11,927
FTSE	4,188	5,284
DAX	4,694	5,951
Nikkei	8,756	10,530
Hang Seng	14,968	20,391

Commodities	2009	2010
Oil	51.1	80.2
Gold	892.9	1184.4

Bond Yields	2009	2010
USA 5 Yr Treasury	1.98	2.29
USA 10 Yr T	3.10	3.56
USA 20 Yr T	4.05	4.20
Moody's Aaa	5.46	5.00
Moody's Baa	8.26	5.98
CAN 5 Yr T	1.99	2.85
CAN 10 Yr T	3.07	3.54

Money Market	2009	2010
USA Fed Funds	0.25	0.25
USA 3 Mo T-B	0.13	0.14
CAN tgt overnight rate	0.25	0.25
CAN 3 Mo T-B	0.21	0.36

Foreign Exchange	2009	2010
USD/EUR	1.32	1.30
USD/GBP	1.47	1.51
CAN/USD	1.20	1.03
JPY/USD	97.40	93.78

2010 Strategy Performance

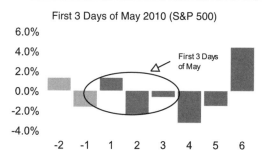

First 3 Days of May 2010 (S&P 500)

MAY

M	T	W	T	F	S	S
						1
2	3	4	5	6	7	8
9	10	11	12	13	14	15
16	17	18	19	20	21	22
23	24	25	26	27	28	29
30	31					

JUNE

M	T	W	T	F	S	S
	1	2	3	4	5
6	7	8	9	10	11	12
13	14	15	16	17	18	19
20	21	22	23	24	25	26
27	28	29	30			

JULY

M	T	W	T	F	S	S
				1	2	3
4	5	6	7	8	9	10
11	12	13	14	15	16	17
18	19	20	21	22	23	24
25	26	27	28	29	30	31

In 2010 the market had already peaked in late April and was showing some serious signs of deteriorating. The first three days continued the same trend, and then the market collapsed briefly on May 6th with the "fat fingers" trade that brought the market down dramatically in the afternoon. Despite the negative performance of the market in the first three days of May, it was still better to be out of the market at the end of the trade, rather than continue to hold a long position in the market. If an investor had to choose between selling at the end of April or holding for a few more days, historically the wiser choice has been to hold for three more days into the beginning of May.

** Weekly avg closing values- except Fed Funds & CAN overnight tgt rate weekly closing values.

6n6 SIX 'N' SIX
Take a Break for Six Months - May 6th to October 27th

Being out of the market feels good when it is going down. And the market has a habit of going down after the beginning of May. Although sometimes a strong market can continue into July and less frequently into autumn, it has historically made sense to reduce your equity exposure in May.

$924,470 gain on $10,000

The accompanying table uses the S&P 500 to compare the returns made from Oct 28th to May 5th (favorable six months), to the returns made during the remainder of the year (unfavorable six months). From 1950 to 2010, the October to May time period has produced stunning results.

Starting with $10,000 and investing from October 28th to May 5th every year (1950 to 2010) has produced a gain of $924,470. On the flip side, being invested from May 6th to October 27th, has actually lost money. An initial investment of $10,000 has lost $3,273 over the same time period.

Investors often worry about being out of the market at a time when the market is rallying, and missing out on profits. In the last sixty years, the S&P 500, during the unfavorable six months, has only had gains of greater than 10%, eight times. This compares with twenty-four times in the favorable six months. Being out of the markets during the unfavorable six months has proven to be a much wiser strategy than being out of the markets during the other six months.

S&P 500 Non-Favorable 6 Month Avg. Gain vs Favorable 6 Month Avg. Gain (1990-2010)

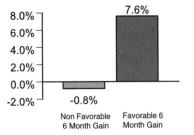

	Non Favorable 6 Month Gain	Favorable 6 Month Gain
	-0.8%	7.6%

(i) *The above growth rates are geometric averages in order to represent the cumulative growth of a dollar investment over time. These figures differ from the arithmetic mean calculations used in the Six 'N' Six Take a Break Strategy, which are used to represent an average year.*

	S&P 500 % May 6 to Oct 27	$10,000 Start	S&P 500 % Oct 28 to May 5	$10,000 Start
1950/51	8.5%	10,851	14.8%	11,477
1951/52	-1.1	10,736	5.4	12,096
1952/53	1.8	10,931	3.9	12,568
1953/54	-3.1	10,595	16.6	14,655
1954/55	13.2	11,992	18.1	17,310
1955/56	12.0	13,425	14.6	19,832
1956/57	-4.6	12,805	0.2	19,862
1957/58	-12.4	11,216	7.9	21,428
1958/59	15.1	12,914	14.5	24,543
1959/60	-0.6	12,840	-4.5	23,449
1960/61	-2.3	12,550	24.1	29,091
1961/62	2.7	12,894	-3.1	28,197
1962/63	-17.7	10,616	28.4	36,205
1963/64	5.7	11,220	9.3	39,566
1964/65	5.1	11,791	5.5	41,758
1965/66	3.1	12,159	-5.0	39,691
1966/67	-8.8	11,094	17.7	46,720
1967/68	0.6	11,155	3.9	48,541
1968/69	5.6	11,782	0.2	48,620
1969/70	-6.1	11,059	-19.8	39,007
1970/71	5.8	11,695	24.9	48,703
1971/72	-9.6	10,570	13.7	55,370
1972/73	3.7	10,965	0.3	55,560
1973/74	0.3	11,003	-18.0	45,539
1974/75	-23.2	8,451	28.5	58,502
1975/76	-0.4	8,418	12.4	65,771
1976/77	0.9	8,492	-1.6	64,705
1977/78	-7.8	7,833	4.5	67,641
1978/79	-2.0	7,675	6.4	72,003
1979/80	-0.1	7,666	5.8	76,162
1980/81	20.2	9,215	1.9	77,616
1981/82	-8.5	8,435	-1.4	76,562
1982/83	15.0	9,699	21.4	92,967
1983/84	0.3	9,732	-3.5	89,736
1984/85	3.9	10,110	8.9	97,765
1985/86	4.1	10,527	26.8	123,942
1986/87	0.4	10,573	23.7	153,307
1987/88	-21.0	8,348	11.0	170,138
1988/89	7.1	8,945	10.9	188,748
1989/90	8.9	9,743	1.0	190,624
1990/91	-10.0	8,773	25.0	238,225
1991/92	0.9	8,852	8.5	258,463
1992/93	0.4	8,887	6.2	274,540
1993/94	4.5	9,288	-2.8	266,722
1994/95	3.2	9,586	11.6	297,794
1995/96	11.5	10,684	10.7	329,608
1996/97	9.2	11,671	18.5	390,445
1997/98	5.6	12,328	27.2	496,632
1998/99	-4.5	11,773	26.5	628,078
1999/00	-3.8	11,331	10.5	693,913
2000/01	-3.7	10,912	-8.2	637,090
2001/02	-12.8	9,516	-2.8	619,107
2002/03	-16.4	7,958	3.2	639,039
2003/04	11.3	8,856	8.8	695,064
2004/05	0.3	8,887	4.2	724,234
2005/06	0.5	8,934	12.5	814,455
2006/07	3.9	9,282	9.3	890,310
2007/08	2.0	9,465	-8.3	816,204
2008/09	-39.7	5,750	6.5	862,619
2009/10	17.7	6,727	9.7	934,470
Total Gain (Loss)		**($-3,273)**		**$924,470**

9 MONDAY	022 / 236

10 TUESDAY	021 / 235

11 WEDNESDAY	020 / 234

12 THURSDAY	019 / 233

13 FRIDAY	018 / 232

WEEK 19

Market Indices & Rates
Weekly Values**

Stock Markets	2009	2010
Dow	8,467	10,767
S&P500	913	1,156
Nasdaq	1,746	2,383
TSX	10,020	12,055
FTSE	4,399	5,360
DAX	4,871	6,110
Nikkei	9,409	10,484
Hang Seng	16,851	20,271

Commodities	2009	2010
Oil	56.0	75.0
Gold	909.8	1226.1

Bond Yields	2009	2010
USA 5 Yr Treasury	2.09	2.25
USA 10 Yr T	3.23	3.54
USA 20 Yr T	4.17	4.23
Moody's Aaa	5.50	5.07
Moody's Baa	8.14	6.12
CAN 5 Yr T	2.06	2.89
CAN 10 Yr T	3.10	3.55

Money Market	2009	2010
USA Fed Funds	0.25	0.25
USA 3 Mo T-B	0.19	0.16
CAN tgt overnight rate	0.25	0.25
CAN 3 Mo T-B	0.18	0.38

Foreign Exchange	2009	2010
USD/EUR	1.34	1.27
USD/GBP	1.51	1.48
CAN/USD	1.17	1.02
JPY/USD	98.84	92.78

MAY

M	T	W	T	F	S	S
						1
2	3	4	5	6	7	8
9	10	11	12	13	14	15
16	17	18	19	20	21	22
23	24	25	26	27	28	29
30	31					

JUNE

M	T	W	T	F	S	S
	1	2	3	4	5	
6	7	8	9	10	11	12
13	14	15	16	17	18	19
20	21	22	23	24	25	26
27	28	29	30			

JULY

M	T	W	T	F	S	S
			1	2	3	
4	5	6	7	8	9	10
11	12	13	14	15	16	17
18	19	20	21	22	23	24
25	26	27	28	29	30	31

2008-10 Strategy Performance

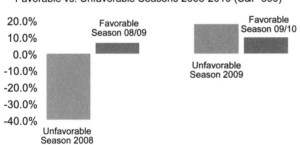

Favorable vs. Unfavorable Seasons 2008-2010 (S&P 500)

Staying out of the market for the unfavourable six months from May 6th to October 27th, paid off handsomely in 2008.

In 2009 it was a different matter as the market rallied almost 18%. To say that the strategy has not worked because of a rally in 2009 is a bit naive as the market lost almost 39% the previous year.

** Weekly avg closing values- except Fed Funds & CAN overnight tgt rate weekly closing values.

In analysing long-term trends for the broad markets such as the S&P 500 or the TSX Composite, a large data set is preferable because it incorporates various economic cycles. The daily data set for the TSX Composite starts in 1977.

Over this time period investors have been rewarded for following the six month cycle of investing from October 28th to May 5th, versus the other unfavorable six months, May 6th to October 27th.

Starting with an investment of $10,000 in 1977, investing in the unfavorable six months has produced a loss of $3,693, versus investing in the favorable six months which has produced a gain of $176,526.

$176,526 gain on $10,000 since 1977

The TSX Composite Average Year 1977 to 2009 (graph below) indicates that the market tended to peak in mid-July or the end of August. In our book Time In Time Out, Outsmart the Stock Market Using Calendar Investment Strategies, Bruce Lindsay and I analyzed a number of markets over different decades.

What we found was that the markets tend to peak at the beginning of May or mid-July. The mid-July peak was usually the result of a strong bull market in place that had a lot of momentum.

The main reason that the TSX Composite data shows a peak occurring in July-August is that the data is primarily from the biggest bull market in history, starting in 1982.

Does a later average peak in the stock market mean that the best six month cycle does not work? No. Dividing the year up into six month intervals, the period from October to May is far superior compared with the other half of the year.

The table below illustrates the superiority of the best six months over the worst six months. Going down the table year by year, the period from October 28 to May 5th outperforms the period from May 6th to October 27.

	TSX Comp May 6 to Oct 27	$10,000 Start	TSX Comp Oct 28 to May 5	$10,000 Start
1977/78	-3.9 %	9,608	13.1 %	11,313
1978/79	12.1	10,775	21.3	13,728
1979/80	2.9	11,084	23.0	16,883
1980/81	22.5	13,579	-2.4	16,479
1981/82	-17.0	11,272	-18.2	13,488
1982/83	16.6	13,138	34.6	18,150
1983/84	-0.9	13,015	-1.9	17,811
1984/85	1.6	13,226	10.7	19,718
1985/86	0.5	13,299	16.5	22,978
1986/87	-1.9	13,045	24.8	28,666
1987/88	-23.4	9,992	15.3	33,050
1988/89	2.7	10,260	5.7	34,939
1989/90	7.9	11,072	-13.3	30,294
1990/91	-8.4	10,148	13.1	34,266
1991/92	-1.6	9,982	-2.0	33,571
1992/93	-2.3	9,750	15.3	38,704
1993/94	10.8	10,801	1.7	39,365
1994/95	-0.1	10,792	0.3	39,483
1995/96	1.3	10,936	18.2	46,671
1996/97	8.3	11,843	10.8	51,725
1997/98	7.3	12,707	17.0	60,510
1998/99	-22.3	9,870	17.1	70,871
1999/00	-0.2	9,853	36.9	97,009
2000/01	-2.9	9,570	-14.4	83,062
2001/02	-12.2	8,399	9.4	90,875
2002/03	-16.4	7,020	4.0	94,476
2003/04	15.1	8,079	10.3	104,252
2004/05	3.9	8,398	7.8	112,379
2005/06	8.1	9,080	19.8	134,587
2006/07	0.0	9,079	12.2	151,053
2007/08	3.8	9,426	-0.2	150,820
2008/09	-40.2	5,638	15.7	174,551
2009/10	11.9	6,307	7.4	187,526
Total Gain (Loss)	**($-3,693)**			**$176,526**

In a strong bull market investors always have the choice of using a stop loss or technical indicators to help time the exit point.

TSX Comp. - Avg. Year 1977 to 2009

16 MONDAY	015 / 229	**17** TUESDAY	014 / 228

18 WEDNESDAY	013 / 227	**19** THURSDAY	012 / 226

20 FRIDAY   011 / 225

* Buy and Sell dates are approximate representations of strategy dates.
** Weekly avg closing values- except Fed Funds & CAN overnight tgt rate weekly closing values.

WEEK 20

Market Indices & Rates
Weekly Values**

Stock Markets	2009	2010
Dow	8,355	10,369
S&P500	895	1,106
Nasdaq	1,696	2,281
TSX	9,899	11,634
FTSE	4,381	5,173
DAX	4,785	5,982
Nikkei	9,290	10,096
Hang Seng	16,927	19,696

Commodities	2009	2010
Oil	58.1	69.1
Gold	921.8	1203.9

Bond Yields	2009	2010
USA 5 Yr Treasury	2.01	2.10
USA 10 Yr T	3.14	3.33
USA 20 Yr T	4.09	4.04
Moody's Aaa	5.44	4.87
Moody's Baa	8.00	6.00
CAN 5 Yr T	2.11	2.68
CAN 10 Yr T	3.11	3.40

Money Market	2009	2010
USA Fed Funds	0.25	0.25
USA 3 Mo T-B	0.18	0.17
CAN tgt overnight rate	0.25	0.25
CAN 3 Mo T-B	0.18	0.37

Foreign Exchange	2009	2010
USD/EUR	1.36	1.24
USD/GBP	1.52	1.44
CAN/USD	1.17	1.05
JPY/USD	96.36	91.49

MAY

M	T	W	T	F	S	S
						1
2	3	4	5	6	7	8
9	10	11	12	13	14	15
16	17	18	19	20	21	22
23	24	25	26	27	28	29
30	31					

JUNE

M	T	W	T	F	S	S
	1	2	3	4	5
6	7	8	9	10	11	12
13	14	15	16	17	18	19
20	21	22	23	24	25	26
27	28	29	30			

JULY

M	T	W	T	F	S	S
				1	2	3
4	5	6	7	8	9	10
11	12	13	14	15	16	17
18	19	20	21	22	23	24
25	26	27	28	29	30	31

2009 Strategy Performance*

6 Month unFavorable Season S&P/TSX 2009

In 2009 the S&P/TSX Composite followed the U.S. markets and started a huge rise in March. The unfavourable time period from May 6th to October 27th produced a positive return of 11.9%. Strong moves during the unfavorable time period are rare. The S&P/TSX or as it was formerly called the TSE, has only risen by 10% or more, five times in the last thirty-four years.

The next occurrence of a gain greater than 10% occurred in 2003 when the market started a substantial bull run. The year 2009 was unique as the stock market rally was created compliments of "Helicopter" Ben Bernanke who dumped liquidity into the markets at an unprecedented rate.

Thackray's 2010 Investor's Guide included a strategy with U.S. Treasuries 7-10 Years. This year's book includes an analysis of the 20+ Year Treasuries which have a very similar seasonal trend.

Since 1982 interest rates have been on a long-term decline and as a result bonds have increased in value. Hidden in this trend is a strong seasonal tendency for bonds to outperform from May 8th to Dec 31st.

8.9% gain & positive 75% of the time

Bonds outperform from the late spring until the end of the year for three reasons. First, companies tend to raise more money through bond issuance at the beginning of the year to meet their needs for the rest of the year. With more bonds competing on the market for money, interest rates tend to increase.

Second, optimistic forecasts at the beginning of the year for stronger GDP growth tend to increase inflation expectations and as a result interest rates respond by going up. As GDP expectations tend to decrease in the summer months, interest rates respond by retreating.

U.S. Treasuries 20+ Yr.*
Total Return 1998 to 2009

	Positive	
	Jan 1- May 7	May 8- Dec 31
1998	2.1 %	11.9 %
1999	-6.3	-4.0
2000	4.9	15.9
2001	-0.7	4.3
2002	2.2	14.5
2003	4.0	-2.1
2004	-3.2	12.6
2005	4.2	4.2
2006	-7.6	9.2
2007	1.9	8.1
2008	-0.5	34.3
2009	-19.4	-2.5
Avg.	-1.5 %	8.9 %

Nevertheless, May has represented a good time to enter the bond market.

The return in the bond market for the last eight months of the year has far exceeded the returns in the first four months.

For the *Barclays U.S. Treasury 20 Plus Year Total Return Index*, the period from January 1st to May 7th produces a loss of 1.5%, compared with the period from May 8th to December 31st, which produces an average gain of 8.9% (1990 to 2009).

The three loses that have occurred from May 8th to December 12th over the last twelve years have been relatively small compared to the size of the gains. The largest loss of 4% occurred in 1999.

In addition the favorable period has been positive 75% of the time and has outperformed the less favorable time 83% of the time.

U.S. Treasuries 20 Yr. Plus Total Return*
Avg. Year 1998 to 2009

Third, the stock market often peaks in May and investors rotate their money into bonds. As the demand for bonds increases, interest rates decrease and bonds increase in value.

Although the beginning of May has been a good time to increase an allocation to bonds, when the stock market has continued to peak in July, the bond market's entry point can be correspondingly delayed.

* *Source: Barclays Capital Inc. The U.S. Treasury: 20+ Year is a total return index, which includes both interest and capital appreciation.*
For more information on fixed income indices, see www.barcap.com.

23 MONDAY	008 / 222	**24** TUESDAY	007 / 221

25 WEDNESDAY	006 / 220	**26** THURSDAY	005 / 219

27 FRIDAY 004 / 218

WEEK 21

Market Indices & Rates
Weekly Values**

Stock Markets	2009	2010
Dow	8,394	10,096
S&P500	899	1,082
Nasdaq	1,716	2,231
TSX	10,069	11,621
FTSE	4,422	5,086
DAX	4,934	5,823
Nikkei	9,233	9,629
Hang Seng	17,261	19,410

Commodities	2009	2010
Oil	60.3	70.6
Gold	936.5	1203.2

Bond Yields	2009	2010
USA 5 Yr Treasury	2.13	2.08
USA 10 Yr T	3.29	3.25
USA 20 Yr T	4.22	3.99
Moody's Aaa	5.57	4.91
Moody's Baa	8.04	6.10
CAN 5 Yr T	2.20	2.61
CAN 10 Yr T	3.18	3.31

Money Market	2009	2010
USA Fed Funds	0.25	0.25
USA 3 Mo T-B	0.18	0.17
CAN tgt overnight rate	0.25	0.25
CAN 3 Mo T-B	0.18	0.45

Foreign Exchange	2009	2010
USD/EUR	1.37	1.23
USD/GBP	1.56	1.44
CAN/USD	1.15	1.06
JPY/USD	95.53	90.26

MAY

M	T	W	T	F	S	S
						1
2	3	4	5	6	7	8
9	10	11	12	13	14	15
16	17	18	19	20	21	22
23	24	25	26	27	28	29
30	31					

JUNE

M	T	W	T	F	S	S
	1	2	3	4	5	
6	7	8	9	10	11	12
13	14	15	16	17	18	19
20	21	22	23	24	25	26
27	28	29	30			

JULY

M	T	W	T	F	S	S
				1	2	3
4	5	6	7	8	9	10
11	12	13	14	15	16	17
18	19	20	21	22	23	24
25	26	27	28	29	30	31

2009 Strategy Performance*

Barclays U.S. Treasury 20 Yr Plus Total Return Index 2009

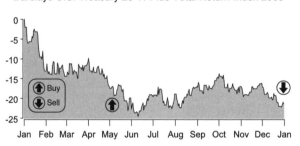

Although long bonds did not do well in 2009, most of the damage was done at the beginning of the year, during the unfavorable season for bonds.

Long bonds started to rally at the start of their seasonal period, but then fell back in the autumn as investors started to believe that the economy was on the mend and the stock market had some "legs" to keep going.

* Buy and Sell dates are approximate representations of strategy dates.
** Weekly avg closing values- except Fed Funds & CAN overnight tgt rate weekly closing values.

MEMORIAL DAY – BE EARLY & STAY LATE
Positive 2 Market Days Before Memorial Day to 5 Market Days into June

A lot of strategies that focus on investing around holidays concentrate on the market performance the day before and the day after a holiday.

Not all holidays were created equal. The typical Memorial Day trade is to invest the day before and sell the day after. If you invested just for these two days you would be missing out on a lot of gains.

1.2% average gain and positive 68% of the time

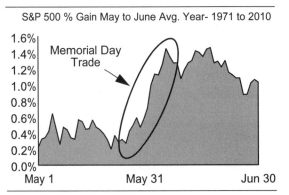

S&P 500 % Gain May to June Avg. Year- 1971 to 2010

Historically, the best strategy has been to invest two market days before Memorial Day and hold until five market days into June. Extending the investment into June makes sense. The first few days in June tend to be positive– so why sell early?

The graph shows the performance of the S&P 500 on a calendar basis for the months of May and June from 1971 to 2010.

The increase from the end of May into June represents the opportunity with the "*Memorial Day - Be Early & Stay Late*" trade. The graph clearly shows a spike in the market that occurs at the end of the month and carries on into June.

Investors using the typical Memorial Day trade, miss out on the majority of the gain. The *Memorial Day - Be Early & Stay Late* strategy has produced an average gain of 1.2% and has been positive 68% of the time (S&P 500, 1971 to 2010). Not a bad gain for being invested an average of ten market days.

The *Memorial Day - Be Early & Stay Late* trade can be extended into June primarily because the first days tend to be positive. These days are part of the end of the month effect. (see *Super Seven* strategy).

2 Market Days Before Memorial Day to 5 Market Days Into June - S&P 500   Positive

		1980	5.1 %	1990	1.1 %	2000	5.2 %	2010	-1.6 %
1971	1.5 %	1981	0.2	1991	0.9	2001	-0.9		
1972	-2.4	1982	-2.6	1992	-0.5	2002	-5.4		
1973	1.7	1983	-2.1	1993	-1.3	2003	7.0		
1974	6.3	1984	1.2	1994	0.4	2004	2.3		
1975	3.8	1985	4.3	1995	0.9	2005	0.6		
1976	-0.7	1986	4.3	1996	0.0	2006	-0.2		
1977	1.0	1987	5.5	1997	2.2	2007	-2.1		
1978	3.1	1988	4.5	1998	-0.5	2008	-2.2		
1979	1.9	1989	2.4	1999	2.3	2009	4.1		
Avg.	1.8 %		2.3 %		0.6 %		0.8 %		-1.6 %

(i) *History of Memorial Day: Originally called Decoration Day in remembrance of those who died in the nation's service. Memorial day was first observed on May 30th 1868 when flowers were placed on the graves of Union and Confederate soldiers at Arlington National Cemetery. The South acknowledged the day after World War I, when the holiday changed from honoring just those who died fighting in the Civil War to honoring Americans who died fighting in any war. In 1971 Congress passed the National Holiday Act recognizing Memorial Day as the last Monday in May.*

30 MONDAY	001 / 215	**31** TUESDAY	000 / 214

1 WEDNESDAY	029 / 213	**2** THURSDAY	028 / 212

3 FRIDAY		027 / 211

WEEK 22

Market Indices & Rates
Weekly Values**

Stock Markets	2009	2010
Dow	8,419	10,115
S&P500	907	1,084
Nasdaq	1,752	2,256
TSX	10,252	11,699
FTSE	4,408	5,163
DAX	4,956	5,984
Nikkei	9,414	9,780
Hang Seng	17,542	19,660

Commodities	2009	2010
Oil	64.3	72.9
Gold	957.3	1215.3

Bond Yields	2009	2010
USA 5 Yr Treasury	2.38	2.10
USA 10 Yr T	3.59	3.31
USA 20 Yr T	4.47	4.05
Moody's Aaa	5.69	4.98
Moody's Baa	8.03	6.23
CAN 5 Yr T	2.45	2.66
CAN 10 Yr T	3.42	3.34

Money Market	2009	2010
USA Fed Funds	0.25	0.25
USA 3 Mo T-B	0.16	0.15
CAN tgt overnight rate	0.25	0.50
CAN 3 Mo T-B	0.19	0.50

Foreign Exchange	2009	2010
USD/EUR	1.40	1.22
USD/GBP	1.60	1.46
CAN/USD	1.12	1.05
JPY/USD	95.59	91.80

JUNE

M	T	W	T	F	S	S
		1	2	3	4	5
6	7	8	9	10	11	12
13	14	15	16	17	18	19
20	21	22	23	24	25	26
27	28	29	30			

JULY

M	T	W	T	F	S	S
			1	2	3	
4	5	6	7	8	9	10
11	12	13	14	15	16	17
18	19	20	21	22	23	24
25	26	27	28	29	30	31

AUGUST

M	T	W	T	F	S	S
1	2	3	4	5	6	7
8	9	10	11	12	13	14
15	16	17	18	19	20	21
22	23	24	25	26	27	28
29	30	31				

2010 Strategy Performance

Memorial Day Strategy 2010 (S&P 500)

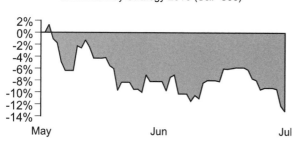

May 2010 was a disastrous month. The "flash crash" occurred, driving some blue chip names down to a few dollars in less than half an hour and the possibility of a global economic slowdown was brought to the forefront.

Additionally the world was starting to realize the extent of the disaster caused by the oil spill in the Gulf of Mexico. There was a brief rise in the markets around the end of May, which helped benefit the Memorial Day trade, but after a few days the negative trend persisted for a terrible June.

** Weekly avg closing values- except Fed Funds & CAN overnight tgt rate weekly closing values.

JUNE

	MONDAY	TUESDAY	WEDNESDAY
WEEK 22	30	31	**1** 29
WEEK 23	**6** 24	**7** 23	**8** 22
WEEK 24	**13** 17	**14** 16	**15** 15
WEEK 25	**20** 10	**21** 9	**22** 8
WEEK 26	**27** 3	**28** 2	**29** 1

THURSDAY	**FRIDAY**
2 28	**3** 27
9 21	**10** 20
16 14	**17** 13
23 7	**24** 6
30	1

JULY

M	T	W	T	F	S	S
				1	2	3
4	5	6	7	8	9	10
11	12	13	14	15	16	17
18	19	20	21	22	23	24
25	26	27	28	29	30	31

AUGUST

M	T	W	T	F	S	S
1	2	3	4	5	6	7
8	9	10	11	12	13	14
15	16	17	18	19	20	21
22	23	24	25	26	27	28
29	30	31				

SEPTEMBER

M	T	W	T	F	S	S
			1	2	3	4
5	6	7	8	9	10	11
12	13	14	15	16	17	18
19	20	21	22	23	24	25
26	27	28	29	30		

OCTOBER

M	T	W	T	F	S	S
					1	2
3	4	5	6	7	8	9
10	11	12	13	14	15	16
17	18	19	20	21	22	23
24	25	26	27	28	29	30
31						

JUNE SUMMARY

S&P500 Cumulative Daily Gains for Avg Month 1950 to 2010

Prob. of Daily Gain

♦ June, on average, is a "see-saw" month. The first half of the month does well and then fades. ♦ The Biotechnology sector usually starts to pick up at the end of the month (see *Biotech Summer Solstice* strategy). ♦ The Nasdaq usually outperforms the S&P 500. ♦ Large Cap Growth (large companies with a growth profile - Russell 1000 Growth) tend to perform well in June. In 2010 virtually all of the sectors of the market suffered as the S&P 500 fell more than 5%.

BEST / WORST JUNE BROAD MKTS. 2001-2010

BEST JUNE MARKETS
- ♦ Russell 2000 (2004) 4.1%
- ♦ Russell 2000 (2005) 3.7%
- ♦ Nasdaq (2009) 3.4%

WORST JUNE MARKETS
- ♦ Dow (2008) -10.2%
- ♦ Russell 3000 Value (2008) -9.8%
- ♦ Nasdaq (2002) -9.4%

Index Values End of Month

	2001	2002	2003	2004	2005	2006	2007	2008	2009	2010
Dow	10,502	9,243	8,985	10,435	10,275	11,150	13,409	11,350	8,447	9,774
S&P 500	1,224	990	975	1,141	1,191	1,270	1,503	1,280	919	1,031
Nasdaq	2,161	1,463	1,623	2,048	2,057	2,172	2,603	2,293	1,835	2,109
TSX	7,736	7,146	6,983	8,546	9,903	11,613	13,907	14,467	10,375	11,294
Russell 1000	1,244	1,007	998	1,171	1,242	1,330	1,573	1,352	966	1,091
Russell 2000	1,275	1,150	1,114	1,470	1,590	1,801	2,072	1,714	1,263	1,515
Russell 3000 Growth	2,148	1,569	1,595	1,876	1,892	2,000	2,350	2,175	1,613	1,810
Russell 3000 Value	2,177	1,967	1,894	2,258	2,515	2,757	3,265	2,574	1,773	2,037

Percent Gain for June

	2001	2002	2003	2004	2005	2006	2007	2008	2009	2010
Dow	-3.8	-6.9	1.5	2.4	-1.8	-0.2	-1.6	-10.2	-0.6	-3.6
S&P 500	-2.5	-7.2	1.1	1.8	0.0	0.0	-1.8	-8.6	0.0	-5.4
Nasdaq	2.4	-9.4	1.7	3.1	-0.5	-0.3	0.0	-9.1	3.4	-6.5
TSX	-5.2	-6.7	1.8	1.5	3.1	-1.1	-1.1	-1.7	0.0	-4.0
Russell 1000	-2.3	-7.5	1.2	1.7	0.3	0.0	-2.0	-8.5	0.1	-5.7
Russell 2000	3.3	-5.1	1.7	4.1	3.7	0.5	-1.6	-7.8	1.3	-7.9
Russell 3000 Growth	-1.9	-9.3	1.3	1.3	-0.1	-0.5	-1.5	-7.2	1.1	-5.7
Russell 3000 Value	-1.9	-5.6	1.1	2.4	1.2	0.5	-2.5	-9.8	-0.9	-6.1

June Market Avg. Performance 2001 to 2010 [1]

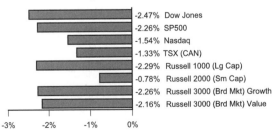

- -2.47% Dow Jones
- -2.26% SP500
- -1.54% Nasdaq
- -1.33% TSX (CAN)
- -2.29% Russell 1000 (Lg Cap)
- -0.78% Russell 2000 (Sm Cap)
- -2.26% Russell 3000 (Brd Mkt) Growth
- -2.16% Russell 3000 (Brd Mkt) Value

Interest Corner Jun[2]

	Fed Funds %[3]	3 Mo. T-Bill %[4]	10 Yr %[5]	20 Yr %[6]
2010	0.25	0.18	2.97	3.74
2009	0.25	0.19	3.53	4.30
2008	2.00	1.90	3.99	4.59
2007	5.25	4.82	5.03	5.21
2006	5.25	5.01	5.15	5.31

(1) Russell Data provided by Russell (2) Federal Reserve Bank of St. Louis- end of month values (3) Target rate set by FOMC (4)(5)(6) Constant yield maturities

THACKRAY SECTOR THERMOMETER

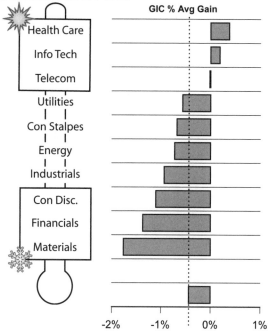

	GIC[2] % Avg Gain	Fq % Gain >S&P 500	
	SP GIC SECTOR 1990-2009[1]		
	0.4 %	55 %	Health Care
	0.2	45	Information Technology
	0.0	60	Telecom
	-0.6	45	Utilities
	-0.7	35	Consumer Staples
	-0.7	40	Energy
	-0.9	40	Industrials
	-1.1	45	Consumer Discretionary
	-1.4	40	Financials
	-1.8 %	30 %	Materials
	-0.4 %	N/A %	S&P 500

Sector Commentary

♦ As described in the *June – Leaderless Month* strategy, the sectors that lead one year to the next vary depending on market conditions. Overall, the defensive sectors have averaged the best gains in June from 1990 to 2009.
♦ The year 2010 very much mirrored the longer term pattern with the defensives at the top of the thermometer. In the month of June the S&P 500 was down 5.4% and all of the major sectors of the market were negative.

Sub-Sector Commentary

♦ After a bad month in May 2010, June followed with an almost equally bad month. The S&P 500 lost 5.4% and most sub-sectors of the market were negative. There were three sub-sectors that were positive: Agriculture, Gold stocks, and Insurance. ♦ Agriculture started its seasonal run a bit early in 2010. It is possible that investors started to favor "soft" commodities, such as wheat, as an alternative to stocks.

SELECTED SUB-SECTORS 1990-2009[3]		
3.0 %	80 %	Software & Services
0.4	60	Pharmaceuticals
-0.2	60	Retail
-0.5	40	Integrated Oil & Gas
-0.6	45	Airlines
-0.6	33	Semiconductor (SOX) 95-2009
-0.7	55	Metals & Mining
-0.7	45	Insurance
-1.0	50	Auto & Components
-1.3	35	Biotech (93-2009)
-1.3	31	Agriculture Products (94-2009)
-1.3	45	Gold (XAU)
-1.3	30	Transportation
-2.7	25	Banks

(1) Sector data provided by Standard and Poors (2) GIC is short form for Global Industry Classification (3) Sub Sector data provided by Standard and Poors, except where marked by symbol.

1ST DAY OF THE MONTH
Best Day of the Month

Not all days are equal. There is one day of the month that has typically been the best – the first day. This day benefits from portfolio managers finishing off their window dressing (making their portfolios look good on the books) and retail investors buying up new positions to start the month on a favorable footing.

0.13% avg. gain & 5 times better than the average market day

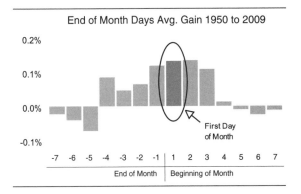

End of Month Days Avg. Gain 1950 to 2009

First Day
of Month

End of Month | Beginning of Month

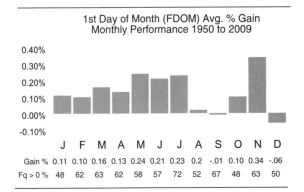

1st Day of Month (FDOM) Avg. % Gain
Monthly Performance 1950 to 2009

	J	F	M	A	M	J	J	A	S	O	N	D
Gain %	0.11	0.10	0.16	0.13	0.24	0.21	0.23	0.2	-.01	0.10	0.34	-.06
Fq > 0 %	48	62	63	62	58	57	72	52	67	48	63	50

From 1950 to 2009, the first day of the month (FDOM) has produced an average return of 0.13% and has been positive 58% of the time. This compares to the average market day (all trading days of the year) over the same time period, which has produced a return of 0.03% and has been positive 53% of the time.

The interesting result is that the average daily gain of the first day of the month was almost five times better than the average market day, and yet it had only a slightly higher frequency of being positive. What this means is that when the first day is positive, it has a much higher likelihood of producing extraordinarily large gains. Examining the returns on a monthly basis, only the "first day" of two months has performed below the average market day from 1950 to 2009. It is not surprising that the months are August and September, two of the worst months in which to invest. On the other hand, the best "first day" of the month has clearly been November: the traditional start of the six month favorable time period to invest and also one of the best months for a stock market gain.

It is interesting to note that a high frequency positive first day of the month does not necessarily mean that the average gain is high. For example, the first day in September has been positive 67% of the time from 1950 to 2009. Yet, although it is positive, it is the second worst month for a first day return (its frequency of being positive is high, but its average return is low).

This indicates that the first day in September has a wide range of returns, with some large down days, but is most of the time positive.

As a side note, the month of September has also proved unfriendly to the market and has produced an average negative return from 1950 to 2009.

> ⚠️ CAUTION:
> Generally, it is not a wise strategy to invest for just one day: the expected rate of return, combined with the risk from volatility do not justify the expected returns.

6 MONDAY	024 / 208	**7** TUESDAY	023 / 207

Market Indices & Rates
Weekly Values**

Stock Markets	2009	2010
Dow	8,730	10,008
S&P500	940	1,069
Nasdaq	1,838	2,193
TSX	10,506	11,555
FTSE	4,438	5,096
DAX	5,097	5,973
Nikkei	9,712	9,549
Hang Seng	18,607	19,598

Commodities	2009	2010
Oil	68.1	73.4
Gold	974.3	1226.4

Bond Yields	2009	2010
USA 5 Yr Treasury	2.58	2.01
USA 10 Yr T	3.70	3.22
USA 20 Yr T	4.55	3.96
Moody's Aaa	5.68	4.90
Moody's Baa	7.80	6.23
CAN 5 Yr T	2.49	2.66
CAN 10 Yr T	3.41	3.36

8 WEDNESDAY	022 / 206	**9** THURSDAY	021 / 205

Money Market	2009	2010
USA Fed Funds	0.25	0.25
USA 3 Mo T-B	0.15	0.10
CAN tgt overnight rate	0.25	0.50
CAN 3 Mo T-B	0.21	0.53

Foreign Exchange	2009	2010
USD/EUR	1.42	1.20
USD/GBP	1.64	1.45
CAN/USD	1.09	1.05
JPY/USD	95.94	91.52

10 FRIDAY	020 / 204

JUNE

M	T	W	T	F	S	S
		1	2	3	4	5
6	7	8	9	10	11	12
13	14	15	16	17	18	19
20	21	22	23	24	25	26
27	28	29	30			

2009 Strategy Performance

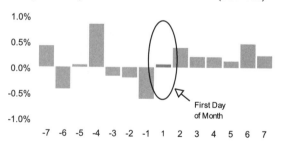

Avg. First Day of Month Performance 2009 (S&P 500)

JULY

M	T	W	T	F	S	S
			1	2	3	
4	5	6	7	8	9	10
11	12	13	14	15	16	17
18	19	20	21	22	23	24
25	26	27	28	29	30	31

Typically it is the first day of the month that averages the largest daily gains. In 2009 the first day of the month was on average positive. The next few days after the first day were also positive.

AUGUST

M	T	W	T	F	S	S
1	2	3	4	5	6	7
8	9	10	11	12	13	14
15	16	17	18	19	20	21
22	23	24	25	26	27	28
29	30	31				

** Weekly avg closing values- except Fed Funds & CAN overnight tgt rate weekly closing values.

JUNE – LEADERLESS MONTH
No Sector Consistently Leads the Pack

June is on average a leaderless month. One year, one sector leads the market, and the next year another sector leads the market. This is somewhat evident by looking at the Thackray Sector Thermometer for the month of June. Out of the ten S&P GIC sectors, from 1990 to 2010 the technology sector has been the top sector five times and the worst sector four times.

This is a disproportionate amount of highs and lows for one sector. Almost all of the top sector performances for information technology occurred in the late 90's and early 2000's, during the technology bubble. Although the other sectors may not have such top and bottom results as the technology sector, they are nevertheless dispersed throughout the ranks.

The June S&P GIC Top/Bottom 3 Ranking Table illustrates the frequency of the GIC sectors placing in the top or bottom three sectors. Other than health care and financials having the largest ratios of top and bottom placement in the ranks and vice versa, there is little to give investors guidance of possible best sectors.

Very often you can judge the strength of a market by which sector is leading. Investors often look to the financial sector to be a leader, and when it is not one of the top sectors, they tend to be cautious. Other investors look at the strength of the semiconductor sector to be a leader. The belief is that if the sector is strong, then investors are bullish on the economy and the stock market.

Using the top ten S&P GIC sectors, there does not seem to be a significant predictive trend. When the technology sector has been a top sector, the subsequent period has been both positive and negative. Likewise, when it has been in the bottom sector, the subsequent period has been positive and negative.

A possible explanation for the lack of leadership in June is that the month is a transition month. As described in the "Six'n'Six" strategy, the market often peaks at the beginning of May. On the other hand, typically in bull markets, the market can peak mid-July. Although the market can peak at any time, on average there are two possible seasonal peaks, May and July - June is the bridge month between the peaks.

With a lot of sectors finishing their period of strength in May, and investors trying to push them higher, there is a struggle with some of the defensive and commodity sectors that are trying to start their rallies. As a result, different sectors of the market lead in different years depending on the extent and nature of the struggle.

The lack of leadership in June is significant for investors as it means there is a lack of seasonal investment opportunities. June falls into the six month unfavorable period and as such the "bank" of the portfolio is in cash waiting for sector opportunities. Although there are sector opportunities in June, there are just not a lot of them. If investors desire market exposure in June, typically they should not over commit to one or two sectors and they should use fundamental and technical analysis to assist in making entry and exit decisions.

June Best / Worst S&P GIC Sectors (1990-2010)		
	Best Sector	Worst Sector
1990	Health Care	Telecom
1991	Telecom	Info Tech
1992	Financials	Health Care
1993	Telecom	Health Care
1994	Telecom	Info Tech
1995	Info Tech	Energy
1996	Utilities	Materials
1997	Health Care	Info Tech
1998	Info Tech	Materials
1999	Info Tech	Utilities
2000	Info Tech	Materials
2001	Info Tech	Utilities
2002	Energy	Telecom
2003	Health Care	Energy
2004	Industrials	Health Care
2005	Energy	Industrials
2006	Telecom	Info Tech
2007	Energy	Utilities
2008	Energy	Financials
2009	Utilities	Materials
2010	Telecom	Consumer Disc.

June Sector Frequency Top/Bottom 3 S&P GIC Sectors (1990-2010)		
	Top 3	Bottom 3
Energy	7	6
Materials	4	8
Industrials	5	6
Consumer Disc	3	4
Consumer Staples	2	4
Health Care	10	6
Financials	5	10
Telecom	10	4
Info Tech	7	8
Utilities	10	7

13 MONDAY	017 / 201	**14** TUESDAY	016 / 200

15 WEDNESDAY	015 / 199	**16** THURSDAY	014 / 198

17 FRIDAY   013 / 197

WEEK 24

Market Indices & Rates
Weekly Values**

Stock Markets	2009	2010
Dow	8,767	10,378
S&P500	942	1,111
Nasdaq	1,855	2,295
TSX	10,611	11,874
FTSE	4,430	5,233
DAX	5,046	6,186
Nikkei	9,952	9,966
Hang Seng	18,556	20,135

Commodities	2009	2010
Oil	70.8	76.7
Gold	947.7	1236.9

Bond Yields	2009	2010
USA 5 Yr Treasury	2.88	2.06
USA 10 Yr T	3.89	3.26
USA 20 Yr T	4.67	4.00
Moody's Aaa	5.80	4.93
Moody's Baa	7.69	6.32
CAN 5 Yr T	2.73	2.71
CAN 10 Yr T	3.55	3.37

Money Market	2009	2010
USA Fed Funds	0.25	0.25
USA 3 Mo T-B	0.19	0.09
CAN tgt overnight rate	0.25	0.50
CAN 3 Mo T-B	0.23	0.53

Foreign Exchange	2009	2010
USD/EUR	1.40	1.23
USD/GBP	1.62	1.48
CAN/USD	1.11	1.03
JPY/USD	98.24	91.36

JUNE

M	T	W	T	F	S	S
		1	2	3	4	5
6	7	8	9	10	11	12
13	14	15	16	17	18	19
20	21	22	23	24	25	26
27	28	29	30			

JULY

M	T	W	T	F	S	S
				1	2	3
4	5	6	7	8	9	10
11	12	13	14	15	16	17
18	19	20	21	22	23	24
25	26	27	28	29	30	31

AUGUST

M	T	W	T	F	S	S
1	2	3	4	5	6	7
8	9	10	11	12	13	14
15	16	17	18	19	20	21
22	23	24	25	26	27	28
29	30	31				

2010 Strategy Performance

June Performance of S&P GICS (2010)

June was not a good month for the stock market in 2010. As a result, the defensive sectors outperformed the cyclical sectors. Generally when the market is pushing strongly to the downside, the defensive sectors will outperform on a relative basis and when the market is in a rally mode, the cyclicals will outperform.

** Weekly avg closing values- except Fed Funds & CAN overnight tgt rate weekly closing values.

BIOTECH SUMMER SOLSTICE
June 23rd to Sep 13th

The *Biotech Summer Solstice* trade starts on June 23rd and lasts until September 13th. The trade is aptly named as its outperformance starts approximately on the day of the summer solstice – the longest day of the year.

There are two main drivers of the trade: biotech is a good substitute for technology stocks in the summer, and investors want to take a position in the biotech sector before the autumn conferences.

12.4% extra & 15 out of 18 times better than the S&P 500

Biotech vs. S&P 500 1992 to 2009

Performance > S&P 500			
Jun 23 to Sep 13	Biotech	S&P 500	Diff
1992	17.9 %	4.0 %	13.8 %
1993	3.6	3.6	0.0
1994	24.2	3.2	21.0
1995	31.5	5.0	26.5
1996	7.0	2.1	4.9
1997	-18.9	2.8	-21.7
1998	20.6	-8.5	29.1
1999	64.3	0.6	63.7
2000	7.6	2.3	5.4
2001	-3.6	-10.8	7.2
2002	8.1	-10.0	18.2
2003	6.4	2.3	4.1
2004	8.9	-0.8	9.6
2005	26.0	1.4	24.5
2006	7.4	5.8	1.6
2007	6.0	-1.2	7.2
2008	11.4	-5.0	16.5
2009	7.7	16.8	-9.1
Avg	13.1 %	0.7 %	12.4 %

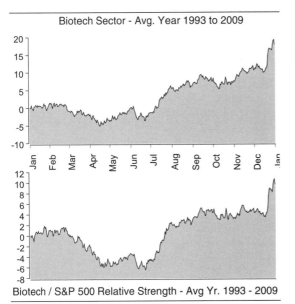

Biotech Sector - Avg. Year 1993 to 2009

Biotech / S&P 500 Relative Strength - Avg Yr. 1993 - 2009

As a result, in the softer summer months, investors are more willing to commit speculative money into the biotech sector, compared with the technology sector.

The biotech sector is one of the few sectors that starts its outperformance in June. This is in part because of the biotech conferences that occur in autumn.

With positive announcements in autumn, the price of biotech companies on the stock market can increase dramatically. As a result, investors try to lock in positions early.

The biotechnology sector is often considered the cousin of the technology sector, a good place for speculative investments. The sectors are similar as both include concept companies (companies without a product but with good potential). Despite their similarity, investors view the sectors differently. The technology sector is viewed as being largely dependent on the economy and conversely the biotech sector as being much less dependent on the economy. The end product of biotechnology companies is mainly medicine, which is not economically sensitive.

> (i) *Biotech SP GIC Sector # 352010: Companies primarily engaged in the research, development, manufacturing and/or marketing of products based on genetic analysis and genetic engineering. This includes companies specializing in protein-based therapeutics to treat human diseases.*

20 MONDAY	010 / 194	**21** TUESDAY	009 / 193

Market Indices & Rates
Weekly Values**

Stock Markets	2009	2010
Dow	8,542	10,266
S&P500	917	1,090
Nasdaq	1,811	2,249
TSX	10,236	11,784
FTSE	4,312	5,174
DAX	4,852	6,191
Nikkei	9,825	9,988
Hang Seng	18,089	20,802

Commodities	2009	2010
Oil	70.6	77.1
Gold	934.5	1241.5

Bond Yields	2009	2010
USA 5 Yr Treasury	2.76	1.96
USA 10 Yr T	3.75	3.17
USA 20 Yr T	4.54	3.92
Moody's Aaa	5.61	4.84
Moody's Baa	7.42	6.22
CAN 5 Yr T	2.66	2.56
CAN 10 Yr T	3.49	3.25

Money Market	2009	2010
USA Fed Funds	0.25	0.25
USA 3 Mo T-B	0.18	0.13
CAN tgt overnight rate	0.25	0.50
CAN 3 Mo T-B	0.23	0.54

Foreign Exchange	2009	2010
USD/EUR	1.39	1.23
USD/GBP	1.63	1.49
CAN/USD	1.13	1.03
JPY/USD	96.80	90.15

22 WEDNESDAY	008 / 192	**23** THURSDAY	007 / 191

24 FRIDAY			006 / 190

JUNE

M	T	W	T	F	S	S
		1	2	3	4	5
6	7	8	9	10	11	12
13	14	15	16	17	18	19
20	21	22	23	24	25	26
27	28	29	30			

JULY

M	T	W	T	F	S	S
				1	2	3
4	5	6	7	8	9	10
11	12	13	14	15	16	17
18	19	20	21	22	23	24
25	26	27	28	29	30	31

AUGUST

M	T	W	T	F	S	S
1	2	3	4	5	6	7
8	9	10	11	12	13	14
15	16	17	18	19	20	21
22	23	24	25	26	27	28
29	30	31				

2009 Strategy Performance*

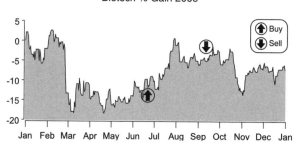

Biotech % Gain 2009

The biotech sector put in a positive performance during its seasonal period, but it failed to outperform the S&P 500.

The S&P 500 was rising strongly in the summer months and in the end there was just not enough excitement in the biotech sector to provide positive stimulus for outperformance.

* Buy and Sell dates are approximate representations of strategy dates.
** Weekly avg closing values- except Fed Funds & CAN overnight tgt rate weekly closing values.

- 74 -

INDEPENDENCE DAY – THE FULL TRADE PROFIT BEFORE & AFTER FIREWORKS

Two Market Days Before June Month End To 5 Market Days After Independence Day

The beginning of July is a time for celebration and the markets tend to agree.

Based on previous market data, the best way to take advantage of this trend is to be invested for the two market days prior to the June month end and hold until five market days after Independence Day. This time period has produced above average returns on a fairly consistent basis.

0.8% avg. gain &
70% of the time positive

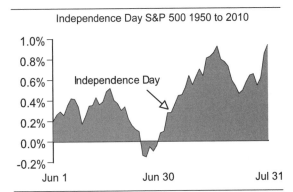

Independence Day S&P 500 1950 to 2010

The typical Independence Day trade put forward by quite a few pundits has been to invest one or two days before the holiday and take profits one or two days after the holiday.

Although this strategy has produced profits, it has left a lot of money on the table. This strategy misses out on the positive days at the end of June and on the full slate of positive days after Independence Day.

The beginning part of the Independence Day positive trend is driven by two combining factors.

First, portfolio managers "window dress" (buying stocks that have a favorable perception in the market); thereby pushing stock prices up at the end of the month.

Second, investors have become "wise" to the Independence Day Trade and try to get into the market before Independence Day to take advantage of rising prices.

> (i) *History of Independence Day:*
> *Independence Day is celebrated on July 4th because that is the day when the Continental Congress adopted the final draft of the Declaration of Independence in 1776. Independence Day was made an official holiday at the end of the War of Independence in 1783. In 1941 Congress declared the 4th of July a federal holiday.*

S&P 500, 2 Market Days Before June Month End To 5 Market Days
after Independence Day % Gain 1950 to 2010   Positive ☐

1950	-4.4 %	1960	-0.1 %	1970	1.5 %	1980	1.4 %	1990	1.7 %	2000	1.8 %	2010	0.4 %
1951	1.5	1961	1.7	1971	3.2	1981	-2.4	1991	1.4	2001	-2.6		
1952	0.9	1962	9.8	1972	0.3	1982	-0.6	1992	2.8	2002	-4.7		
1953	0.8	1963	0.5	1973	2.1	1983	1.5	1993	-0.6	2003	1.2		
1954	2.9	1964	2.3	1974	-8.8	1984	-0.7	1994	0.4	2004	-1.7		
1955	4.9	1965	5.0	1975	-0.2	1985	1.5	1995	1.8	2005	1.5		
1956	3.4	1966	2.1	1976	2.4	1986	-2.6	1996	-2.8	2006	2.1		
1957	3.8	1967	1.3	1977	-0.6	1987	0.4	1997	3.7	2007	0.8		
1958	2.0	1968	2.3	1978	0.6	1988	-0.6	1998	2.7	2008	-3.4		
1959	3.3	1969	-1.5	1979	1.3	1989	0.9	1999	5.1	2009	-4.3		
Avg.	1.9 %		2.3 %		0.2 %		-0.1 %		1.8 %		-0.9 %		0.4 %

27 MONDAY	003 / 187	**28** TUESDAY	002 / 186

29 WEDNESDAY	001 / 185	**30** THURSDAY	000 / 184

1 FRIDAY   030 / 183

Market Indices & Rates
Weekly Values**

Stock Markets	2009	2010
Dow	8,375	9,840
S&P500	906	1,039
Nasdaq	1,798	2,132
TSX	10,115	11,340
FTSE	4,248	4,909
DAX	4,763	5,953
Nikkei	9,728	9,409
Hang Seng	18,073	20,252

Commodities	2009	2010
Oil	68.5	75.0
Gold	930.6	1235.0

Bond Yields	2009	2010
USA 5 Yr Treasury	2.66	1.80
USA 10 Yr T	3.63	2.99
USA 20 Yr T	4.37	3.76
Moody's Aaa	5.43	4.69
Moody's Baa	7.20	6.06
CAN 5 Yr T	2.54	2.36
CAN 10 Yr T	3.43	3.10

Money Market	2009	2010
USA Fed Funds	0.25	0.25
USA 3 Mo T-B	0.19	0.17
CAN tgt overnight rate	0.25	0.50
CAN 3 Mo T-B	0.24	0.51

Foreign Exchange	2009	2010
USD/EUR	1.40	1.23
USD/GBP	1.64	1.51
CAN/USD	1.15	1.05
JPY/USD	95.71	88.57

JULY

M	T	W	T	F	S	S
				1	2	3
4	5	6	7	8	9	10
11	12	13	14	15	16	17
18	19	20	21	22	23	24
25	26	27	28	29	30	31

AUGUST

M	T	W	T	F	S	S
1	2	3	4	5	6	7
8	9	10	11	12	13	14
15	16	17	18	19	20	21
22	23	24	25	26	27	28
29	30	31				

SEPTEMBER

M	T	W	T	F	S	S
		1	2	3	4	
5	6	7	8	9	10	11
12	13	14	15	16	17	18
19	20	21	22	23	24	25
26	27	28	29	30		

2010 Strategy Performance*

Independence Day Trade June to July S&P 500 (2010)

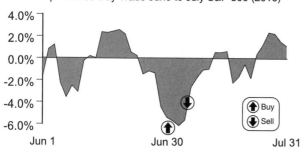

The Independence Day Trade in 2010 was not stellar, but it was positive. The end of June was decidely negative, giving the trade a bad start into the beginning of July.

Once Independence Day arrived, the market celebrated and put all of its troubles behind itself (at least for a while). July ended up being a strong month, producing a return of almost 4%. The bulk of the gains came in the first eighteen days of the month, which is consistent with the positive trend of the *18 Day Earnings Months Effect* strategy for strong gains.

** Weekly avg closing values- except Fed Funds & CAN overnight tgt rate weekly closing values.

JULY

	MONDAY	TUESDAY	WEDNESDAY
WEEK 26	27	28	29
WEEK 27	**4** 27 USA Market Closed - Independence Day	**5** 26	**6** 25
WEEK 28	**11** 20	**12** 19	**13** 18
WEEK 29	**18** 13	**19** 12	**20** 11
WEEK 30	**25** 6	**26** 5	**27** 4

THURSDAY	FRIDAY
30 30	**1** 30

1 CAN   Market Closed-
Canada Day

7 24	**8** 23
14 17	**15** 16
21 10	**22** 9
28 3	**29** 2

AUGUST

M	T	W	T	F	S	S
1	2	3	4	5	6	7
8	9	10	11	12	13	14
15	16	17	18	19	20	21
22	23	24	25	26	27	28
29	30	31				

SEPTEMBER

M	T	W	T	F	S	S
			1	2	3	4
5	6	7	8	9	10	11
12	13	14	15	16	17	18
19	20	21	22	23	24	25
26	27	28	29	30		

OCTOBER

M	T	W	T	F	S	S
					1	2
3	4	5	6	7	8	9
10	11	12	13	14	15	16
17	18	19	20	21	22	23
24	25	26	27	28	29	30
31						

NOVEMBER

M	T	W	T	F	S	S
	1	2	3	4	5	6
7	8	9	10	11	12	13
14	15	16	17	18	19	20
21	22	23	24	25	26	27
28	29	30				

JULY
S U M M A R Y

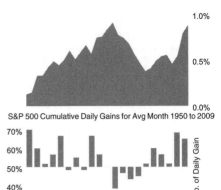

S&P 500 Cumulative Daily Gains for Avg Month 1950 to 2009

STRATEGIES	PAGE
STRATEGIES STARTING	
18 Day Earnings Month Effect	43
Utilities – Summer Bounce	81
Gold (Metal) Shines	83
Golden Times	85
Oil – Summer/Autumn Strategy II of II	95
STRATEGIES FINISHING	
18 Day Earnings Month Effect	43
Independence Day – Full Trade Profit	75

♦ When a summer rally does occur, the bulk of the gains are made in July. ♦ In the last half of the month the energy, gold and utility stocks tend to start their seasonal rallies (see strategies in this month). ♦ In 2010 the market shot up like a rocket after Independence Day as the earnings of companies were better than expected. Gold started its rally on que and energy turned in a lack lustre performance.

BEST / WORST JULY BROAD MKTS. 2000-2009

BEST JULY MARKETS
♦ Russell 2000 (2009) 9.5%
♦ Dow (2009) 8.6%
♦ Russell 3000 Value (2009) 8.2%

WORST JULY MARKETS
♦ Russell 2000 (2002) -15.2%
♦ Russell 3000 Value (2002) -9.9%
♦ Nasdaq (2002) -9.2%

Index Values End of Month

	2000	2001	2002	2003	2004	2005	2006	2007	2008	2009
Dow	10,522	10,523	8,737	9,234	10,140	10,641	11,186	13,212	11,378	9,172
S&P 500	1,431	1,211	912	990	1,102	1,234	1,277	1,455	1,267	987
Nasdaq	3,767	2,027	1,328	1,735	1,887	2,185	2,091	2,546	2,326	1,979
TSX	10,406	7,690	6,605	7,258	8,458	10,423	11,831	13,869	13,593	10,787
Russell 1000	1,454	1,225	931	1,016	1,129	1,288	1,331	1,523	1,334	1,038
Russell 2000	1,244	1,205	975	1,183	1,370	1,689	1,741	1,929	1,776	1,384
Russell 3000 Growth	3,183	2,084	1,471	1,639	1,764	1,988	1,955	2,305	2,139	1,727
Russell 3000 Value	2,012	2,166	1,773	1,922	2,216	2,589	2,809	3,099	2,570	1,920

Percent Gain for July

	2000	2001	2002	2003	2004	2005	2006	2007	2008	2009
Dow	0.7	0.2	-5.5	2.8	-2.8	3.6	0.3	-1.5	0.2	8.6
S&P 500	-1.6	-1.1	-7.9	1.6	-3.4	3.6	0.5	-3.2	-1.0	7.4
Nasdaq	-5.0	-6.2	-9.2	6.9	-7.8	6.2	-3.7	-2.2	1.4	7.8
TSX	2.1	-0.6	-7.6	3.9	-1.0	5.3	1.9	-0.3	-6.0	4.0
Russell 1000	-1.7	-1.5	-7.5	1.8	-3.6	3.8	0.1	-3.2	-1.3	7.5
Russell 2000	-3.3	-5.5	-15.2	6.2	-6.8	6.3	-3.3	-6.9	3.6	9.5
Russell 3000 Growth	-4.5	-3.0	-6.2	2.8	-6.0	5.0	-2.2	-1.9	-1.6	7.1
Russell 3000 Value	1.3	-0.5	-9.9	1.5	-1.9	2.9	1.9	-5.1	-0.2	8.2

July Market Avg. Performance 2000 to 2009 [1]

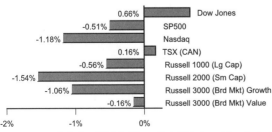

Interest Corner Jul[2]

	Fed Funds % [3]	3 Mo. T-Bill % [4]	10 Yr % [5]	20 Yr % [6]
2009	0.25	0.18	3.52	4.29
2008	2.00	1.68	3.99	4.63
2007	5.25	4.96	4.78	5.00
2006	5.25	5.10	4.99	5.17
2005	3.25	3.42	4.28	4.56

(1) Russell Data provided by Russell (2) Federal Reserve Bank of St. Louis - end of month values (3) Target rate set by FOMC (4)(5)(6) Constant yield maturities.

THACKRAY SECTOR THERMOMETER

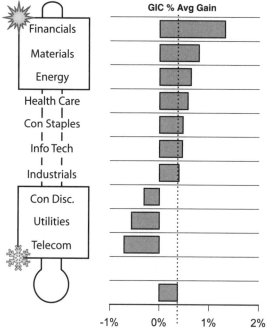

GIC[2] % Avg Gain	Fq % Gain >S&P 500	
SP GIC SECTOR 1990-2009[1]		
1.3 %	55 %	Financials
0.8	65	Materials
0.6	60	Energy
0.6	45	Health Care
0.5	60	Consumer Staples
0.5	45	Information Technology
0.4	50	Industrials
-0.3	45	Consumer Discretionary
-0.6	40	Utilities
-0.7 %	45 %	Telecom
0.4 %	N/A %	S&P 500

Sector Commentary

♦ July's performance is really the tale of two half months. In the first half of the month, the broad market tends to do very well (see *18 Day Earnings Month Effect*). In the second half the performance tends to wither away. ♦ In 2009 the S&P 500 gained 7.4% in July, mainly on the back of better than expected earnings. As a result the defensive sectors were the bottom performers and the cyclical sectors the top performers. Materials, Consumer Discretionary and Industrials were the top performing sectors with gains of 13.3%, 9.3% and 9.2% respectively.

Sub-Sector Commentary

♦ The Biotech sector has the best long-term average gain and has the highest frequency of beating the S&P 500. In 2009 the S&P 500 performed strongly at 7.4%, but the Biotech sector managed to outperform with a gain of 10.2%. ♦ The Auto & Components sector is the second highest rated sector in the sub-sector thermometer with an average gain of 1.3% from 1990 to 2009. In 2009 it gained 29.2% as the economy rebounded and car companies that not too long ago were bound for the scrap yard were emerging with strong prospects.

SELECTED SUB-SECTORS 1990-2009[3]		
6.8 %	82 %	Biotech (93-2009)
1.3	55	Auto & Components
1.3	65	Banks
1.2	45	Airlines
1.1	65	Insurance
1.0	50	Transportation
0.8	55	Integrated Oil & Gas
0.5	53	Semiconductor (SOX) 95-2009
0.2	55	Retail
0.2	50	Metals & Mining
-0.1	50	Pharmaceuticals
-1.2	40	Gold (XAU)
-1.9	44	Agriculture Products (94-2009)
-2.7	20	Software & Services

(1) Sector data provided by Standard and Poors (2) GIC is short form for Global Industry Classification (3) Sub Sector data provided by Standard and Poors, except where marked by symbol.

UTILITIES – SUMMER BOUNCE
July 17th to Oct 3rd

Utility stocks are a long forgotten part of the market. Very seldom do you hear pundits singing their virtues. They lost out to the hype of tech stocks in the 90's and are still shunned by a large number of investors because of the fear of rising interest rates. Despite the environment of neglect, utility stocks have managed to outperform the S&P 500 on a fairly consistent basis from July 17th to October 3rd.

2.8% extra and positive at a time when the S&P 500 has been negative

Utilities' outperformance from the end of July to the beginning of October fits in very well with the theme of investors taking a defensive position during this time of year. At this time the broad market tends to produce a negative return and investors are looking for a safe place to invest. Utilities fit the bill.

S&P Utilities Sector vs. S&P 500 1990 to 2009			
Jul 17 to Oct 3	Utilities	Positive	Diff
		SP500	
1990	-3.4 %	-15.6 %	12.2 %
1991	9.2	0.8	8.5
1992	-0.9	-1.7	0.8
1993	3.6	3.5	0.1
1994	-1.6	1.7	-3.3
1995	6.6	4.0	2.5
1996	-0.9	10.3	-11.2
1997	2.6	3.0	-0.4
1998	6.8	-15.3	22.1
1999	-5.5	-9.6	4.1
2000	23.0	-5.5	28.5
2001	-13.6	-10.8	-2.8
2002	-12.0	-9.1	-2.9
2003	7.2	3.6	3.6
2004	5.1	2.7	2.4
2005	6.0	-0.1	6.1
2006	5.3	7.9	-2.6
2007	0.6	-0.6	1.2
2008	-17.6	-11.7	-5.9
2009	1.1	9.0	-7.9
Avg.	1.1 %	-1.7 %	2.8 %

Utilities Sector - Avg. Year 1990 to 2009

Utilities / S&P 500 Relative Strength - Avg Yr. 1990 - 2009

From July 17th to October 3rd, during the years 1990 to 2009, the utilities sector has produced an average return of 1.1%, while the S&P 500 reached into the negative territory with an average loss of 1.7%. Utilities have produced 2.8% more when the S&P 500 has typically been negative. Also, during this time period the utilities sector beat the S&P 500, 12 out of 20 times. Not bad for a defensive sector. The utilities sector is considered defensive because it is a slow growth mature industry that has stable income from long term contracts. When the market gets "spooked," investors typically switch their money into companies with stable earnings. There is an added bonus of investing in utilities – dividends. Because the sector is mature with stable earnings they tend to pay out a higher dividend yield.

In the last two decades there have been two periods of two back-to-back years of negative performance. In 1996 and 1997 the utilities sector under performed as dividends and defensive positions did not matter much. In 2001 and 2002 the utilities sector under performed as a few scandal ridden utilities companies hit the newspaper headlines. The most notorious being Enron.

It appears the utilities trade is once again back on track as the companies have "cleaned house" and moved back to their core business: providing utilities services.

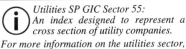

Utilities SP GIC Sector 55: An index designed to represent a cross section of utility companies.
For more information on the utilities sector, see www.standardandpoors.com.

4 MONDAY	027 / 180	**5** TUESDAY	026 / 179

6 WEDNESDAY	025 / 178	**7** THURSDAY	024 / 177

8 FRIDAY   023 / 176

WEEK 27

Market Indices & Rates
Weekly Values**

Stock Markets	2008	2009
Dow	11,309	8,440
S&P500	1,272	917
Nasdaq	2,274	1,830
TSX	14,164	10,345
FTSE	5,484	4,271
DAX	6,333	4,805
Nikkei	13,347	9,875
Hang Seng	21,618	18,322

Commodities	2008	2009
Oil	142.5	69.4
Gold	933.7	934.1

Bond Yields	2008	2009
USA 5 Yr Treasury	3.32	2.50
USA 10 Yr T	4.00	3.53
USA 20 Yr T	4.59	4.30
Moody's Aaa	5.60	5.40
Moody's Baa	7.06	7.18
CAN 5 Yr T	3.45	2.45
CAN 10 Yr T	3.74	3.37

Money Market	2008	2009
USA Fed Funds	2.00	0.25
USA 3 Mo T-B	1.86	0.18
CAN tgt overnight rate	3.00	0.25
CAN 3 Mo T-B	2.44	0.23

Foreign Exchange	2008	2009
USD/EUR	1.58	1.41
USD/GBP	1.99	1.64
CAN/USD	1.02	1.16
JPY/USD	106.11	96.20

2009 Strategy Performance*

Utilities % Average Gain 2009

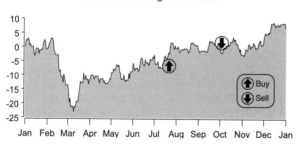

Although the utilities sector produced a positive result during its seasonally strong period, it was no contest for the S&P 500.

When the market is really strong, generally the defensive utilities sector under performs. The year 2009 was no exception. Investors were more interested in sectors with higher betas that could provide them with bigger returns.

JULY

M	T	W	T	F	S	S
				1	2	3
4	5	6	7	8	9	10
11	12	13	14	15	16	17
18	19	20	21	22	23	24
25	26	27	28	29	30	31

AUGUST

M	T	W	T	F	S	S
1	2	3	4	5	6	7
8	9	10	11	12	13	14
15	16	17	18	19	20	21
22	23	24	25	26	27	28
29	30	31				

SEPTEMBER

M	T	W	T	F	S	S
			1	2	3	4
5	6	7	8	9	10	11
12	13	14	15	16	17	18
19	20	21	22	23	24	25
26	27	28	29	30		

* Buy and Sell dates are approximate representations of strategy dates.
** Weekly avg closing values- except Fed Funds & CAN overnight tgt rate weekly closing values.

GOLD SHINES

(Metal) Gold (Metal) Outperforms – July 12th to October 9th

"Foul cankering rust the hidden treasure frets, but gold that's put to use more gold begets."

(William Shakespeare, *Venus and Adonis*)

For many years gold was thought to be a dead investment. It was only the "gold bugs" that espoused the virtues of investing in the precious metal. Investors were mesmerized with technology stocks and central bankers, confident of their currencies, were selling gold, "left, right and center."

3.6% gain & positive 70% of the time

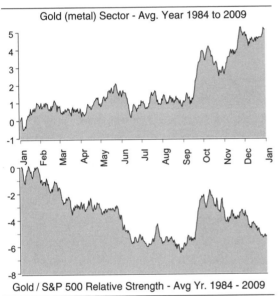

Gold (metal) Sector - Avg. Year 1984 to 2009

Gold / S&P 500 Relative Strength - Avg Yr. 1984 - 2009

Jul 12 to Oct 9th	Gold	S&P 500	Positive Diff
1984	0.5 %	7.4 %	-6.9 %
1985	4.1	-5.4	9.5
1986	25.2	-2.6	27.8
1987	3.9	0.9	3.0
1988	-7.5	2.8	-10.3
1989	-4.2	9.4	-13.6
1990	12.1	-15.5	27.6
1991	-2.9	0.0	-2.8
1992	0.4	-2.9	3.3
1993	-8.8	2.7	-11.5
1994	1.6	1.6	0.0
1995	-0.1	4.3	-4.3
1996	-0.4	7.9	-8.3
1997	4.4	5.9	-1.5
1998	2.8	-15.5	18.2
1999	25.6	-4.8	30.4
2000	-4.5	-5.3	0.8
2001	8.4	-10.5	18.8
2002	1.7	-16.2	17.9
2003	7.8	4.1	3.8
2004	3.8	0.8	2.9
2005	11.4	-1.9	13.4
2006	-8.8	6.1	-14.9
2007	11.0	3.1	8.0
2008	-8.2	-26.6	18.4
2009	15.2	21.9	- 6.7
Avg.	3.6 %	- 1.1 %	4.7 %

Times have changed and investors have taken a shine to gold (metal). In the last few years gold has substantially outperformed the stock market. On a seasonal basis, on average from 1984 to 2009, gold has done well relative to the stock market from July 12th to October 9th. The reasons for gold's seasonal changes in price, are related to jewellery production and European Central banks selling cycles (see *Golden Times* strategy page).

The movement of gold stock prices, represented by the index (XAU) on the Philadelphia Exchange, coincides closely with the price of gold (metal). Although there is a strong correlation between gold and gold stocks, there are other factors, such as company operations and hedging policies which determine each company's price in the market. Gold (metal) has typ-ically started its seasonal strong period a few weeks earlier than gold stocks and finished just after gold stocks have turned down.

Investors should know that gold can have a run from October 28th to the end of the year. Although this is a positive time for gold, on average it does not perform as well as the S&P 500. From Oct. 28th to Dec. 31st (1984 to 2009), gold has an average return of 2.2% and has been positive 62% of the time. In this time period it has only outperformed the S&P 500 42% of the time, which has averaged a return of 4.9%. Investors should use technical analysis to determine the relative strength of both markets.

> *Source: Bank of England*
> *London PM is recognized as the world benchmark for gold prices.*
> *London PM represents the close value of gold in afternoon trading in London.*

11 MONDAY	020 / 173

12 TUESDAY	019 / 172

13 WEDNESDAY	018 / 171

14 THURSDAY	017 / 170

15 FRIDAY	016 / 169

WEEK 28

Market Indices & Rates
Weekly Values**

Stock Markets	2008	2009
Dow	11,219	8,199
S&P500	1,253	884
Nasdaq	2,254	1,758
TSX	13,717	9,809
FTSE	5,430	4,162
DAX	6,309	4,606
Nikkei	13,110	9,466
Hang Seng	21,789	17,812

Commodities	2008	2009
Oil	140.0	61.5
Gold	933.5	918.3

Bond Yields	2008	2009
USA 5 Yr Treasury	3.18	2.31
USA 10 Yr T	3.90	3.42
USA 20 Yr T	4.51	4.22
Moody's Aaa	5.53	5.34
Moody's Baa	7.03	7.10
CAN 5 Yr T	3.39	2.41
CAN 10 Yr T	3.72	3.31

Money Market	2008	2009
USA Fed Funds	2.00	0.25
USA 3 Mo T-B	1.77	0.19
CAN tgt overnight rate	3.00	0.25
CAN 3 Mo T-B	2.35	0.23

Foreign Exchange	2008	2009
USD/EUR	1.57	1.39
USD/GBP	1.97	1.62
CAN/USD	1.02	1.16
JPY/USD	107.18	94.02

JULY

M	T	W	T	F	S	S
				1	2	3
4	5	6	7	8	9	10
11	12	13	14	15	16	17
18	19	20	21	22	23	24
25	26	27	28	29	30	31

AUGUST

M	T	W	T	F	S	S
1	2	3	4	5	6	7
8	9	10	11	12	13	14
15	16	17	18	19	20	21
22	23	24	25	26	27	28
29	30	31				

SEPTEMBER

M	T	W	T	F	S	S
			1	2	3	4
5	6	7	8	9	10	11
12	13	14	15	16	17	18
19	20	21	22	23	24	25
26	27	28	29	30		

2009 Strategy Performance*

Gold % Gain 2009

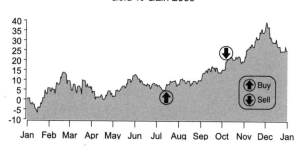

In 2009 gold had a good run in its seasonal period, but under performed the S&P 500. At the end of its seasonal period, gold paused before resuming its run to early December.

At the same time that gold was running at the end of the year, the S&P 500 was also rising. Gold soared a lot higher than the S&P 500 before pulling back at the end of the year.

* Buy and Sell dates are approximate representations of strategy dates.
** Weekly avg closing values- except Fed Funds & CAN overnight tgt rate weekly closing values.

Gold stocks were shunned for many years. It is only recently that interest has sparked again. What few investors know is that even during the twenty year bear market in gold that started in 1981, it was possible to make money in gold stocks.

6.8% when the S&P 500 has been negative

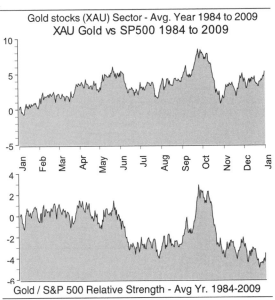

Gold stocks (XAU) Sector - Avg. Year 1984 to 2009
XAU Gold vs SP500 1984 to 2009

Gold / S&P 500 Relative Strength - Avg Yr. 1984-2009

Jul 27 to Sep 25	XAU	Positive		
		S&P 500	Diff	
1984	20.8 %	10.4 %	10.4	%
1985	-5.5	-6.1	0.6	
1986	36.9	-3.5	40.4	
1987	23.0	3.5	19.5	
1988	-11.9	1.7	-13.7	
1989	10.5	1.8	8.7	
1990	3.8	-13.4	17.2	
1991	-11.9	1.6	-13.5	
1992	-3.8	0.7	-4.5	
1993	-7.3	1.9	-9.2	
1994	18.2	1.4	16.8	
1995	-1.0	3.6	-4.6	
1996	-1.0	7.9	-8.9	
1997	8.7	-0.1	8.8	
1998	12.0	-8.4	20.5	
1999	16.9	-5.2	22.1	
2000	-2.8	-0.9	-1.9	
2001	3.2	-15.8	19.0	
2002	29.8	-1.5	31.4	
2003	11.0	0.5	10.5	
2004	16.5	2.4	14.1	
2005	20.5	-1.3	21.8	
2006	-11.9	4.6	-16.8	
2007	14.0	2.3	11.7	
2008	-18.5	-3.9	-14.6	
2009	6.0	6.7	-0.6	
Avg.	6.8 %	-0.4 %	7.1	%

XAU (Gold Stocks) vs S&P 500 1984 to 2009

On average from 1984 (start of the XAU index) to 2009, gold stocks as represented by the XAU index, have outperformed the S&P 500 from July 27th to September 25th. One factor that has led to a rise in the price of gold stocks in August and September is the Indian festival and wedding season that starts in October and finishes in November during Diwali. The Asian culture places a great emphasis on gold as a store of value and a lot of it is "consumed" as jewellery during the festival and wedding season. The price of gold tends to increase in the months preceding this season as the jewellery fabricators purchase gold to make their final product.

The August-September increase in gold stocks coincides with the time that a lot of investors are pulling their money out of the broad market and are looking for a place to invest. If you believe in the merits of gold stocks, this is definitely a great time to consider.

Be careful. Just as the gold stocks tend to go up in August-September, they also tend to go down in Oc-

tober. Historically, this negative trend in October has been caused by European Central banks selling some of their gold holdings in autumn when their annual allotment of possible sales is renewed yearly. In recent years most European Central banks either dramatically reduced their sales of gold or stopped selling gold altogether. This has muted the negative trend in October.

In addition, investors can take advantage of the positive trend in gold from October 28th to December 31st, depending on the relative strength of the sector. In this time period gold stocks (XAU) have produced an average return of 6.1%, been positive 50% of the time, but only managed to beat the S&P 500 42% of the time (1984-2009).

 XAU is an index traded on the Philadelphia exchange. It consists of 12 precious metal mining companies.

18 MONDAY	013 / 166	**19** TUESDAY	012 / 165

20 WEDNESDAY	011 / 164	**21** THURSDAY	010 / 163

22 FRIDAY			009 / 162

WEEK 29

Market Indices & Rates
Weekly Values**

Stock Markets	2008	2009
Dow	11,240	8,553
S&P500	1,242	924
Nasdaq	2,262	1,845
TSX	13,516	10,153
FTSE	5,257	4,307
DAX	6,218	4,874
Nikkei	12,843	9,264
Hang Seng	21,604	18,113

Commodities	2008	2009
Oil	135.3	61.3
Gold	971.4	928.8

Bond Yields	2008	2009
USA 5 Yr Treasury	3.26	2.43
USA 10 Yr T	3.98	3.55
USA 20 Yr T	4.62	4.39
Moody's Aaa	5.67	5.44
Moody's Baa	7.18	7.19
CAN 5 Yr T	3.34	2.52
CAN 10 Yr T	3.74	3.43

Money Market	2008	2009
USA Fed Funds	2.00	0.25
USA 3 Mo T-B	1.44	0.18
CAN tgt overnight rate	3.00	0.25
CAN 3 Mo T-B	2.25	0.22

Foreign Exchange	2008	2009
USD/EUR	1.59	1.41
USD/GBP	2.00	1.63
CAN/USD	1.00	1.13
JPY/USD	105.47	93.37

JULY

M	T	W	T	F	S	S
				1	2	3
4	5	6	7	8	9	10
11	12	13	14	15	16	17
18	19	20	21	22	23	24
25	26	27	28	29	30	31

AUGUST

M	T	W	T	F	S	S
1	2	3	4	5	6	7
8	9	10	11	12	13	14
15	16	17	18	19	20	21
22	23	24	25	26	27	28
29	30	31				

SEPTEMBER

M	T	W	T	F	S	S
			1	2	3	4
5	6	7	8	9	10	11
12	13	14	15	16	17	18
19	20	21	22	23	24	25
26	27	28	29	30		

2009 Strategy Performance*

XAU % Average Gain 2009

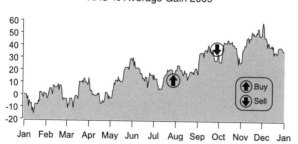

Gold stocks did well in 2009 rising up over 50% during the year and ending up 36% higher on the year. During its seasonal time period, gold stocks (XAU) produced a moderate gain of 6.0%, which was just under the performance of the S&P 500.

Gold stocks paused just after their seasonally strong period, but then resumed their run into the beginning of December, before correcting into the end of the year.

* Buy and Sell dates are approximate representations of strategy dates.
** Weekly avg closing values- except Fed Funds & CAN overnight tgt rate weekly closing values.

In the past my writings on the transportation sector have focused on the positive seasonal period. This is only half the story. Preceding transportation's positive seasonal period is a weak period, giving investors an opportunity to sell short the sector and profit from its decline. This weak period from August 1st to October 9 is followed by the strong period from October 10th to November 13th.

5.7% extra & positive 16 times out of 20

The transportation sector is very sensitive to economic expectations. Typically, when the economy is showing signs of improving, the transportation sector outperforms. When it is showing signs of deteriorating, the sector tends to underperform.

In the late summer months investors question the strength of an economic run which tends to put pressure on the transportation sector. On average since 1990, the sector has lost 4.9% from August 1st to October 9th.

In autumn the market generally becomes positive about the expectations for the stock market's final months of the year which helps propel the transportation sector into positive territory. In addition, the price of oil tends to retreat in autumn. Since oil is one of the primary input costs for transportation, the sector benefits. From October 10th to November 13th (1990 to 2009), the transportation sector has gained an average of 6.5%.

(i) *The SP GICS Transportation Sector encompasses a wide range transportation based companies.*
For more information on the information technology sector, see www.standardandpoors.com

Transportation Sector vs. S&P 500 1990 to 2009
Negative [ ]   Positive [ ]

	SHORT Aug 1 to Oct 9		LONG Oct 10 to Nov 13		Compound Growth	
Year	S&P 500	Trans port	S&P 500	Trans port	S&P 500	Trans port
1990	-14.3 %	-19.2 %	4.1 %	3.3 %	19.0 %	23.1 %
1991	-2.8	0.5	5.5	9.6	8.5	9.1
1992	-5.1	-9.1	4.9	14.1	10.2	24.5
1993	2.7	-0.3	1.1	6.4	-1.6	6.8
1994	-0.7	-9.3	1.6	0.8	2.3	10.2
1995	2.9	-1.3	2.4	5.0	-0.6	6.4
1996	8.9	4.9	4.9	6.1	-4.4	0.9
1997	1.7	0.9	-5.6	-5.4	-7.2	-6.3
1998	-12.2	-16.5	14.4	12.5	28.3	31.0
1999	0.6	-11.0	4.5	4.0	3.9	15.4
2000	-2.0	-6.0	-3.6	13.0	-1.7	19.7
2001	-12.8	-20.0	7.8	14.1	21.5	36.9
2002	-14.8	-11.2	13.6	8.2	30.4	20.3
2003	4.9	4.9	1.9	8.0	-3.1	2.7
2004	1.9	6.6	5.5	11.1	3.6	3.7
2005	-3.1	-0.5	3.3	9.0	6.5	9.5
2006	5.8	6.4	2.5	3.8	-3.4	-2.9
2007	7.6	-0.2	-5.4	-2.9	-12.5	-2.7
2008	-28.2	-23.5	0.2	4.0	28.4	28.4
2009	8.5	6.7	2.1	5.9	-6.6	-1.2
Avg.	-2.5 %	-4.9 %	3.3 %	6.5 %	6.1 %	11.8 %

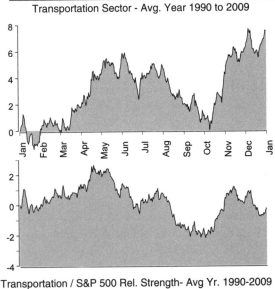

Transportation Sector - Avg. Year 1990 to 2009

Transportation / S&P 500 Rel. Strength- Avg Yr. 1990-2009

25 MONDAY   006 / 159

26 TUESDAY   005 / 158

27 WEDNESDAY   004 / 157

28 THURSDAY   003 / 156

29 FRIDAY   002 / 155

WEEK 30

Market Indices & Rates
Weekly Values**

Stock Markets	2008	2009
Dow	11,484	8,962
S&P500	1,266	963
Nasdaq	2,300	1,938
TSX	13,486	10,570
FTSE	5,387	4,511
DAX	6,456	5,144
Nikkei	13,359	9,778
Hang Seng	22,805	19,611

Commodities	2008	2009
Oil	126.0	65.1
Gold	939.4	950.1

Bond Yields	2008	2009
USA 5 Yr Treasury	3.44	2.48
USA 10 Yr T	4.11	3.62
USA 20 Yr T	4.72	4.46
Moody's Aaa	5.78	5.46
Moody's Baa	7.27	7.13
CAN 5 Yr T	3.43	2.57
CAN 10 Yr T	3.83	3.48

Money Market	2008	2009
USA Fed Funds	2.00	0.25
USA 3 Mo T-B	1.60	0.19
CAN tgt overnight rate	3.00	0.25
CAN 3 Mo T-B	2.39	0.23

Foreign Exchange	2008	2009
USD/EUR	1.58	1.42
USD/GBP	2.00	1.64
CAN/USD	1.01	1.10
JPY/USD	107.17	94.28

JULY

M	T	W	T	F	S	S
				1	2	3
4	5	6	7	8	9	10
11	12	13	14	15	16	17
18	19	20	21	22	23	24
25	26	27	28	29	30	31

AUGUST

M	T	W	T	F	S	S
1	2	3	4	5	6	7
8	9	10	11	12	13	14
15	16	17	18	19	20	21
22	23	24	25	26	27	28
29	30	31				

SEPTEMBER

M	T	W	T	F	S	S
			1	2	3	4
5	6	7	8	9	10	11
12	13	14	15	16	17	18
19	20	21	22	23	24	25
26	27	28	29	30		

2009 Strategy Performance*

Transportation % Gain 2009

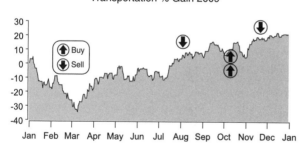

In 2009 the transportation sector rallied with the market off the bottom low in March. It made a small gain in the time period when the sector is typically weak, as the market continued to rally.

The gain that was made during the time when the sector is usually positive was a bit smaller than the loss during the best time to short the sector. Overall, the strategy produced a small loss in 2009.

* Buy and Sell dates are approximate representations of strategy dates.
** Weekly avg closing values- except Fed Funds & CAN overnight tgt rate weekly closing values.

Seasonal Investment Time Line*

Investment	Season
Core Positions	
S&P 500	Oct 28 - May 5
TSX Comp	Oct 28 - May 5
Cash	May 6 - Oct 27
Primary Sectors	
Small Cap (Russell 2000)	Dec 19 - Mar 7
Information Tech	Oct 9 - Jan 17
Consumer Discretionary	Oct 28 - Apr 22
Industrials	Jan 23- May 5
	Oct 28 - Dec 31
Materials	Jan 23 - May 5
	Oct 28 - Jan 6
Financial	Jan 19 - Apr 13
Energy	Feb 25 - May 9
	Jul 24 - Oct 3
Consumer Staples	Jan 1 - Jan 22 (Short)
	Apr 23 - Oct 27
Utilities	Jul 17 - Oct 3
Health Care	Aug 15 - Oct 18
Secondary Sectors	
Transportation	Aug 1 - Oct 9 (Short)
	Oct 10 - Nov 13
Canadian Banks	Oct 10 - Dec 31
	Jan 23 - Apr 13
Retail	Oct 28 - Nov 29
	Jan 21 - Apr 12
Metals & Mining	Nov 19 - Jan 5
	Jan 23 - May 5
U.S. Dollar	Dec 1 - Dec 31 (Short)
	Jan 1 - Jan 31
Platinum	Jan 1 - May 31
Oil E & P	Jan 30 - Apr 13
Oil E & S	Apr 14 - May 17
Canadian Dollar	Apr 1 - Apr 30
Bonds	May 8 - Dec 31
Biotech	Jun 23 - Sep 13
Gold Bullion	Jul 12 - Oct 9
Gold Stocks (XAU)	Jul 27 - Sep 25
Natural Gas	Aug 1 - Dec 21
Agriculture	Aug 1 - Dec 31

2010   2011

OCT NOV DEC JAN FEB MAR APR MAY JUN JUL AUG SEP OCT NOV DEC

Long Investment   Short Investment

* Holiday, End of Month, Witches' Hangover, Yearly Cycles (Presidential Cycle), Predictor Trades (January Predictor), Value - Growth Trades - et al not included.

AUGUST

	MONDAY	TUESDAY	WEDNESDAY
WEEK 31	**1** 30 CAN Market Closed- Civic Day	**2** 29	**3** 28
WEEK 32	**8** 23	**9** 22	**10** 21
WEEK 33	**15** 16	**16** 15	**17** 14
WEEK 34	**22** 9	**23** 8	**24** 7
WEEK 35	**29** 2	**30** 1	**31**

THURSDAY	FRIDAY
4 27	**5** 26
11 20	**12** 19
18 13	**19** 12
25 6	**26** 5
1	2

SEPTEMBER

M	T	W	T	F	S	S
			1	2	3	4
5	6	7	8	9	10	11
12	13	14	15	16	17	18
19	20	21	22	23	24	25
26	27	28	29	30		

OCTOBER

M	T	W	T	F	S	S
					1	2
3	4	5	6	7	8	9
10	11	12	13	14	15	16
17	18	19	20	21	22	23
24	25	26	27	28	29	30
31						

NOVEMBER

M	T	W	T	F	S	S
	1	2	3	4	5	6
7	8	9	10	11	12	13
14	15	16	17	18	19	20
21	22	23	24	25	26	27
28	29	30				

DECEMBER

M	T	W	T	F	S	S
			1	2	3	4
5	6	7	8	9	10	11
12	13	14	15	16	17	18
19	20	21	22	23	24	25
26	27	28	29	30	31	

AUGUST
S U M M A R Y

S&P 500 Cumulative Daily Gains for Avg Month 1950 to 2009

STRATEGIES	PAGE
STRATEGIES STARTING	
Transportation – On a Roll - SHORT	87
Agriculture Moooves	99
Gas For 5 Months	101
Health Care August Prescription Renewal	103
STRATEGIES FINISHING	
None	

♦ If there is a summer rally, it is often in jeopardy in August. ♦ The best August over the last ten years occurred in 2000 (Nasdaq 11.7%; Russell 3000, 9.1%, and the TSX (Canada) 8.1%. ♦ Since 1950 the S&P 500 has produced an average gain of 0.1% and has been positive 57% of the time. Over the same time period it is ranked as the 9th best month. ♦ In 2009 the S&P 500 returned 3.4% in August, but this occurred in the middle of a very strong bull run. This is in contrast to the 4.7% loss in 2010.

BEST / WORST AUGUST BROAD MKTS. 2000-2009

BEST AUGUST MARKETS
- ♦ Nasdaq (2000) 11.7%
- ♦ Russell 3000 Gr (2000) 9.1%
- ♦ TSX (2000) 8.1%

WORST AUGUST MARKETS
- ♦ Nasdaq (2001) -10.9%
- ♦ Russell 3000 Gr (2001) -8.1%
- ♦ S&P500 (2001) -6.4%

Index Values End of Month

	2000	2001	2002	2003	2004	2005	2006	2007	2008	2009
Dow	11,215	9,950	8,664	9,416	10,174	10,482	11,381	13,358	11,544	9,496
S&P 500	1,518	1,134	916	1,008	1,104	1,220	1,304	1,474	1,283	1,021
Nasdaq	4,206	1,805	1,315	1,810	1,838	2,152	2,184	2,596	2,368	2,009
TSX	11,248	7,399	6,612	7,510	8,377	10,669	12,074	13,660	13,771	10,868
Russell 1000	1,559	1,149	934	1,035	1,132	1,275	1,360	1,540	1,350	1,073
Russell 2000	1,337	1,165	972	1,236	1,362	1,656	1,791	1,970	1,838	1,422
Russell 3000 Growth	3,473	1,915	1,474	1,682	1,751	1,959	2,013	2,341	2,162	1,758
Russell 3000 Value	2,118	2,080	1,780	1,951	2,242	2,567	2,851	3,127	2,613	2,014

Percent Gain for August

	2000	2001	2002	2003	2004	2005	2006	2007	2008	2009
Dow	6.6	-5.4	-0.8	2.0	0.3	-1.5	1.7	1.1	1.5	3.5
S&P 500	6.1	-6.4	0.5	1.8	0.2	-1.1	2.1	1.3	1.2	3.4
Nasdaq	11.7	-10.9	-1.0	4.3	-2.6	-1.5	4.4	2.0	1.8	1.5
TSX	8.1	-3.8	0.1	3.5	-1.0	2.4	2.1	-1.5	1.3	0.8
Russell 1000	7.3	-6.2	0.4	1.9	0.3	-1.1	2.2	1.1	1.2	3.4
Russell 2000	7.5	-3.3	-0.4	4.5	-0.6	-1.9	2.8	2.2	3.5	2.8
Russell 3000 Growth	9.1	-8.1	0.2	2.6	-0.8	-1.4	3.0	1.5	1.0	1.8
Russell 3000 Value	5.3	-4.0	0.4	1.5	1.2	-0.9	1.5	0.9	1.7	4.9

August Market Avg. Performance 2000 to 2009[1]

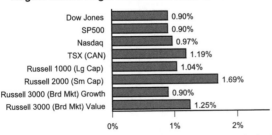

Dow Jones	0.90%
SP500	0.90%
Nasdaq	0.97%
TSX (CAN)	1.19%
Russell 1000 (Lg Cap)	1.04%
Russell 2000 (Sm Cap)	1.69%
Russell 3000 (Brd Mkt) Growth	0.90%
Russell 3000 (Brd Mkt) Value	1.25%

Interest Corner Aug[2]

	Fed Funds % [3]	3 Mo. T-Bill % [4]	10 Yr % [5]	20 Yr % [6]
2009	0.25	0.15	3.40	4.14
2008	2.00	1.72	3.83	4.47
2007	5.25	4.01	4.54	4.87
2006	5.25	5.05	4.74	4.95
2005	3.50	3.52	4.02	4.30

(1) Russell Data provided by Russell (2) Federal Reserve Bank of St. Louis- end of month values (3) Target rate set by FOMC (4)(5)(6) Constant yield maturities.

THACKRAY SECTOR THERMOMETER

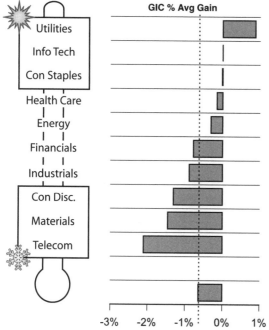

GIC[2] % Avg Gain	Fq % Gain >S&P 500	
SP GIC SECTOR 1990-2009[1]		
0.9 %	65 %	Utilities
0.0	55	Information Technology
0.0	65	Consumer Staples
-0.2	70	Health Care
-0.3	45	Energy
-0.8	40	Financial
-0.9	35	Industrials
-1.3	30	Consumer Discretionary
-1.5	40	Materials
-2.1 %	40 %	Telecom
-0.6 %	N/A %	S&P 500

Sector Commentary

♦ From 1990 to 2009, other than the Telecom sector it is typically the defensive sectors that dominate the relative performance in August. In 2009 the market was on "fire" and rallied throughout the summer. ♦ In August, typically one of the weaker months of the year, the S&P 500 gained 3.6%. ♦ In 2009 the top three sectors were the Financial, Industrial and Consumer Discretionary with returns of 12.8%, 4.1% and 3.3% respectively. ♦ The Financial sector was still getting a boost emerging from the depths of almost collapsing and as a result any long-term optimism in the markets tended to be lever-aged in this sector.

Sub-Sector Commentary

♦ In 2009 the major driver of the gains in the market was the Financial sector which gained 12.9%, substantially higher than the S&P 500. This performance showed up in the sub-sectors with the Insurance sector gaining 15.9% and the banks gaining 12.9%.

SELECTED SUB-SECTORS 1990-2009[3]		
1.0 %	53 %	Biotech (93-2009)
0.6	53	Semiconductor (SOX) 95-2009
0.2	55	Gold (XAU)
0.0	50	Agriculture Products (94-2009)
-0.3	45	Banks
-0.3	65	Pharmaceuticals
-0.4	40	Integrated Oil & Gas
-0.5	55	Software & Services
-0.7	55	Retail
-1.1	40	Insurance
-1.6	45	Metals & Mining
-2.8	25	Transportation
-3.3	30	Auto & Components
-5.0	25	Airlines

(1) Sector data provided by Standard and Poors (2) GIC is short form for Global Industry Classification (3) Sub Sector data provided by Standard and Poors, except where marked by symbol.

OIL – SUMMER/AUTUMN STRATEGY
IInd of II Oil Stock Strategies for the Year
July 24th to October 3rd

Oil stocks tend to outperform the market from July 24th to October 3rd. Earlier in the year there is a first wave of outperformance from late February to early May. Although the first wave has had an incredible record of outperformance, the second wave in July is still noteworthy.

While the first wave has more to do with inventories during the switch from producing heating oil to gasoline, the second wave is more related to the conversion of production from gasoline to heating oil and the effects of the hurricane season.

Extra 2.4% &
58% of the time better than S&P 500

Jul 24 to Oct 3	XOI	Positive S&P 500	Diff
1984	9.0	9.1	-0.1
1985	6.7	-4.3	11.0
1986	15.7	-2.1	17.7
1987	-1.2	6.6	-7.8
1988	-3.6	3.0	-6.6
1989	5.7	5.6	0.1
1990	-0.5	-12.4	11.8
1991	0.7	1.3	-0.7
1992	2.9	-0.4	3.3
1993	7.8	3.2	4.6
1994	-3.6	1.9	-5.5
1995	-2.2	5.2	-7.4
1996	7.7	10.5	-2.8
1997	8.9	3.0	5.9
1998	1.4	-12.0	13.5
1999	-2.1	-5.5	3.3
2000	12.2	-3.6	15.8
2001	-5.1	-10.0	4.8
2002	7.3	2.7	4.6
2003	5.5	4.2	1.4
2004	10.9	4.2	6.7
2005	14.3	-0.6	14.9
2006	-8.5	7.6	-16.9
2007	-4.2	-0.1	-4.1
2008	-18.1	-14.3	-3.8
2009	3.0	5.0	-2.0
Avg	2.7 %	0.3 %	2.4 %

XOI vs. S&P 500
1984 to 2009

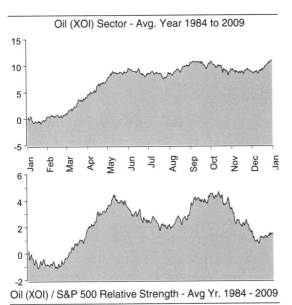

Oil (XOI) Sector - Avg. Year 1984 to 2009

Oil (XOI) / S&P 500 Relative Strength - Avg Yr. 1984 - 2009

start switching from gasoline to heating oil, dropping their inventory levels and boosting prices.

Second, hurricane season can play havoc with the production of oil and drive up prices substantially. The official duration of the hurricane season in the Gulf of Mexico is from June 1st to November 30th, but most major hurricanes occur in September and early October.

The threat of a strong hurricane can shut down the oil platforms temporarily, interrupting production. If a strong hurricane strikes the oil platforms it can do significant damage and put the platform out of commission for an extended period of time.

First, there is a large difference between how heating oil and gasoline are stored and consumed. For the average individual and business, gasoline is consumed in a fairly immediate fashion. It is stored by the local distributor and the supplies are drawn upon as needed. Heating oil, on the other hand is largely inventoried by individuals, farms and business operations in rural areas in large amounts.

The inventory process starts well before the cold weather arrives. The production facilities have to

1 MONDAY	030 / 152

2 TUESDAY	029 / 151

3 WEDNESDAY	028 / 150

4 THURSDAY	027 / 149

5 FRIDAY	026 / 148

WEEK 31

Market Indices & Rates
Weekly Values**

Stock Markets	2008	2009
Dow	11,363	9,120
S&P500	1,262	982
Nasdaq	2,310	1,975
TSX	13,484	10,649
FTSE	5,364	4,580
DAX	6,417	5,278
Nikkei	13,270	10,162
Hang Seng	22,646	20,364

Commodities	2008	2009
Oil	124.6	67.1
Gold	913.7	940.4

Bond Yields	2008	2009
USA 5 Yr Treasury	3.31	2.63
USA 10 Yr T	4.04	3.67
USA 20 Yr T	4.66	4.47
Moody's Aaa	5.73	5.40
Moody's Baa	7.21	6.91
CAN 5 Yr T	3.31	2.67
CAN 10 Yr T	3.75	3.54

Money Market	2008	2009
USA Fed Funds	2.00	0.25
USA 3 Mo T-B	1.70	0.19
CAN tgt overnight rate	3.00	0.25
CAN 3 Mo T-B	2.40	0.24

Foreign Exchange	2008	2009
USD/EUR	1.57	1.42
USD/GBP	1.98	1.65
CAN/USD	1.02	1.08
JPY/USD	107.80	94.93

2009 Strategy Performance*

XOI % Gain 2009

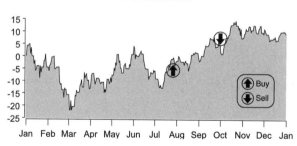

In its seasonal summer strong period in 2009, the oil sector produced a small positive result and under performed the S&P 500 by 2.0%. The oil sector started its run before its seasonal start date and ended it a bit later.

Although the buy and sell dates in the book have worked on average for the strategy, often there is room to adjust the dates based upon technical indicators.

AUGUST

M	T	W	T	F	S	S
1	2	3	4	5	6	7
8	9	10	11	12	13	14
15	16	17	18	19	20	21
22	23	24	25	26	27	28
29	30	31				

SEPTEMBER

M	T	W	T	F	S	S
			1	2	3	4
5	6	7	8	9	10	11
12	13	14	15	16	17	18
19	20	21	22	23	24	25
26	27	28	29	30		

OCTOBER

M	T	W	T	F	S	S
					1	2
3	4	5	6	7	8	9
10	11	12	13	14	15	16
17	18	19	20	21	22	23
24	25	26	27	28	29	30
31						

* Buy and Sell dates are approximate representations of strategy dates.
** Weekly avg closing values- except Fed Funds & CAN overnight tgt rate weekly closing values.

Over the long-term, small companies have produced better returns than large companies.

Most pundits agree that this outcome is a result of investors being rewarded for taking on greater risks.

From 1979 to 2009, if an investor had invested in small value companies for the first eight months of the year and then switched to small growth companies for the last four months, they would have increased their returns even more.

For definitions of value and growth, information on the Russell small cap indices, and the trend of value out-performing growth at the beginning of the year and growth outperform-ing at the end, see *Value For First Four Months of Year - Growth For Last 3 Months* strategy.

It is important to note that the perform-ance for this strategy has been very volatile.

Sometimes value or growth small caps can outperform significantly in their seasonal time and other times not. Even within the year there can be a large difference in performance.

	Small Cap Value & Small Cap Growth Switch Strategy*					
	Val>Gr		Gr>Val		8n4> S&P 500	
	Jan to Aug		Sep to Dec		Yr. % Gain	
Year	Sm Cap Gr	Sm Cap Val	Sm Cap Val	Sm Cap Gr	S&P 500	Sm Cap 8n4
1979	36.2%	35.7%	-5.0%	8.1%	12.3%	46.7%
1980	27.4	15.6	2.9	17.3	25.8	35.6
1981	-8.9	9.4	1.0	-1.8	-9.7	7.5
1982	-12.4	-1.6	24.4	35.2	14.8	33.1
1983	28.2	31.8	1.7	-7.3	17.3	22.2
1984	-9.3	-1.2	-0.1	-8.5	1.4	-9.6
1985	19.4	17.2	8.0	8.2	26.3	26.8
1986	10.9	10.4	-5.0	-7.4	14.6	2.2
1987	31.2	28.2	-29.1	-32.5	2.0	-13.5
1988	17.0	24.7	1.0	1.5	12.4	26.6
1989	22.4	18.8	-7.7	-2.8	27.3	15.5
1990	-16.1	-18.0	-7.7	-2.8	-6.6	-20.3
1991	36.6	34.6	2.5	9.6	26.3	47.4
1992	-10.9	10.3	14.5	19.8	4.5	32.2
1993	6.4	16.4	4.4	5.8	7.1	23.1
1994	-2.6	1.2	-4.8	-0.6	-1.5	0.6
1995	25.9	18.5	3.6	3.3	34.1	22.4
1996	5.1	5.7	12.1	5.3	20.3	11.2
1997	13.6	19.7	7.6	-1.0	31.0	18.5
1998	-25.9	-19.9	14.2	36.0	26.7	8.9
1999	5.0	-2.6	-1.4	35.8	19.5	32.3
2000	2.1	12.3	6.5	-24.2	-10.1	-14.9
2001	-14.4	8.2	3.0	5.7	-13.0	14.3
2002	-30.3	-10.2	-3.4	-0.6	-23.4	-10.7
2003	34.6	25.3	14.3	9.6	26.4	37.4
2004	-6.1	2.8	16.8	21.3	9.0	24.6
2005	1.4	3.0	-0.2	2.2	3.0	5.3
2006	3.2	10.9	9.3	9.3	13.6	21.2
2007	5.9	-4.3	-7.6	0.5	3.5	-3.7
2008	-4.9	-2.1	-29.1	-35.8	-38.5	-37.5
2009	20.6	9.0	8.0	10.7	23.5	20.7
Avg.	6.8%	10.0%	1.8%	9.7%	9.7%	13.8%
Fq >		58%		61%		61%

* Small Cap Growth (Russell 2000 Growth)
Small Cap Value (Russell 2000 Value)

⚠ CAUTION: The small cap sector can be very volatile. There can also be large performance differences be-tween the two different styles of management, value and growth. Like all strategies in this book, proper care should be taken so that risk tolerances are not exceeded.

Russell 2000 Growth less Russell 2000 Value 1979-2009

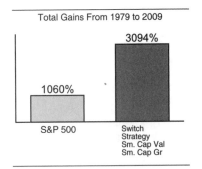

Total Gains From 1979 to 2009

3094%

1060%

S&P 500

Switch Strategy Sm. Cap Val Sm. Cap Gr

8 MONDAY	023 / 145	**9** TUESDAY	022 / 144

10 WEDNESDAY	021 / 143	**11** THURSDAY	020 / 142

12 FRIDAY	019 / 141

WEEK 32

Market Indices & Rates
Weekly Values**

Stock Markets	2008	2009
Dow	11,544	9,303
S&P500	1,277	1,004
Nasdaq	2,357	1,997
TSX	13,356	10,936
FTSE	5,446	4,685
DAX	6,507	5,405
Nikkei	13,079	10,356
Hang Seng	22,114	20,675

Commodities	2008	2009
Oil	118.9	71.6
Gold	878.3	960.2

Bond Yields	2008	2009
USA 5 Yr Treasury	3.24	2.73
USA 10 Yr T	3.99	3.77
USA 20 Yr T	4.63	4.50
Moody's Aaa	5.74	5.34
Moody's Baa	7.22	6.71
CAN 5 Yr T	3.17	2.68
CAN 10 Yr T	3.66	3.55

Money Market	2008	2009
USA Fed Funds	2.00	0.25
USA 3 Mo T-B	1.70	0.18
CAN tgt overnight rate	3.00	0.25
CAN 3 Mo T-B	2.48	0.26

Foreign Exchange	2008	2009
USD/EUR	1.54	1.43
USD/GBP	1.95	1.69
CAN/USD	1.05	1.07
JPY/USD	108.76	95.63

2009 Strategy Performance

Russell 2000 Growth minus Russell 2000 Value (2009)

The beginning of the year was dominated by the performance of growth stocks as investors looked for stability in earnings.

In addition small companies bounced off the March low and turned in stronger gains for the remainder of the year, compared to the S&P 500.

AUGUST

M	T	W	T	F	S	S
1	2	3	4	5	6	7
8	9	10	11	12	13	14
15	16	17	18	19	20	21
22	23	24	25	26	27	28
29	30	31				

SEPTEMBER

M	T	W	T	F	S	S
			1	2	3	4
5	6	7	8	9	10	11
12	13	14	15	16	17	18
19	20	21	22	23	24	25
26	27	28	29	30		

OCTOBER

M	T	W	T	F	S	S
					1	2
3	4	5	6	7	8	9
10	11	12	13	14	15	16
17	18	19	20	21	22	23
24	25	26	27	28	29	30
31						

** Weekly avg closing values- except Fed Funds & CAN overnight tgt rate weekly closing values.

AGRICULTURE MOOOVES
LAST 5 MONTHS OF THE YEAR – Aug to Dec

Agriculture, one of the hot sectors in recent years, has typically been hot during the last five months of the year (August to December).

This is the result of the major summer growing season in the northern hemisphere producing cash for the growers and subsequently increasing sales for the farming suppliers (fertilizer, farming machinery - see note at bottom of page for description of sector).

75% of the time better than the S&P 500

Although this sector can represent a good opportunity, investors should be wary of the wide performance swings. Out of the fifteen cycles from August to December (1994 to 2009), there have been six years with absolute returns greater than +25% or less than -25%, and ten years of returns greater than +10% or less than -10%. In other words, this sector is very volatile.

Agriculture vs. S&P 500 1994 to 2009

| Aug 1 to Dec 31 | Agri | Positive | |
		S&P 500	Diff
1994 %	8.0 %	0.2 %	7.8 %
1995	31.7	9.6	22.1
1996	30.2	15.7	14.5
1997	14.6	1.7	13.0
1998	-3.4	9.7	-13.1
1999	-2.6	10.6	-13.2
2000	68.0	-7.7	75.7
2001	12.5	-5.2	17.7
2002	6.0	-3.5	9.5
2003	15.8	12.3	3.5
2004	44.6	10.0	34.6
2005	7.5	1.1	6.4
2006	-27.4	11.1	-38.5
2007	38.2	0.9	37.3
2008	0.7	-28.7	29.4
2009	4.0	12.9	-9.0
Avg.	15.5 %	3.2 %	12.4 %

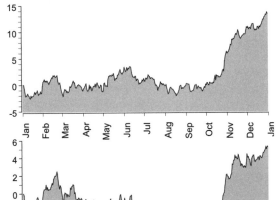

Agriculture Sector - Avg. Year 1994 to 2009

Agriculture / S&P 500 Relative Strength - Avg Yr. 1994-2009

performance of worldwide stock markets.

There was a negative performance in 2006 which was a correction from the rapid rise of the sector in the first half of the year. This time period was the start of investors having an epiphany that the world might be running out of food and as the market marched upwards, it produced some big swings.

In 2007 and the first half of 2008, the agriculture sector rocketed upwards due to the increase in prices of agricultural products, which in turn were a result of worldwide food shortages.

Although food prices have had some reprieve with the global slowdown, the world population is still increasing and imbalances in food supply and demand will continue to exist in the future.

On a year by year basis, the year 2000 produced the biggest return at 68%; the same year that the technology bubble burst.

The agriculture sector benefited from the market correction because investors were looking for a safe haven to invest in – people need to eat, regardless of the

Investors should consider "mooov-ing" into the agriculture sector for the last five months of the year.

> *The SP GICS Agriculture Sector # 30202010*
> *For more information on the agriculture sector, see www.standardandpoors.com*

15 MONDAY   016 / 138

16 TUESDAY   015 / 137

17 WEDNESDAY   014 / 136

18 THURSDAY   013 / 135

19 FRIDAY   012 / 134

WEEK 33

Market Indices & Rates
Weekly Values**

Stock Markets	2008	2009
Dow	11,647	9,332
S&P500	1,294	1,005
Nasdaq	2,441	1,991
TSX	13,241	10,751
FTSE	5,495	4,716
DAX	6,501	5,353
Nikkei	13,147	10,532
Hang Seng	21,469	20,839

Commodities	2008	2009
Oil	114.4	69.6
Gold	818.7	948.4

Bond Yields	2008	2009
USA 5 Yr Treasury	3.18	2.65
USA 10 Yr T	3.91	3.67
USA 20 Yr T	4.58	4.42
Moody's Aaa	5.68	5.34
Moody's Baa	7.17	6.62
CAN 5 Yr T	3.11	2.62
CAN 10 Yr T	3.60	3.51

Money Market	2008	2009
USA Fed Funds	2.00	0.25
USA 3 Mo T-B	1.86	0.18
CAN tgt overnight rate	3.00	0.25
CAN 3 Mo T-B	2.49	0.23

Foreign Exchange	2008	2009
USD/EUR	1.49	1.42
USD/GBP	1.89	1.65
CAN/USD	1.07	1.09
JPY/USD	109.83	96.15

AUGUST

M	T	W	T	F	S	S
1	2	3	4	5	6	7
8	9	10	11	12	13	14
15	16	17	18	19	20	21
22	23	24	25	26	27	28
29	30	31				

SEPTEMBER

M	T	W	T	F	S	S
			1	2	3	4
5	6	7	8	9	10	11
12	13	14	15	16	17	18
19	20	21	22	23	24	25
26	27	28	29	30		

OCTOBER

M	T	W	T	F	S	S
					1	2
3	4	5	6	7	8	9
10	11	12	13	14	15	16
17	18	19	20	21	22	23
24	25	26	27	28	29	30
31						

2009 Strategy Performance*

Agricultural Sector % Gain 2009

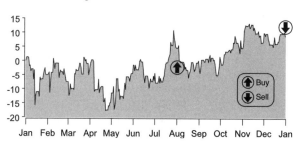

During its seasonally strong period in 2009, the agriculture sector under performed the S&P 500. At this time, the world was not focused on food shortages and the need to produce more food – it was focused on the economy coming back to life and a rising stock market.

The real sweet spot for the agriculture trade is from the beginning of October to the end of the year. In 2009, this is the time period where the majority of the seasonal gains were made.

* Buy and Sell dates are approximate representations of strategy dates.
** Weekly avg closing values- except Fed Funds & CAN overnight tgt rate weekly closing values.

GAS FOR 5 MONTHS
Natural Gas (Commodity) – Outperforms last 5 months
Cash price increases from Aug 1st to Dec 21st

We may not use natural gas ourselves, but most of us depend on it in one way or another. It is used for furnaces and hot water tanks and is usually responsible for producing some portion of the electrical power that we consume.

As a result, there are two high consumption times for natural gas: winter and summer. The colder it gets in winter, the more natural gas is consumed to keep the furnaces going. The warmer it gets in the summer, the more natural gas is used to produce power for air conditioners.

On the supply side, weather also plays a large factor in determining price. During the hurricane season in the Gulf of Mexico, the price of natural gas is effected by the forecast for the number, severity and impact of hurricanes.

The tail end of the hurricane season occurs in late autumn and early winter, at the same time distributors are accumulating natural gas inventories for the winter heating season.

As a result the price of natural gas tends to rise from the beginning of September. As the price is very dependent on the weather, it is also extremely volatile. Large percentage moves are not uncommon.

Caution and a shorting possibility should be noted. As a result of the hurricane season ending and the slowdown in accumulating natural gas inventories for winter heating, the price of natural gas frequently decreases during the last part of December.

Natural Gas (Cash) Henry Hub LA
Seasonal Gains 1995 to 2009

	Negative	Positive	Negative
	Jan 1 to Jul 31	Aug 1 to Dec 21	Dec 22 to Dec 31
1995		144.6 %	-24.0 %
1996	-16.0 %	90.0	-7.7
1997	-45.2	6.8	-4.6
1998	-18.1	10.8	-5.9
1999	32.1	1.2	-10.9
2000	62.6	180.8	-0.9
2001	-68.2	-20.6	4.0
2002	11.1	66.4	-9.0
2003	0.8	49.5	-16.7
2004	4.5	13.3	-11.9
2005	29.0	74.7	-29.8
2006	-15.5	-24.3	-9.7
2007	18.7	7.7	6.1
2008	24.1	-38.8	-0.6
2009	-40.7	73.2	0.6
Avg.	-1.5 %	42.3 %	-8.1 %

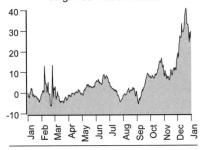

Natural Gas (Cash) Henry Hub LA
Avg. Year 1996 to 2009

⚠ *Caution:*
The cash price for natural gas is extremely volatile and extreme caution should be used. Care must be taken to ensure that investments are within risk tolerances.

ⓘ *Source: New York Mercantile Exchange. NYMX is an exchange provider of futures and options.*

	Jan	Feb	Mar	Apr	May	Jun	Jul	Aug	Sep	Oct	Nov	Dec	Year
1997	-28	-39	6	13	6	-6	3	22	16	3	-25	-6	-44
1998	-6	3	5	-5	-4	12	-22	-14	38	-19	-9	18	-15
1999	-6	-8	19	13	0	4	10	13	-20	21	-22	6	19
2000	17	0	7	8	45	-4	-14	27	8	-15	46	64	353
2001	-44	-11	3	-12	-21	-21	12	-34	-17	68	-40	47	-74
2002	-21	16	28	15	-14	2	-6	3	31	7	-5	10	69
2003	22	94	-54	5	14	-11	-13	5	-4	-15	22	19	25
2004	1	-9	7	3	11	-7	0	-16	26	1	6	-11	5
2005	2	8	13	-11	-5	11	11	64	17	-18	-4	-19	58
2006	-8	-23	4	-5	-10	-2	38	-28	-37	81	25	-34	-42
2007	41	-7	4	3	1	-18	2	-16	12	18	0	-2	29
2008	9	12	8	10	6	15	-30	-11	-13	-13	4	-13	-21
2009	-15	-15	-11	-9	21	-5	-10	-28	34	27	7	32	3
Avg	-1 %	0 %	3 %	0 %	4 %	-1 %	-2 %	-2 %	7 %	13 %	5 %	10 %	29 %

Natural Gas (Cash Price) Henry Hub Louisiana % Month Gain

22 MONDAY	009 / 131	**23** TUESDAY	008 / 130

24 WEDNESDAY	007 / 129	**25** THURSDAY	006 / 128

26 FRIDAY	005 / 127

WEEK 34

Market Indices & Rates
Weekly Values**

Stock Markets	2008	2009
Dow	11,461	9,298
S&P500	1,278	1,000
Nasdaq	2,397	1,973
TSX	13,304	10,685
FTSE	5,404	4,726
DAX	6,322	5,292
Nikkei	12,860	10,276
Hang Seng	20,685	20,185

Commodities	2008	2009
Oil	115.5	70.8
Gold	811.7	940.8

Bond Yields	2008	2009
USA 5 Yr Treasury	3.07	2.47
USA 10 Yr T	3.83	3.48
USA 20 Yr T	4.48	4.26
Moody's Aaa	5.58	5.24
Moody's Baa	7.11	6.56
CAN 5 Yr T	3.10	2.54
CAN 10 Yr T	3.58	3.42

Money Market	2008	2009
USA Fed Funds	2.00	0.25
USA 3 Mo T-B	1.75	0.17
CAN tgt overnight rate	3.00	0.25
CAN 3 Mo T-B	2.49	0.21

Foreign Exchange	2008	2009
USD/EUR	1.47	1.42
USD/GBP	1.86	1.64
CAN/USD	1.06	1.10
JPY/USD	109.59	94.53

AUGUST

M	T	W	T	F	S	S
1	2	3	4	5	6	7
8	9	10	11	12	13	14
15	16	17	18	19	20	21
22	23	24	25	26	27	28
29	30	31				

SEPTEMBER

M	T	W	T	F	S	S
			1	2	3	4
5	6	7	8	9	10	11
12	13	14	15	16	17	18
19	20	21	22	23	24	25
26	27	28	29	30		

OCTOBER

M	T	W	T	F	S	S
					1	2
3	4	5	6	7	8	9
10	11	12	13	14	15	16
17	18	19	20	21	22	23
24	25	26	27	28	29	30
31						

2009 Strategy Performance*

Natural Gas (Henry Hub) 2009

In 2009 very large gains were made for natural gas during its seasonal period. Coming into September a lot of investors were short natural gas as the price had been falling since the beginning of the year.

The "short" investors were caught off guard as supply and economic reports indicated higher prices ahead. The price of natural gas rocketed upwards as a lot of the "short" investors were forced to cover their positions. It is important to note that the price of natural gas peaked at the end of its strong seasonal period.

* Buy and Sell dates are approximate representations of strategy dates.
** Weekly avg closing values- except Fed Funds & CAN overnight tgt rate weekly closing values.

HEALTH CARE
AUGUST PRESCRIPTION RENEWAL
August 15th to October 18th

Health care stocks have traditionally been classified as defensive stocks because of the stability of their earnings. Pharmaceutical and other health care companies typically still do well in an economic downturn.

Even in tough times, people still need to take their medication. As a result, investors have typically found comfort in this sector starting in the late summer doldrums and riding the momentum into early December.

*3.1% more & 14 out of 20
times better than the S&P 500*

Aug 15 to Oct 18	Health Care	Positive	S&P 500	Diff
1990	-1.3 %		-9.9 %	8.6 %
1991	1.3		0.7	0.6
1992	-9.0		-1.9	-7.1
1993	13.5		4.1	9.5
1994	7.2		1.2	6.0
1995	11.7		4.9	6.7
1996	9.4		7.4	2.1
1997	5.8		2.1	3.7
1998	3.0		-0.6	3.6
1999	-0.5		-5.5	5.0
2000	6.9		-10.0	16.9
2001	-0.4		-10.0	9.6
2002	2.4		-3.8	6.2
2003	-0.5		4.9	-5.4
2004	-0.8		4.6	-5.4
2005	-3.1		-4.2	1.2
2006	6.4		7.7	-1.3
2007	6.0		8.0	-2.0
2008	-20.4		-27.3	6.8
2009	5.1		8.3	-3.3
Avg	2.1 %		-1.0 %	3.1 %

Health Care vs. S&P 500 Performance 1990 to 2009

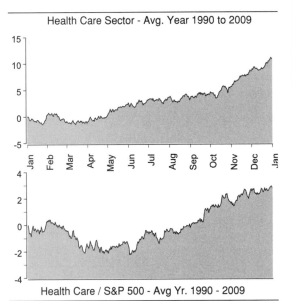

Health Care Sector - Avg. Year 1990 to 2009

Health Care / S&P 500 - Avg Yr. 1990 - 2009

The real benefit of investing in the health care sector has been the positive returns that have been generated when the market has typically been negative.

Since 1950, August and September have been the worst two-month combination for gains in the broad stock market.

Having an alternative sector to invest in during the summer and early autumn is a valuable asset.

From August 15th to October 18th (1990 to 2009), health care stocks have had a tendency to outperform the S&P 500 on a yearly basis.

During this time period, the broad market (S&P 500) produced a loss of 1.0%, compared with the health care stocks that produced a gain of 2.1%.

Despite competing with a runaway market in 2003 and legal problems which required drugs to be withdrawn from the market in 2004, the sector has beaten the S&P 500 fourteen out of twenty times from 1990 to 2009.

Alternate Strategy—As the health care sector has had a tendency to perform at par with the broad market from late October to early December, an alternative strategy is to continue holding the health care sector during this time period if the fundamentals or technicals are favorable.

*Health Care SP GIC Sector# 35: An index designed to represent a cross section of utility companies.
For more information on the materials sector, see www.standardandpoors.com.*

29 MONDAY   002 / 124   **30** TUESDAY   001 / 123

31 WEDNESDAY   000 / 122   **1** THURSDAY   029 / 121

2 FRIDAY   028 / 120

WEEK 35

Market Indices & Rates
Weekly Values**

Stock Markets	2008	2009
Dow	11,512	9,543
S&P500	1,281	1,028
Nasdaq	2,378	2,025
TSX	13,528	10,907
FTSE	5,559	4,896
DAX	6,360	5,517
Nikkei	12,850	10,545
Hang Seng	21,172	20,354

Commodities	2008	2009
Oil	116.0	72.4
Gold	831.3	948.2

Bond Yields	2008	2009
USA 5 Yr Treasury	3.06	2.48
USA 10 Yr T	3.79	3.46
USA 20 Yr T	4.43	4.18
Moody's Aaa	5.54	5.14
Moody's Baa	7.09	6.45
CAN 5 Yr T	3.06	2.61
CAN 10 Yr T	3.54	3.41

Money Market	2008	2009
USA Fed Funds	2.00	0.25
USA 3 Mo T-B	1.72	0.16
CAN tgt overnight rate	3.00	0.25
CAN 3 Mo T-B	2.43	0.20

Foreign Exchange	2008	2009
USD/EUR	1.47	1.43
USD/GBP	1.84	1.63
CAN/USD	1.05	1.09
JPY/USD	109.28	94.08

2009 Strategy Performance*

Health Care Sector 2009

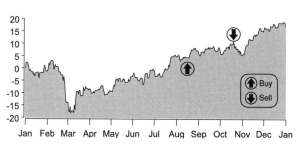

In 2009 the health care sector turned in a lackluster performance during its seasonally strong period.

With the health care sector being a defensive, investors were just not interested when other sectors with higher betas were benefiting from investors renewed interest in the rising stock market.

SEPTEMBER

M	T	W	T	F	S	S
			1	2	3	4
5	6	7	8	9	10	11
12	13	14	15	16	17	18
19	20	21	22	23	24	25
26	27	28	29	30		

OCTOBER

M	T	W	T	F	S	S
					1	2
3	4	5	6	7	8	9
10	11	12	13	14	15	16
17	18	19	20	21	22	23
24	25	26	27	28	29	30
31						

NOVEMBER

M	T	W	T	F	S	S
	1	2	3	4	5	6
7	8	9	10	11	12	13
14	15	16	17	18	19	20
21	22	23	24	25	26	27
28	29	30				

* Buy and Sell dates are approximate representations of strategy dates.
** Weekly avg closing values- except Fed Funds & CAN overnight tgt rate weekly closing values.

SEPTEMBER

	MONDAY	TUESDAY	WEDNESDAY
WEEK 35	29	30	31
WEEK 36	**5** 25 USA Market Closed- Labour Day CAN Market Closed- Labour Day	**6** 24	**7** 23
WEEK 37	**12** 18	**13** 17	**14** 16
WEEK 38	**19** 11	**20** 10	**21** 9
WEEK 39	**26** 4	**27** 3	**28** 2

THURSDAY	FRIDAY
1 29	**2** 28
8 22	**9** 21
15 15	**16** 14
22 8	**23** 7
29 1	**30**

OCTOBER

M	T	W	T	F	S	S
					1	2
3	4	5	6	7	8	9
10	11	12	13	14	15	16
17	18	19	20	21	22	23
24	25	26	27	28	29	30
31						

NOVEMBER

M	T	W	T	F	S	S
	1	2	3	4	5	6
7	8	9	10	11	12	13
14	15	16	17	18	19	20
21	22	23	24	25	26	27
28	29	30				

DECEMBER

M	T	W	T	F	S	S
			1	2	3	4
5	6	7	8	9	10	11
12	13	14	15	16	17	18
19	20	21	22	23	24	25
26	27	28	29	30	31	

JANUARY

M	T	W	T	F	S	S
						1
2	3	4	5	6	7	8
9	10	11	12	13	14	15
16	17	18	19	20	21	22
23	24	25	26	27	28	29
30	31					

SEPTEMBER
S U M M A R Y

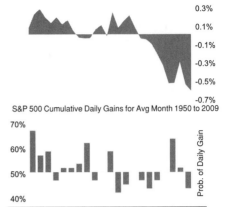

S&P 500 Cumulative Daily Gains for Avg Month 1950 to 2009

♦ September earns the sad face award (see *September Not A Favorable Month*). ♦ Although it is not always negative, overall it has not fared well. ♦ Gold is golden until month end when it tends to lose its shine (see *Golden Times* strategy). ♦ Biotech sector typically finishes its season of outperformance mid-month (see *Biotech Summer Solstice* strategy). ♦ In 2009 the S&P 500 produced a strong 3.6% return in September.

BEST / WORST SEPTEMBER BROAD MKTS. 2000-2009

BEST SEPTEMBER MARKETS
- ♦ Nasdaq (2009) 5.6%
- ♦ Russell 2000 (2009) 5.6%
- ♦ TSX (2009) 4.8%

WORST SEPTEMBER MARKETS
- ♦ Nasdaq (2001) -17.0%
- ♦ TSX (2008) -14.7%
- ♦ Russell 2000 (2001) -13.6%

Index Values End of Month

	2000	2001	2002	2003	2004	2005	2006	2007	2008	2009
Dow	10,651	8,848	7,592	9,275	10,080	10,569	11,679	13,896	10,851	9,712
S&P 500	1,437	1,041	815	996	1,115	1,229	1,336	1,527	1,166	1,057
Nasdaq	3,673	1,499	1,172	1,787	1,897	2,152	2,258	2,702	2,092	2,122
TSX	10,378	6,839	6,180	7,421	8,668	11,012	11,761	14,099	11,753	11,395
Russell 1000	1,486	1,050	833	1,023	1,145	1,285	1,391	1,597	1,219	1,115
Russell 2000	1,296	1,006	900	1,212	1,424	1,660	1,803	2,002	1,689	1,502
Russell 3000 Growth	3,154	1,714	1,322	1,660	1,772	1,967	2,063	2,434	1,910	1,834
Russell 3000 Value	2,132	1,925	1,584	1,928	2,277	2,595	2,901	3,220	2,420	2,090

Percent Gain for September

	2000	2001	2002	2003	2004	2005	2006	2007	2008	2009
Dow	-5.0	-11.1	-12.4	-1.5	-0.9	0.8	2.6	4.0	-6.0	2.3
S&P 500	-5.3	-8.2	-11.0	-1.2	0.9	0.7	2.5	3.6	-9.1	3.6
Nasdaq	-12.7	-17.0	-10.9	-1.3	3.2	0.0	3.4	4.0	-11.6	5.6
TSX	-7.7	-7.6	-6.5	-1.2	3.5	3.2	-2.6	3.2	-14.7	4.8
Russell 1000	-4.7	-8.6	-10.9	-1.2	1.1	0.8	2.3	3.7	-9.7	3.9
Russell 2000	-3.1	-13.6	-7.3	-2.0	4.6	0.2	0.7	1.6	-8.1	5.6
Russell 3000 Growth	-9.2	-10.5	-10.3	-1.3	1.2	0.4	2.5	4.0	-11.7	4.3
Russell 3000 Value	0.7	-7.5	-11.0	-1.2	1.5	1.1	1.7	3.0	-7.4	3.8

September Market Avg. Performance 2000 to 2009 [1]

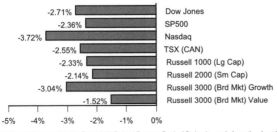

	-2.71%	Dow Jones
	-2.36%	SP500
-3.72%		Nasdaq
	-2.55%	TSX (CAN)
	-2.33%	Russell 1000 (Lg Cap)
	-2.14%	Russell 2000 (Sm Cap)
-3.04%		Russell 3000 (Brd Mkt) Growth
	-1.52%	Russell 3000 (Brd Mkt) Value

Interest Corner Sep[2]

	Fed Funds % [3]	3 Mo. T-Bill % [4]	10 Yr % [5]	20 Yr % [6]
2009	0.25	0.14	3.31	4.02
2008	2.00	0.92	3.85	4.43
2007	4.75	3.82	4.59	4.89
2006	5.25	4.89	4.64	4.84
2005	3.75	3.55	4.34	4.62

(1) Russell Data provided by Russell (2) Federal Reserve Bank of St. Louis - end of month values (3) Target rate set by FOMC (4)(5)(6) Constant yield maturities

THACKRAY SECTOR THERMOMETER

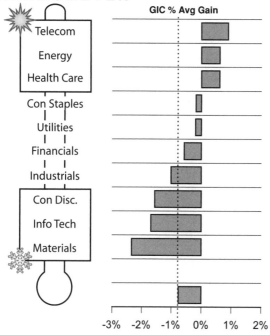

	GIC % Avg Gain	GIC[2] % Avg Gain	Fq % Gain >S&P 500	
		SP GIC SECTOR 1990-2009[1]		
Telecom		0.9 %	65 %	Telecom
Energy		0.6	60	Energy
Health Care		0.6	60	Health Care
Con Staples		-0.2	60	Consumer Staples
Utilities		-0.2	35	Utilities
Financials		-0.6	60	Financial
Industrials		-1.0	45	Industrials
Con Disc.		-1.6	45	Consumer Discretionary
Info Tech		-1.7	65	Information Technology
Materials		-2.3 %	20 %	Materials
		-0.8 %	N/A %	S&P 500

-3% -2% -1% 0% 1% 2%

Sector Commentary

♦ September is usually a weak month and ranks the worst performing month for the S&P 500 since 1950. As a result, investors look for a safe place to park their money and typically turn to the defensive sectors. In 2009 September proved to be a strong month and the S&P 500 gained 3.6%. The cyclicals dominated the top half of the thermometer and the defensives were relegated to the bottom half. The top performing sectors were the Consumer Discretionary, Industrials and Materials sectors, producing gains of 6.6%, 5.2% and 4.7%, respectively.

Sub-Sector Commentary

♦ Gold stocks are the "solid" winner with an average 5.7% gain and 75% frequency of out performance. ♦ Caution should be used because the sector tends to peak before the end of the month (see Golden Times strategy). ♦ In 2009 Gold stocks were the second best performing sector producing a gain of 12.5%. September is typically the strongest month for gold and gold stocks.

		SELECTED SUB-SECTORS 1990-2009[3]
5.7 %	75 %	Gold (XAU)
1.3	65	Biotech (93-2009)
0.9	60	Integrated Oil & Gas
0.7	65	Pharmaceuticals
0.2	65	Software & Services
0.1	63	Agriculture Products (94-2009)
-0.5	55	Insurance
-1.1	50	Transportation
-1.2	55	Banks
-1.4	40	Retail
-1.9	40	Metals & Mining
-2.7	40	Airlines
-2.9	30	Auto & Components
-4.7	27	Semiconductor (SOX) 95-2009

(1) Sector data provided by Standard and Poors (2) GIC is short form for Global Industry Classification (3) Sub Sector data provided by Standard and Poors, except where marked by symbol.

SEPTEMBER – THE STORY OF TWO PARTS
First 19 Days — Last 11 Days

The media often publishes articles about the poor perform-ance of stock markets in September. They are correct; on av-erage it has been the worst month of the year (S&P 500, 1950 to 2009). For more details, see *September Not a Favorable Month* strategy. Nevertheless, it is important to know that the first part of the month has performed differently than the sec-ond part of the month. The S&P 500 from 1950 to 2009, has produced an average gain of 0.2% from September 1st to September 19th and has been positive 53% of the time. On the other hand, the S&P 500 has produced a loss of 0.8%, on average from September 20th to September 30th and has only been positive 40% of the time.

1st Part of September – on average "flat"
2nd Part of September – on average negative

The end result is that the first part of the month is "flat" or slightly positive and the second half of the month is, on av-erage negative. This does not make the first part of the month a great time to invest, especially since the second part of the month does not have a great track record.

S&P 500 - Avg. % Gain September 1950 to 2009

The second part of the month has half the number of days as the first part, is negative more often, and produces an average loss. The second part of September is overwhelmingly the worst part of the month.

S&P 500	Negative Sep 1-19	Sep 20-30
1950's	0.7%	-0.4%
1960's	0.7	-1.1
1970's	-0.2	-0.6
1980's	-0.9	-0.3
1990's	1.8	-1.0
2000's	-0.9	-1.5

Measuring across decades, the first part of the month of Sep-tember has been positive for 50% of the decades since 1950 and the second part of the month has been negative for 100% of the decades. The second part of the month has been con-sistently worse than the first part.

	Negative	
S&P 500	S&P 500 Sep 1-19	S&P 500 Sep 20-30
1950	4.8%	0.7%
1951	1.3	-1.4
1952	-1.8	-0.1
1953	-1.6	1.7
1954	6.3	1.9
1955	4.6	-3.3
1956	-2.7	-1.9
1957	-1.8	-4.5
1958	3.5	1.3
1959	-5.9	1.4
1960	-5.4	-0.6
1961	-2.0	0.1
1962	-0.3	-4.6
1963	1.0	-2.1
1964	2.0	0.8
1965	3.3	-0.1
1966	3.2	-3.8
1967	2.7	0.6
1968	2.8	1.1
1969	-0.3	-2.2
1970	1.4	1.9
1971	0.9	-1.6
1972	-2.3	1.8
1974	1.6	2.4
1974	-2.9	-9.4
1975	-1.2	-2.3
1976	3.3	-1.0
1977	-1.0	0.7
1978	-0.7	0.0
1979	-1.0	1.0
1980	5.6	-2.9
1981	-5.3	-0.1
1982	2.5	-1.7
1983	2.0	-0.9
1984	0.2	-0.5
1985	-2.8	-0.7
1986	-8.2	-0.4
1987	-4.5	2.2
1988	2.8	1.2
1989	-1.4	0.8
1990	-1.9	-3.3
1991	-2.0	0.1
1992	2.2	-1.2
1993	-1.0	0.0
1994	-1.0	-1.7
1995	4.0	0.0
1996	4.8	0.6
1997	5.7	-0.3
1998	6.6	-0.3
1999	1.1	-4.0
2000	-3.8	-1.6
2001	-10.4	2.4
2002	-7.9	-3.3
2003	2.8	-3.9
2004	2.2	-1.2
2005	0.9	-0.2
2006	1.1	1.3
2007	3.7	-0.2
2008	-2.2	-7.1
2009	4.7	-1.1
AVG.	0.2%	-0.8%

5 MONDAY	025 / 117	**6** TUESDAY	024 / 116

7 WEDNESDAY	023 / 115	**8** THURSDAY	022 / 114

9 FRIDAY   021 / 113

WEEK 36

Market Indices & Rates
Weekly Values**

Stock Markets	2008	2009
Dow	11,365	9,375
S&P500	1,258	1,007
Nasdaq	2,299	1,989
TSX	13,017	10,840
FTSE	5,465	4,821
DAX	6,363	5,360
Nikkei	12,581	10,341
Hang Seng	20,571	19,840

Commodities	2008	2009
Oil	108.3	68.4
Gold	807.7	972.9

Bond Yields	2008	2009
USA 5 Yr Treasury	2.93	2.33
USA 10 Yr T	3.69	3.37
USA 20 Yr T	4.34	4.12
Moody's Aaa	5.49	5.12
Moody's Baa	7.04	6.37
CAN 5 Yr T	2.99	2.59
CAN 10 Yr T	3.49	3.35

Money Market	2008	2009
USA Fed Funds	2.00	0.25
USA 3 Mo T-B	1.70	0.14
CAN tgt overnight rate	3.00	0.25
CAN 3 Mo T-B	2.39	0.21

Foreign Exchange	2008	2009
USD/EUR	1.44	1.43
USD/GBP	1.78	1.63
CAN/USD	1.07	1.10
JPY/USD	108.01	92.89

2009 Strategy Performance

September % Gain S&P 500 (2009)

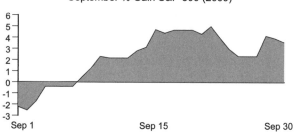

In 2009 the market was on a roll, including the first part of September. The second part of September was a different story, and ended up negative.

Overall the pattern of September in 2009 was very much like the average September, up the first part and down the second part. The only difference was that in 2009, September ended up being positive.

SEPTEMBER

M	T	W	T	F	S	S
			1	2	3	4
5	6	7	8	9	10	11
12	13	14	15	16	17	18
19	20	21	22	23	24	25
26	27	28	29	30		

OCTOBER

M	T	W	T	F	S	S
					1	2
3	4	5	6	7	8	9
10	11	12	13	14	15	16
17	18	19	20	21	22	23
24	25	26	27	28	29	30
31						

NOVEMBER

M	T	W	T	F	S	S
	1	2	3	4	5	6
7	8	9	10	11	12	13
14	15	16	17	18	19	20
21	22	23	24	25	26	27
28	29	30				

** Weekly avg closing values- except Fed Funds & CAN overnight tgt rate weekly closing values.

SEPTEMBER NOT A FAVORABLE MONTH

Wake Me Up When September Ends...
Green Day (2005)

A lot of investors feel the same way as the rock group Green Day. September has not been the best month for the markets: in fact it has been the worst.

-0.6% return & only positive 43% of the time

You have to ask yourself why you would want to be invested up to your risk tolerance during the month of September. It has been positive less than half the time from 1950 to 2009 and has produced an average loss of 0.6%.

Over the years, numerous explanations have been suggested as to why September is a poor performer.

The most commonly accepted reason is that in the month of September investors return from their summer vacations and get serious about their portfolios. They sell off securities that they had previously intended to sell, and generally "clean house." The result has been an under performing September.

Another reason that the markets tend to under perform in September is that mutual fund companies clean their bad stocks from their books in September in order to purchase "good" stocks in October. This

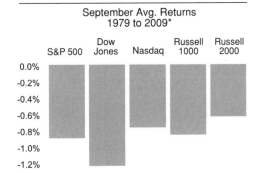

September Avg. Returns
1979 to 2009*

* 1979 inception year for Russell indices

makes their year end holdings on the annual statements look good at the end of October.

The good news is that there are parts of the market in which you can hide. The basic defensive sectors: telecom, energy, health care and utilities have all produced an average positive return from 1990 to 2009 (see *September Sector/Sub-Sector Performance* page).

September's negative performance has been fairly well spread out over the decades. There have only been two decades with an average positive performance: the 1950s and the 1990s. September's performance in the 1950s was barely positive and in the 1990s it was influenced by an extremely strong bull market.

S&P 500 September Monthly % Gain 1950 to 2009   ☐ Negative

Year	%	Year	%	Year	%	Year	%	Year	%	Year	%
1950	5.6 %	1960	-6.0 %	1970	3.4 %	1980	2.5 %	1990	-5.1 %	2000	-5.3 %
1951	-0.1	1961	-2.0	1971	-0.7	1981	-5.4	1991	-1.9	2001	-8.2
1952	-2.0	1962	-4.8	1972	-0.5	1982	0.8	1992	0.9	2002	-11.0
1953	0.1	1963	-1.1	1973	4.0	1983	1.0	1993	-1.0	2003	-1.2
1954	8.3	1964	2.9	1974	-11.9	1984	-0.3	1994	-2.7	2004	0.9
1955	1.1	1965	3.2	1975	-3.5	1985	-3.5	1995	4.0	2005	0.7
1956	-4.5	1966	-0.7	1976	2.3	1986	-8.5	1996	5.4	2006	2.5
1957	-6.2	1967	3.3	1977	-0.2	1987	-2.4	1997	5.3	2007	3.6
1958	4.8	1968	3.9	1978	-0.7	1988	4.0	1998	6.2	2008	-9.1
1959	-4.6	1969	-2.5	1979	0.0	1989	-0.7	1999	-2.9	2009	3.6
Average	0.3 %		-0.4 %		-0.8 %		-1.3 %		0.8 %		-2.4 %

12 MONDAY	018 / 110	**13** TUESDAY	017 / 109

14 WEDNESDAY	016 / 108	**15** THURSDAY	015 / 107

16 FRIDAY	014 / 106

WEEK 37

Market Indices & Rates
Weekly Values**

Stock Markets	2008	2009
Dow	11,373	9,569
S&P500	1,245	1,036
Nasdaq	2,246	2,066
TSX	12,532	11,128
FTSE	5,393	4,977
DAX	6,224	5,548
Nikkei	12,338	10,397
Hang Seng	20,005	20,956

Commodities	2008	2009
Oil	102.8	70.9
Gold	771.3	998.5

Bond Yields	2008	2009
USA 5 Yr Treasury	2.92	2.34
USA 10 Yr T	3.66	3.41
USA 20 Yr T	4.28	4.18
Moody's Aaa	5.46	5.18
Moody's Baa	7.05	6.39
CAN 5 Yr T	3.01	2.60
CAN 10 Yr T	3.50	3.37

Money Market	2008	2009
USA Fed Funds	2.00	0.25
USA 3 Mo T-B	1.62	0.14
CAN tgt overnight rate	3.00	0.25
CAN 3 Mo T-B	2.37	0.21

Foreign Exchange	2008	2009
USD/EUR	1.41	1.45
USD/GBP	1.76	1.65
CAN/USD	1.07	1.08
JPY/USD	107.69	92.13

SEPTEMBER

M	T	W	T	F	S	S
			1	2	3	4
5	6	7	8	9	10	11
12	13	14	15	16	17	18
19	20	21	22	23	24	25
26	27	28	29	30		

OCTOBER

M	T	W	T	F	S	S
					1	2
3	4	5	6	7	8	9
10	11	12	13	14	15	16
17	18	19	20	21	22	23
24	25	26	27	28	29	30
31						

NOVEMBER

M	T	W	T	F	S	S
	1	2	3	4	5	6
7	8	9	10	11	12	13
14	15	16	17	18	19	20
21	22	23	24	25	26	27
28	29	30				

2009 Strategy Performance

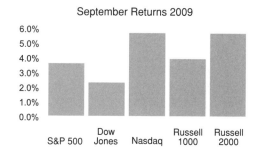

September Returns 2009

In 2009 the market had rallied during the summer months and investors were wondering if September would turn in a negative performance. Was this the month that was going to break the back of the rally? When the market is in strong rally mode, investors keep piling into the markets, waiting for a reason not to get into the markets. With the Federal Reserve dumping liquidity into the market the rally never let up.

It is interesting to note that the best two markets for the month, Russell 2000 and Nasdaq are also the best two markets over the long-term (since 1979, see preceding page).

** Weekly avg closing values- except Fed Funds & CAN overnight tgt rate weekly closing values.

SEPTEMBER PAIR TRADE
Long Gold – Short Metals and Mining in September

How a pair trade works
The trade requires buying one security in the expectation that it will go up (long position) and buying a second security in the expectation that it will go down (short position). The short position can be achieved by selling a position short (selling a position before buying it), or buying a bear fund that buys the short positions.

Most retail investors shy away from taking a short position because of the perceived risk. But selling a position short can help reduce risk, especially when it is used in a pair trade.

Taking a long position in gold (expecting the price of gold to increase), and taking a short position in the metals and mining sector (expecting a decrease in price), has paid handsome rewards in the month of September from 1990 to 2009.

This trade has netted an average return of 3.7% and has been positive 80% of the time. The pair trade results have been better than if you just entered a long position for gold or a short position for the metals and mining sector.

There is a good reason that this pair trade makes sense. The metals and mining and the gold sector have a lot of the same factors driving their performance, at least on the supply side of the equation. If it costs more to get "stuff" out of the ground, then both sectors are effected.

Where the metals and mining sector and gold differ is in their demand cycle. Demand in the metals and mining sector slows down in the summer months as industrial production decreases during the holiday months. Gold on the other hand has a large spike in

demand in the late summer from the gold fabricators having to buy enough gold for the Indian wedding and festival season.

Over the long-term, gold and the metals and mining sector have monthly averages that generally move together.

September presents an exception to this trend and a profitable opportunity for a pair trade.

Gold vs. Metals and Mining
Performance 1990 to 2009

Sept	Gold	Positive M&M	Diff
1990	5.3 %	-4.0 %	9.3 %
1991	2.2	-2.9	5.0
1992	2.6	-1.2	3.9
1993	-4.3	-8.0	3.6
1994	2.4	3.7	-1.4
1995	0.4	-1.7	2.1
1996	-1.9	-2.1	0.2
1997	2.1	1.3	0.8
1998	7.5	26.8	-19.3
1999	17.3	3.0	14.3
2000	-1.2	-15.3	14.1
2001	7.4	-13.0	20.4
2002	3.5	-16.7	20.1
2003	3.3	-4.2	7.5
2004	2.1	5.5	-3.4
2005	9.2	7.3	1.9
2006	-3.9	-5.4	1.5
2007	10.6	11.9	-1.3
2008	6.2	-31.1	37.3
2009	4.2	7.9	-3.7
Avg	3.7 %	-1.9 %	5.6 %

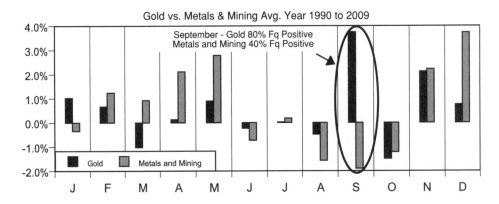

Gold vs. Metals & Mining Avg. Year 1990 to 2009

September - Gold 80% Fq Positive
Metals and Mining 40% Fq Positive

19 MONDAY — 011 / 103

20 TUESDAY — 010 / 102

21 WEDNESDAY — 009 / 101

22 THURSDAY — 008 / 100

23 FRIDAY — 007 / 099

WEEK 38

Market Indices & Rates
Weekly Values**

Stock Markets	2008	2009
Dow	10,999	9,741
S&P500	1,205	1,061
Nasdaq	2,192	2,117
TSX	12,267	11,472
FTSE	5,067	5,104
DAX	5,989	5,677
Nikkei	11,692	10,301
Hang Seng	18,224	21,319

Commodities	2008	2009
Oil	97.3	71.4
Gold	819.9	1008.3

Bond Yields	2008	2009
USA 5 Yr Treasury	2.69	2.43
USA 10 Yr T	3.54	3.46
USA 20 Yr T	4.20	4.19
Moody's Aaa	5.63	5.15
Moody's Baa	7.28	6.36
CAN 5 Yr T	2.95	2.61
CAN 10 Yr T	3.50	3.37

Money Market	2008	2009
USA Fed Funds	2.00	0.25
USA 3 Mo T-B	0.62	0.11
CAN tgt overnight rate	3.00	0.25
CAN 3 Mo T-B	1.85	0.21

Foreign Exchange	2008	2009
USD/EUR	1.43	1.47
USD/GBP	1.80	1.65
CAN/USD	1.07	1.07
JPY/USD	105.51	90.89

SEPTEMBER

M	T	W	T	F	S	S
				1	2	3	4
5	6	7	8	9	10	11
12	13	14	15	16	17	18
19	20	21	22	23	24	25
26	27	28	29	30		

OCTOBER

M	T	W	T	F	S	S
					1	2
3	4	5	6	7	8	9
10	11	12	13	14	15	16
17	18	19	20	21	22	23
24	25	26	27	28	29	30
31						

NOVEMBER

M	T	W	T	F	S	S
	1	2	3	4	5	6
7	8	9	10	11	12	13
14	15	16	17	18	19	20
21	22	23	24	25	26	27
28	29	30				

2009 Strategy Performance

Gold and Metals & Mining % Gain by Month 2009

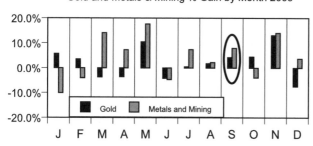

In 2009 both the gold sector and the metals and mining sector produced positive returns during the month of September. The pair trade did not work because both sectors increased.

In the 2009 rally, most sectors increased in the market, it was just a degree of which sectors increased more than others.

CANADIAN BANKS — IN-OUT-IN AGAIN
➔IN (Oct 10 - Dec 31) ➔OUT ➔IN (Jan 23 - Apr 13)

During the financial crisis of 2007/08 the Canadian banks were touted as being the best in the world. Canadians love to invest in their banks because they operate in a regulated environment and for long periods of time have grown their earnings and dividends. Although a lot of sectors in the Canadian market have very similar seasonally strong periods compared with the US, the seasonality for Canadian banks starts earlier than the US banks.

The difference in seasonally strong periods is driven by the difference in fiscal year ends. The US banks have their yearend on December 31st and the Canadian banks on October 31st. Why does this make a difference? Typically, banks clean up their "books" at their yearend, by announcing any bad news. In addition, this is often the time period when the banks announce their positive news, including increases in dividends.

4.9% extra & and positive 76% of the time

The Canadian Bank sector, from October 10th to December 31st for the years 1989 to 2009 has been positive 86% of the time and has produced an average gain of 5.9%. From January 23rd to April 13th, the sector has been positive 71% of the time and has produced an average gain of 6.3%. On a compounded basis the strategy has been positive 76% of the time and produced an average gain of 12.5%.

Basically the strategy does well until mid-April which is the start of the earnings season. Investors have a choice of whether to bridge the two seasonal time periods for the Canadian Bank sector and hold for the entire October 10th to April 13th time period. Investors should consider that from January 1st to the 22nd, from 1990 to 2010, the sector has produced an average loss of 2.3% and has only been positive 38% of the time.

CDN Banks* vs. S&P/TSX Comp 1989 to 2009   Positive ▢

Year	Oct 10 to Dec 31		Jan 23 to Apr 13		Compound Growth	
	TSX Comp	CDN Banks	TSX Comp	CDN Banks	TSX Comp	CDN Banks
1989/90	-1.7%	-1.8%	-6.3%	-9.1%	-7.9%	-10.8%
1990/91	3.7	8.9	9.8	14.6	13.9	24.8
1991/92	5.2	10.2	-6.8	-11.6	-2.0	-2.6
1992/93	4.1	2.5	10.7	14.4	15.2	17.3
1993/94	6.3	6.8	-5.6	-13.3	0.3	-7.4
1994/95	-1.8	3.4	5.0	10.0	3.1	13.8
1995/96	4.9	3.5	3.6	-3.2	8.6	0.1
1996/97	9.0	15.1	-6.2	0.7	2.3	15.9
1997/98	-6.1	7.6	19.9	38.8	12.6	49.4
1998/99	18.3	28.0	4.8	13.0	24.0	44.6
1999/00	18.2	5.1	3.8	22.1	22.8	28.3
2000/01	-14.4	1.7	-14.1	-6.7	-26.4	-5.1
2001/02	11.9	6.5	2.3	8.2	14.5	15.1
2002/03	16.1	21.3	-4.3	2.6	11.1	24.4
2003/04	8.1	5.1	2.0	2.1	10.3	7.4
2004/05	4.9	6.2	4.5	6.9	9.6	13.5
2005/06	6.2	8.4	5.5	2.7	12.1	11.3
2006/07	10.4	8.4	6.9	3.2	18.0	11.8
2007/08	-3.0	-10.4	8.2	-3.5	5.0	-13.5
2008/09	-6.4	-14.8	9.4	24.4	2.4	6.1
2009/10	2.7	2.4	6.7	15.2	9.6	18.0
Avg.	4.6%	5.9%	2.8%	6.3%	7.6%	12.5%

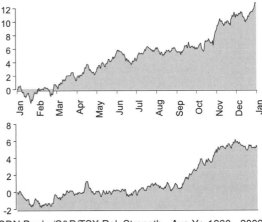

CDN Bank Sector* S&P GIC- Avg. Year 1990 to 2009

CDN Banks/S&P/TSX Rel. Strength - Avg Yr. 1990 - 2009

> Ⓨ *Alternate Strategy—*
> *Investors can bridge the gap between the two positive seasonal trends for the bank sector by holding from October 10th to April 13th. Longer term investors may prefer this strategy, shorter term investors can use technical tools to determine the appropriate strategy.*

> ⓘ * *Banks SP GIC Canadian Sector Level 2*
> *An index designed to represent a cross section of banking companies For more information on the bank sector, see www.standardandpoors.com.*

26 MONDAY	004 / 096	**27** TUESDAY	003 / 095

Market Indices & Rates
Weekly Values**

Stock Markets	2008	2009
Dow	10,972	9,746
S&P500	1,201	1,058
Nasdaq	2,172	2,123
TSX	12,471	11,405
FTSE	5,151	5,116
DAX	6,093	5,653
Nikkei	12,026	10,405
Hang Seng	19,017	21,369

Commodities	2008	2009
Oil	110.4	68.3
Gold	894.9	1004.5

Bond Yields	2008	2009
USA 5 Yr Treasury	3.02	2.41
USA 10 Yr T	3.84	3.43
USA 20 Yr T	4.48	4.15
Moody's Aaa	5.91	5.14
Moody's Baa	7.66	6.27
CAN 5 Yr T	3.15	2.63
CAN 10 Yr T	3.67	3.40

Money Market	2008	2009
USA Fed Funds	2.00	0.25
USA 3 Mo T-B	0.84	0.11
CAN tgt overnight rate	3.00	0.25
CAN 3 Mo T-B	1.98	0.23

Foreign Exchange	2008	2009
USD/EUR	1.47	1.47
USD/GBP	1.85	1.62
CAN/USD	1.04	1.08
JPY/USD	105.83	91.07

28 WEDNESDAY	002 / 094	**29** THURSDAY	001 / 093

30 FRIDAY	000 / 092

2009 Strategy Performance*

Canadian Bank Sector 2009

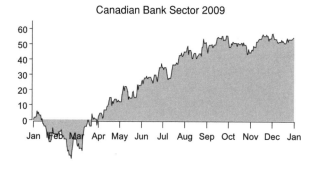

In 2009 the banking sector followed the same pattern as the rest of the stock market, bottoming in March and rallying throughout the year.

The rally in the markets was largely a relief rally based upon the improving conditions in the financial sector, so naturally the financial sector did very well for the year.

SEPTEMBER

M	T	W	T	F	S	S
			1	2	3	4
5	6	7	8	9	10	11
12	13	14	15	16	17	18
19	20	21	22	23	24	25
26	27	28	29	30		

OCTOBER

M	T	W	T	F	S	S
					1	2
3	4	5	6	7	8	9
10	11	12	13	14	15	16
17	18	19	20	21	22	23
24	25	26	27	28	29	30
31						

NOVEMBER

M	T	W	T	F	S	S
	1	2	3	4	5	6
7	8	9	10	11	12	13
14	15	16	17	18	19	20
21	22	23	24	25	26	27
28	29	30				

** Weekly avg closing values- except Fed Funds & CAN overnight tgt rate weekly closing values.

OCTOBER

	MONDAY	TUESDAY	WEDNESDAY
WEEK 40	**3** 28	**4** 27	**5** 26
WEEK 41	**10** 21 USA Bond Market Closed- Columbus Day CAN Market Closed- Thanksgiving Day	**11** 20	**12** 19
WEEK 42	**17** 14	**18** 13	**19** 12
WEEK 43	**24** 7	**25** 6	**26** 5
WEEK 44	**31**	1	2

THURSDAY		FRIDAY	
6	25	**7**	24
13	18	**14**	17
20	11	**21**	10
27	4	**28**	3
3		4	

NOVEMBER

M	T	W	T	F	S	S
	1	2	3	4	5	6
7	8	9	10	11	12	13
14	15	16	17	18	19	20
21	22	23	24	25	26	27
28	29	30				

DECEMBER

M	T	W	T	F	S	S
		1	2	3	4
5	6	7	8	9	10	11
12	13	14	15	16	17	18
19	20	21	22	23	24	25
26	27	28	29	30	31	

JANUARY

M	T	W	T	F	S	S
						1
2	3	4	5	6	7	8
9	10	11	12	13	14	15
16	17	18	19	20	21	22
23	24	25	26	27	28	29
30	31					

FEBRUARY

M	T	W	T	F	S	S
		1	2	3	4	5
6	7	8	9	10	11	12
13	14	15	16	17	18	19
20	21	22	23	24	25	26
27	28	29				

OCTOBER
S U M M A R Y

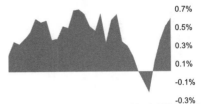

S&P 500 Cumulative Daily Gains for Avg Month 1950 to 2009

BEST / WORST OCTOBER BROAD MKTS. 2000-2009

BEST OCTOBER MARKETS

- ◆ Nasdaq (2002) 13.5%
- ◆ Nasdaq (2001) 12.8%
- ◆ Dow (2002) 10.6%

WORST OCTOBER MARKETS

- ◆ Russell 2000 (2008) -20.9%
- ◆ Russell 3000 Gr (2008) -18.0%
- ◆ Russell 3000 Value (2008) -17.8%

Index Values End of Month

	2000	2001	2002	2003	2004	2005	2006	2007	2008	2009
Dow	10,971	9,075	8,397	9,801	10,027	10,440	12,081	13,930	9,325	9,713
S&P 500	1,429	1,060	886	1,051	1,130	1,207	1,378	1,549	969	1,036
Nasdaq	3,370	1,690	1,330	1,932	1,975	2,120	2,367	2,859	1,721	2,045
TSX	9,640	6,886	6,249	7,773	8,871	10,383	12,345	14,625	9,763	10,911
Russell 1000	1,467	1,071	900	1,081	1,162	1,261	1,437	1,623	1,004	1,089
Russell 2000	1,237	1,064	928	1,313	1,451	1,607	1,906	2,058	1,336	1,399
Russell 3000 Growth	2,997	1,808	1,439	1,756	1,800	1,942	2,140	2,518	1,566	1,800
Russell 3000 Value	2,178	1,910	1,691	2,045	2,310	2,526	2,996	3,219	1,991	2,017

Percent Gain for October

	2000	2001	2002	2003	2004	2005	2006	2007	2008	2009
Dow	3.0	2.6	10.6	5.7	-0.5	-1.2	3.4	0.2	-14.1	0.0
S&P 500	-0.5	1.8	8.6	5.5	1.4	-1.8	3.2	1.5	-16.9	-2.0
Nasdaq	-8.3	12.8	13.5	8.1	4.1	-1.5	4.8	5.8	-17.7	-3.6
TSX	-7.1	0.7	1.1	4.7	2.3	-5.7	5.0	3.7	-16.9	-4.2
Russell 1000	-1.3	2.0	8.1	5.7	1.5	-1.9	3.3	1.6	-17.6	-2.3
Russell 2000	-4.6	5.8	3.1	8.3	1.9	-3.2	5.7	2.8	-20.9	-6.9
Russell 3000 Growth	-5.0	5.5	8.8	5.8	1.6	-1.3	3.7	3.4	-18.0	-1.9
Russell 3000 Value	2.1	-0.8	6.7	6.1	1.5	-2.7	3.3	-0.1	-17.8	-3.5

October Market Avg. Performance 2000 to 2009[1]

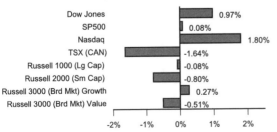

Interest Corner Oct[2]

	Fed Funds % [3]	3 Mo. T-Bill % [4]	10 Yr % [5]	20 Yr % [6]
2009	0.25	0.05	3.41	4.19
2008	1.00	0.46	4.01	4.74
2007	4.50	3.94	4.48	4.79
2006	5.25	5.08	4.61	4.81
2005	3.75	3.98	4.57	4.84

(1) Russell Data provided by Russell (2) Federal Reserve Bank of St. Louis- end of month values (3) Target rate set by FOMC (4)(5)(6) Constant yield maturities

THACKRAY SECTOR THERMOMETER

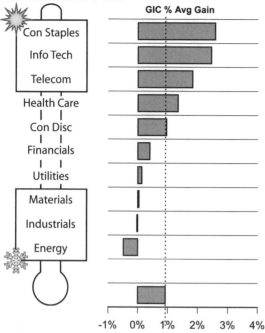

	GIC[2] % Avg Gain	Fq % Gain >S&P 500	
	SP GIC SECTOR 1990-2009[1]		
Con Staples	2.6 %	60 %	Consumer Staples
Info Tech	2.5	50	Information Technology
Telecom	1.8	45	Telecom
Health Care	1.3	50	Health Care
Con Disc	1.0	45	Consumer Discretionary
Financials	0.4	40	Financials
Utilities	0.1	40	Utilities
Materials	0.0	45	Materials
Industrials	0.0	30	Industrials
Energy	-0.5 %	40 %	Energy
	0.9 %	N/A %	S&P 500

Sector Commentary

♦ Consumer Staples and Information Technology live together in the top rank for this month (see *Odd Couple* strategy). ♦ Information Technology, although it has a better average return than the S&P 500, outperforms the market half of the time in the month of October. The sector's outperformance has typically started after September's spell has worn off- October 9th (see Information Technology Use It Or Lose It strategy). In 2009 both the Consumer Staples and Information Technology sectors outperformed the S&P 500. The Consumer Staples produced a gain of 1.0% and Information Technology sectors suffered a mild loss of 1.4%

Sub-Sector Commentary

♦ The agriculture sector is the top performing sub-sector producing an average gain of 6.3% for the month of October, from 1990 to 2009, and beating the S&P 500, 75% of the time. In 2009 it was the second best sector and produced a gain of 3.1%. Gold stocks typically do not do well in the month of October. In 2009 they suffered a loss of 5.3%, which is much bigger than the loss of 2.0% that the S&P 500 suffered.

SELECTED SUB-SECTORS 1990-2009[3]		
6.3 %	75 %	Agriculture Products (94-2009)
4.2	70	Software & Services
3.6	65	Airlines
3.3	70	Transportation
2.1	60	Pharmaceuticals
1.4	55	Retail
1.1	40	Semiconductor (SOX) 95-2009
0.8	47	Biotech (93-2009)
0.4	45	Banks
0.2	40	Insurance
-0.2	40	Integrated Oil & Gas
-1.2	30	Metals & Mining
-1.8	35	Auto & Components
-5.3	30	Gold (XAU)

(1) Sector data provided by Standard and Poors (2) GIC is short form for Global Industry Classification (3) Sub Sector data provided by Standard and Poors, except where marked by symbol.

ODD COUPLE
CONSUMER STAPLES & INFO TECH
Live Together for the Month of October

The consumer staples and information technology sectors make an odd couple for the month of October.

Usually stocks of a similar type move together. For example, the growth sectors of the market tend to rise and fall together. The defensive sectors tend to rise and fall together. Although this relationship is not always true, it is true more often than not.

1.6% extra and 70% of the time better than the S&P 500

October is considered a transition month, where the market bottoms and new sectors tend to rotate into positions of outperformance.

It also tends to be the most volatile month of the year. In this month two unlikely sectors tend to outperform the market: consumer staples and information technology.

Consumer Staples & Information Technology
October Performance vs S&P 500- 1990-2009

% Gain > S&P 500			
		Consumer	
	Consumer	Info	Staples &
	Staples	Tech	Info Tech	S&P 500
1990	5.1 %	-4.2 %	0.5 %	-0.7 %
1991	-0.1	-0.1	-0.1	1.2
1992	-0.1	-0.4	-0.3	0.2
1993	6.8	2.6	4.7	1.9
1994	3.1	8.9	6.0	2.1
1995	2.5	3.8	3.2	-0.5
1996	1.5	1.1	1.3	2.6
1997	-2.1	-9.2	-5.6	-3.4
1998	14.9	6.7	10.8	8.0
1999	7.1	1.8	4.5	6.3
2000	11.6	-5.8	2.9	-0.5
2001	-0.6	17.4	8.4	1.8
2002	3.4	22.3	12.9	8.6
2003	4.8	8.1	6.5	5.5
2004	0.6	5.2	2.9	1.4
2005	-0.4	-2.2	-1.3	-1.8
2006	1.8	4.1	3.0	3.2
2007	1.7	7.1	4.4	1.5
2008	-11.1	-17.8	-14.4	-16.9
2009	1.0	-0.4	0.3	-2.0
Avg	2.6 %	2.5 %	2.5 %	0.9 %

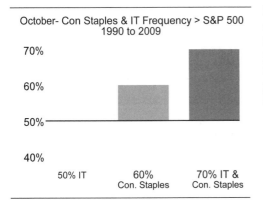

October- Con Staples & IT Frequency > S&P 500
1990 to 2009

70%		
60%		
50%		
40%		
50% IT	60% Con. Staples	70% IT & Con. Staples

In the transition month of October the *Odd Couple* sectors of consumer staples and information technology have the same approximate gain, 2.6% and 2.5% respectively. The real value of the odd couple comes in its combined performance of how often it outperforms the S&P 500.

Why does this odd couple outperform? It is a combination of two factors.

First, investors seek the stability of earnings from the consumer staples sector during volatile times.

Second, investors desire to establish a position in information technology before the best three months of the market in a row- November, December and January.

> (i) *Odd Couple Strategy is similar to a Barbell Strategy- The term barbell strategy is usually reserved for fixed income managers who overweight both short-term and long-term bonds. The odd couple strategy is similar in that it combines sectors that are totally different.*

3 MONDAY	028 / 089	**4** TUESDAY	027 / 088

---

5 WEDNESDAY	026 / 087	**6** THURSDAY	025 / 086

---

7 FRIDAY 024 / 085

WEEK 40

Market Indices & Rates
Weekly Values**

Stock Markets	2008	2009
Dow	10,571	9,648
S&P500	1,129	1,047
Nasdaq	2,014	2,097
TSX	11,291	11,232
FTSE	4,906	5,099
DAX	5,780	5,629
Nikkei	11,293	9,991
Hang Seng	17,948	20,733

Commodities	2008	2009
Oil	96.7	69.0
Gold	869.9	997.1

Bond Yields	2008	2009
USA 5 Yr Treasury	2.77	2.28
USA 10 Yr T	3.70	3.28
USA 20 Yr T	4.30	4.00
Moody's Aaa	5.96	5.00
Moody's Baa	7.86	6.14
CAN 5 Yr T	3.03	2.55
CAN 10 Yr T	3.64	3.30

Money Market	2008	2009
USA Fed Funds	2.00	0.25
USA 3 Mo T-B	0.77	0.12
CAN tgt overnight rate	3.00	0.25
CAN 3 Mo T-B	1.55	0.22

Foreign Exchange	2008	2009
USD/EUR	1.41	1.46
USD/GBP	1.78	1.60
CAN/USD	1.06	1.08
JPY/USD	105.58	89.73

OCTOBER

M	T	W	T	F	S	S
					1	2
3	4	5	6	7	8	9
10	11	12	13	14	15	16
17	18	19	20	21	22	23
24	25	26	27	28	29	30
31						

NOVEMBER

M	T	W	T	F	S	S
	1	2	3	4	5	6
7	8	9	10	11	12	13
14	15	16	17	18	19	20
21	22	23	24	25	26	27
28	29	30				

DECEMBER

M	T	W	T	F	S	S
			1	2	3	4
5	6	7	8	9	10	11
12	13	14	15	16	17	18
19	20	21	22	23	24	25
26	27	28	29	30	31	

2009 Strategy Performance

Odd Couple Strategy 2009

In October 2009, both sectors of the odd couple strategy outperformed the S&P 500. The S&P 500 produced a loss of 2.0%, compared with information technology's loss of 0.4% and consumer staples' gain of 1.0%.

This combination worked once again because of the offsetting characteristics of both sectors. Typically, when the market has been negative, consumer staples has outperformed the S&P 500 and the information technology sector. When the market has been positive, the information technology sector has outperformed. For 2009 it was consumer staples that saved the day.

** Weekly avg closing values- except Fed Funds & CAN overnight tgt rate weekly closing values.

INFORMATION TECHNOLOGY
USE IT OR LOSE IT
October 9th to January 17th

Information technology– the sector that investors love to love and love to hate. In recent times most investors have made and lost money in this sector. When the sector is good, it can be really good. When it is bad, it can be really bad.

5.7% extra compared with the S&P 500

Technology stocks get bid up at the end of the year for three reasons:

First, a lot of companies operate with year end budgets and if they do not spend the money in their budget, they lose it.

In the last few months of the year, whatever money they have they spend. Hence, the saying "use it or lose it."

The number one purchase item for this budget flush is technology equipment. An upgrade in technology equipment is something which a large number of employees in the company can benefit from and is easy to justify.

Second, consumers indirectly help push up technology stocks by purchasing electronic items during the holiday season.

Retail sales ramp up significantly on Black Friday, the Friday after Thanksgiving. Investors anticipate the upswing in sales and increase money flows into technology stocks.

Third, the "Conference Effect" helps maintain the momentum in January. This phenomenon is the result of investors increasing positions ahead of major conferences in order to benefit from positive announcements.

In the case of Information Technology, investors increase their holdings ahead of the Las Vegas Consumer Electronics Conference that typically occurs in the second week of January.

Info Tech & Nasdaq vs S&P 500
Oct 9 to Jan 17, 1989/90-2009/10

	Info Tech	Nas daq	S&P 500	Positive ▢
				Diff IT to S&P	Diff Nas to S&P
1989/90	-6.9 %	-9.3 %	-6.0 %	-1.0 %	-3.3 %
1990/91	13.4	8.0	4.6	8.8	3.3
1991/92	16.4	21.2	10.0	6.4	11.2
1992/93	11.2	21.5	7.2	4.0	14.3
1993/94	12.5	3.7	2.8	9.7	0.8
1994/95	16.0	3.0	3.3	12.7	-0.3
1995/96	-8.9	-1.4	4.1	-13.0	-5.5
1996/97	21.2	8.8	10.8	10.4	-2.0
1997/98	-14.2	-10.3	-1.3	-12.9	-9.0
1998/99	71.8	65.5	29.6	42.2	35.9
1999/00	29.2	40.8	9.7	19.5	31.1
2000/01	-21.7	-20.2	-5.6	-16.1	-14.5
2001/02	26.8	23.7	7.2	19.6	16.5
2002/03	30.0	21.9	12.9	17.0	8.9
2003/04	14.2	13.0	10.3	4.0	2.8
2004/05	6.8	8.7	5.6	1.2	3.2
2005/06	9.7	10.2	7.3	2.4	2.9
2006/07	7.1	7.8	6.0	1.1	1.8
2007/08	-14.9	-15.8	-14.1	-0.7	-1.7
2008/09	-12.0	-12.1	-13.7	1.6	1.6
2009/10	9.9	7.7	6.6	3.3	1.1
Avg	10.4 %	9.3 %	4.6 %	5.7 %	4.7 %

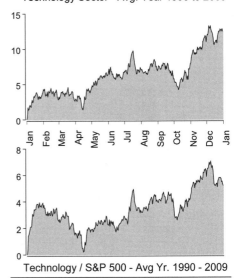

Technology Sector - Avg. Year 1990 to 2009

Technology / S&P 500 - Avg Yr. 1990 - 2009

> ⓘ *Information Technology SP GIC Sector 45: An index designed to represent a cross section of information technology companies.*
> *For more information on the information technology sector, see www.standardandpoors.com.*

10 MONDAY	021 / 082	**11** TUESDAY	020 / 081

12 WEDNESDAY	019 / 080	**13** THURSDAY	018 / 079

14 FRIDAY		017 / 078

WEEK 41

Market Indices & Rates
Weekly Values**

Stock Markets	2008	2009
Dow	9,138	9,742
S&P500	969	1,058
Nasdaq	1,731	2,109
TSX	9,756	11,324
FTSE	4,361	5,118
DAX	5,032	5,647
Nikkei	9,453	9,803
Hang Seng	15,744	21,095

Commodities	2008	2009
Oil	86.2	70.9
Gold	888.0	1036.2

Bond Yields	2008	2009
USA 5 Yr Treasury	2.63	2.24
USA 10 Yr T	3.69	3.28
USA 20 Yr T	4.28	4.04
Moody's Aaa	6.12	5.06
Moody's Baa	8.25	6.22
CAN 5 Yr T	2.81	2.61
CAN 10 Yr T	3.59	3.34

Money Market	2008	2009
USA Fed Funds	1.50	0.25
USA 3 Mo T-B	0.58	0.08
CAN tgt overnight rate	2.50	0.25
CAN 3 Mo T-B	0.73	0.20

Foreign Exchange	2008	2009
USD/EUR	1.36	1.47
USD/GBP	1.73	1.59
CAN/USD	1.12	1.06
JPY/USD	100.80	89.13

2009-2010 Strategy Performance*

Information Technology % Gain June 2009 to May 2010

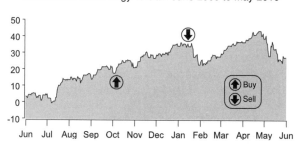

In 2009 the information technology sector started its outperformance right on schedule towards the beginning of October. It then went on to peak in mid-January 2010, where once again it peaked out. It is always good to see when the buy and sell dates line up so closely with the long-term trend dates.

When the S&P 500 is positive during technology's strong period (which is usually the case), typically technology outperforms. Essentially, technology stocks provide a higher beta to the market. In the 2009-2010 seasonal cycle, technology outperformed the S&P 500.

* Buy and Sell dates are approximate representations of strategy dates.
** Weekly avg closing values- except Fed Funds & CAN overnight tgt rate weekly closing values.

OCTOBER

M	T	W	T	F	S	S
					1	2
3	4	5	6	7	8	9
10	11	12	13	14	15	16
17	18	19	20	21	22	23
24	25	26	27	28	29	30
31						

NOVEMBER

M	T	W	T	F	S	S
	1	2	3	4	5	6
7	8	9	10	11	12	13
14	15	16	17	18	19	20
21	22	23	24	25	26	27
28	29	30				

DECEMBER

M	T	W	T	F	S	S
			1	2	3	4
5	6	7	8	9	10	11
12	13	14	15	16	17	18
19	20	21	22	23	24	25
26	27	28	29	30	31	

CONSUMER SWITCH
SELL CONSUMER STAPLES
BUY CONSUMER DISCRETIONARY
Con. Discretionary Outperforms From Oct 28 to Apr 22

This is the time to sell the sector of "need" and buy the sector of "want."

Companies that are classified as consumer staples sell products to the consumer that they need for their everyday life.

Consumers will generally still buy products from a consumer staples company, such as a drugstore, even if the economy and the stock market turns down.

On the other hand, consumer discretionary companies sell products that consumers do not necessarily need, such as furniture.

Why is this important? Consumer discretionary companies tend to outperform in the six favorable months of the market.

The discretionary sector benefits from the positive market forces and positive market forecasts that tend to take place in this period.

The consumer staples and discretionary sectors average year graphs illustrate the individual trends of the sectors.

The discretionary sector tends to outperform strongly from the end of December to April. Although the staples sector in the summer months has a slightly average negative performance, it still outperforms the discretionary sector.

At the end of the year, both sectors do well, but investing in the right sector at the right time can make a substantial difference in an investor's profits.

Consumer Discretionary Avg. Year 1990 to 2009

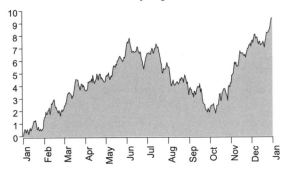

Consumer Staples Avg. Year 1990 to 2009

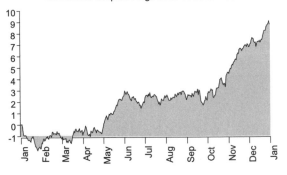

Con. Discretionary / Staples - Relative Strength Avg. Year 1990 to 2009

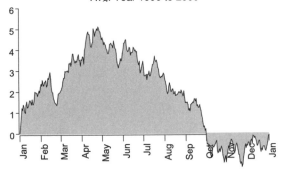

> *Alternate Strategy — The consumer discretionary stocks have dramatically outperformed the consumer staples stocks from December 27th to April 22nd. With both the discretionary and staples sectors performing well in November and December, depending on market conditions, investors can delay some or all of their allocation to the discretionary sector until the end of December.*

17 MONDAY	014 / 075	**18** TUESDAY	013 / 074

19 WEDNESDAY	012 / 073	**20** THURSDAY	011 / 072

21 FRIDAY   010 / 071

WEEK 42

Market Indices & Rates
Weekly Values**

Stock Markets	2008	2009
Dow	9,022	9,966
S&P500	959	1,085
Nasdaq	1,736	2,156
TSX	9,528	11,489
FTSE	4,131	5,207
DAX	4,905	5,785
Nikkei	9,037	10,158
Hang Seng	15,786	21,716

Commodities	2008	2009
Oil	75.2	75.7
Gold	819.6	1055.4

Bond Yields	2008	2009
USA 5 Yr Treasury	2.90	2.36
USA 10 Yr T	4.02	3.43
USA 20 Yr T	4.60	4.23
Moody's Aaa	6.47	5.21
Moody's Baa	9.09	6.38
CAN 5 Yr T	2.96	2.85
CAN 10 Yr T	3.77	3.51

Money Market	2008	2009
USA Fed Funds	1.50	0.25
USA 3 Mo T-B	0.46	0.07
CAN tgt overnight rate	2.50	0.25
CAN 3 Mo T-B	1.63	0.23

Foreign Exchange	2008	2009
USD/EUR	1.36	1.49
USD/GBP	1.74	1.60
CAN/USD	1.17	1.03
JPY/USD	101.13	90.00

2009-2010 Strategy Performance*

Consumer Discretionary / Consumer Staples July 2009 to June 2010

The consumer switch strategy worked great in 2009 and into 2010. The consumer discretionary sector started to outperform the consumer staples sector at the end of October and maintained its outperformance into April.

The above graph shows the ratio of outperformance between the two sectors. When the line is rising, the discretionary sector is outperforming. When it is falling, the staples sector is outperforming.

* Buy and Sell dates are approximate representations of strategy dates.
** Weekly avg closing values- except Fed Funds & CAN overnight tgt rate weekly closing values.

OCTOBER

M	T	W	T	F	S	S
					1	2
3	4	5	6	7	8	9
10	11	12	13	14	15	16
17	18	19	20	21	22	23
24	25	26	27	28	29	30
31						

NOVEMBER

M	T	W	T	F	S	S
	1	2	3	4	5	6
7	8	9	10	11	12	13
14	15	16	17	18	19	20
21	22	23	24	25	26	27
28	29	30				

DECEMBER

M	T	W	T	F	S	S
		1	2	3	4	
5	6	7	8	9	10	11
12	13	14	15	16	17	18
19	20	21	22	23	24	25
26	27	28	29	30	31	

Although the *Retail – Shop Early* strategy is the second retail sector strategy of the year, it occurs before the biggest shopping season of the year – the Christmas holiday season.

2.9% extra & 75% of the time better than S&P 500

The time to go shopping for retail stocks is at the end of October, which is about one month before Thanksgiving. It is the time when two favorable influences happen at the same time.

Retail Sector - Avg. Year 1990 to 2009

Retail / S&P 500 Relative Strength - Avg Yr. 1990 - 2009

First, the three best months in a row for the market have been November, December and January. The end of October usually represents an excellent buying opportunity, not only for the next three months, but the next six months.

Second, investors tend to buy retail stocks in anticipation of a strong holiday sales season. At the same time that the market tends to increase, investors are attracted back into the retail sector.

Retail sales tend to be lower in the summer and a lot of investors view investing in retail stocks at this time as dead money. During the summertime investors prefer not to invest in this sector until it comes back

into favor towards the end of October.

The trick to investing is not to be too early, but early. If an investor gets into a sector too early they can suffer from the frustration of having dead money (having an investment that goes nowhere, while the rest of the market increases).

If an investor moves into a sector too late there is very little upside potential. In fact, this can be a dangerous strategy because if the sales or earnings numbers disappoint the analysts, the sector can severely correct.

For the *Retail – Shop Early* strategy the time to enter is approximately one month before Black Friday.

Coincidentally the end of October is also typically a good time to enter the broad market.

Retail Sector vs. S&P 500 1990 to 2009

Oct 28 to Nov 29	Positive		
	Retail	S&P500	Diff
1990	9.9 %	3.8 %	6.0 %
1991	2.7	-2.3	5.0
1992	5.5	2.8	2.8
1993	6.3	-0.6	6.9
1994	0.4	-2.3	2.7
1995	9.5	4.8	4.7
1996	0.4	8.0	-7.6
1997	16.9	8.9	7.9
1998	20.4	11.9	8.4
1999	14.1	8.6	5.5
2000	9.9	-2.7	12.6
2001	7.9	3.2	4.7
2002	-1.7	4.3	-6.0
2003	2.5	2.6	-0.1
2004	7.0	4.7	2.3
2005	9.9	6.7	3.2
2006	0.2	1.6	-1.4
2007	-7.5	-4.3	-3.2
2008	7.5	5.6	1.9
2009	3.6	2.6	1.0
Avg.	6.3 %	3.4 %	2.9 %

24 MONDAY	007 / 068	**25** TUESDAY	006 / 067

26 WEDNESDAY	005 / 066	**27** THURSDAY	004 / 065

28 FRIDAY	003 / 064

WEEK 43

Market Indices & Rates
Weekly Values**

Stock Markets	2008	2009
Dow	8,778	10,027
S&P500	924	1,089
Nasdaq	1,648	2,162
TSX	9,582	11,487
FTSE	4,105	5,247
DAX	4,601	5,800
Nikkei	8,619	10,291
Hang Seng	14,202	22,341

Commodities	2008	2009
Oil	68.3	80.1
Gold	748.7	1056.2

Bond Yields	2008	2009
USA 5 Yr Treasury	2.64	2.38
USA 10 Yr T	3.74	3.43
USA 20 Yr T	4.46	4.20
Moody's Aaa	6.32	5.17
Moody's Baa	9.29	6.31
CAN 5 Yr T	2.82	2.75
CAN 10 Yr T	3.65	3.47

Money Market	2008	2009
USA Fed Funds	1.50	0.25
USA 3 Mo T-B	1.05	0.07
CAN tgt overnight rate	2.25	0.25
CAN 3 Mo T-B	1.92	0.22

Foreign Exchange	2008	2009
USD/EUR	1.30	1.50
USD/GBP	1.65	1.64
CAN/USD	1.23	1.05
JPY/USD	98.33	91.09

2009 Strategy Performance*

Retail % Gain 2009

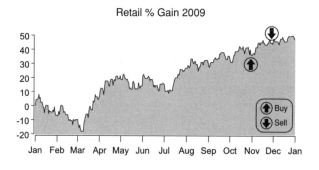

OCTOBER

M	T	W	T	F	S	S
					1	2
3	4	5	6	7	8	9
10	11	12	13	14	15	16
17	18	19	20	21	22	23
24	25	26	27	28	29	30
31						

NOVEMBER

M	T	W	T	F	S	S
	1	2	3	4	5	6
7	8	9	10	11	12	13
14	15	16	17	18	19	20
21	22	23	24	25	26	27
28	29	30				

DECEMBER

M	T	W	T	F	S	S
			1	2	3	4
5	6	7	8	9	10	11
12	13	14	15	16	17	18
19	20	21	22	23	24	25
26	27	28	29	30	31	

The retail sector performed well in 2009. By the time autumn rolled around, it was quite evident that the consumer was not dead yet. The retail sector benefited from a drop in the market just before the start of its seasonal autumn period. On the bounce it managed to outperform the S&P 500, as expected, until Black Friday.

At the end of its seasonal autumn cycle, the retail sector started to under perform the S&P 500, once again, as expected.

* Buy and Sell dates are approximate representations of strategy dates.
** Weekly avg closing values- except Fed Funds & CAN overnight tgt rate weekly closing values.

LAST 4 MARKET DAYS IN OCTOBER
The 1% Difference

The adage "buy at the beginning of November and sell at the end of April" has been around a long time. A lot of prudent investors believe in the merits of this strategy and have profited handsomely.

Nevertheless, if they entered the market four market days earlier they would have received, on average, an extra 1% per year from 1950 to 2009.

Average Return of 1% &
Positive 58% of the time

It is not just the four days gain that is attractive; the seasonal safety net that follows has been very solid.

The last four days is followed by one of the best months: November. This month is also the first month of the best three months in a row and the first month of the six favorable months.

Although October has a reputation for being a "tough month," its average return has been positive from 1950 to 2009. It is October's volatility that shakes investors up.

The interesting fact is that almost all of the gains for October can be attributed to the last four market days. The average daily gain for all days in October, except the last four, is 0.02%. This pales in comparison to the average daily gain for the last four days of the market, 0.25%.

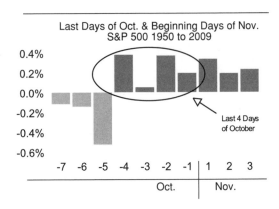

Last Days of Oct. & Beginning Days of Nov. S&P 500 1950 to 2009

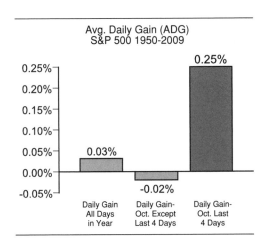

Avg. Daily Gain (ADG) S&P 500 1950-2009

Last 4 Market Days in October % Gain 1950 to 2009 — Positive

Year	%	Year	%	Year	%	Year	%	Year	%	Year	%
1950	-0.4 %	1960	2.3 %	1970	-0.1 %	1980	-0.3 %	1990	-2.0 %	2000	4.7 %
1951	0.6	1961	0.4	1971	-0.9	1981	3.2	1991	2.1	2001	-3.7
1952	1.8	1962	3.3	1972	0.8	1982	0.3	1992	0.1	2002	-1.3
1953	0.9	1963	0.0	1973	-2.0	1983	-1.8	1993	0.8	2003	1.9
1954	-0.9	1964	-0.2	1974	5.4	1984	-0.1	1994	2.3	2004	3.2
1955	-0.7	1965	0.8	1975	-0.8	1985	1.2	1995	-0.2	2005	0.9
1956	-0.6	1966	1.6	1976	2.8	1986	2.2	1996	0.6	2006	-0.3
1957	1.2	1967	-1.3	1977	1.5	1987	10.6	1997	4.3	2007	2.3
1958	1.8	1968	-0.4	1978	-4.3	1988	-1.2	1998	2.5	2008	14.1
1959	1.0	1969	-0.9	1979	1.8	1989	-0.6	1999	5.4	2009	-2.9
Average	0.5 %		0.6 %		0.4 %		1.3 %		1.6 %		1.9 %

31 MONDAY   000 / 061

1 TUESDAY   029 / 060

2 WEDNESDAY   028 / 059

3 THURSDAY   027 / 058

4 FRIDAY   026 / 057

WEEK 44

Market Indices & Rates
Weekly Values**

Stock Markets	2008	2009
Dow	8,948	9,838
S&P500	928	1,055
Nasdaq	1,646	2,092
TSX	9,362	11,016
FTSE	4,138	5,131
DAX	4,765	5,555
Nikkei	8,121	10,115
Hang Seng	12,923	21,737

Commodities	2008	2009
Oil	65.4	78.5
Gold	742.2	1040.6

Bond Yields	2008	2009
USA 5 Yr Treasury	2.77	2.41
USA 10 Yr T	3.92	3.49
USA 20 Yr T	4.59	4.27
Moody's Aaa	6.42	5.22
Moody's Baa	9.49	6.34
CAN 5 Yr T	2.80	2.74
CAN 10 Yr T	3.71	3.48

Money Market	2008	2009
USA Fed Funds	1.00	0.25
USA 3 Mo T-B	0.62	0.07
CAN tgt overnight rate	2.25	0.25
CAN 3 Mo T-B	1.99	0.22

Foreign Exchange	2008	2009
USD/EUR	1.27	1.48
USD/GBP	1.60	1.64
CAN/USD	1.25	1.07
JPY/USD	96.07	91.11

NOVEMBER

M	T	W	T	F	S	S
	1	2	3	4	5	6
7	8	9	10	11	12	13
14	15	16	17	18	19	20
21	22	23	24	25	26	27
28	29	30				

DECEMBER

M	T	W	T	F	S	S
			1	2	3	4
5	6	7	8	9	10	11
12	13	14	15	16	17	18
19	20	21	22	23	24	25
26	27	28	29	30	31	

JANUARY

M	T	W	T	F	S	S
						1
2	3	4	5	6	7	8
9	10	11	12	13	14	15
16	17	18	19	20	21	22
23	24	25	26	27	28	29
30	31					

2009 Strategy Performance

October Last Days of Month and Beginning of Nov. S&P 500 (2009)

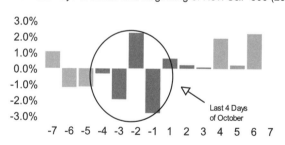

Last 4 Days of October

In 2008 if an investor had not been in the market the last four days of October, a gain of over 14% would have been missed. In 2009 entering the market four days before the end of the month cost 2.9%. The market bottomed on the last day of October.

It is very difficult to pick the exact bottom of the market, but getting into the market four days before the end of October has proven to be a wise strategy over the long-term.

** Weekly avg closing values- except Fed Funds & CAN overnight tgt rate weekly closing values.

NOVEMBER

	MONDAY	TUESDAY	WEDNESDAY
WEEK 44	31	1 29	2 28
WEEK 45	7 23	8 22	9 21
WEEK 46	14 16	15 15	16 14
WEEK 47	21 9	22 8	23 7
WEEK 48	28 2	29 1	30

	THURSDAY		FRIDAY
3	27	**4**	26
10	20	**11**	19
17	13	**18**	12
24	6	**25**	5
	USA Market Closed- Thanksgiving Day		USA Early Market Close Thanksgiving
1		2	

DECEMBER

M	T	W	T	F	S	S
			1	2	3	4
5	6	7	8	9	10	11
12	13	14	15	16	17	18
19	20	21	22	23	24	25
26	27	28	29	30	31	

JANUARY

M	T	W	T	F	S	S
						1
2	3	4	5	6	7	8
9	10	11	12	13	14	15
16	17	18	19	20	21	22
23	24	25	26	27	28	29
30	31					

FEBRUARY

M	T	W	T	F	S	S
		1	2	3	4	5
6	7	8	9	10	11	12
13	14	15	16	17	18	19
20	21	22	23	24	25	26
27	28	29				

MARCH

M	T	W	T	F	S	S
			1	2	3	4
5	6	7	8	9	10	11
12	13	14	15	16	17	18
19	20	21	22	23	24	25
26	27	28	29	30	31	

NOVEMBER
S U M M A R Y

S&P 500 Cumulative Daily Gains for Avg Month 1950 to 2009

Prob. of Daily Gain

♦ November typically performs well, but when it is negative it tends to have large losses. It lost 8.0%, 4.4% and 7.5% in 2000, 2007 and 2008 respectively. ♦ The day before and the day after the U.S. Thanksgiving tend to be very good (see *Thanksgiving - Give Thanks and Take Returns* strategy). In 2009 the Thanksgiving trade produced a loss. ♦ The Metals and Mining sector tends to start its ascent mid-November.

BEST / WORST NOVEMBER BROAD MKTS. 2000-2009

BEST NOVEMBER MARKETS
♦ Nasdaq (2001) 14.2%
♦ Nasdaq (2002) 11.2%
♦ Russell 3000 Gr (2001) 9.5%

WORST NOVEMBER MARKETS
♦ Nasdaq (2000) -22.9%
♦ Russell 3000 Gr (2000) -15.0%
♦ Russell 2000 (2008) -12.0%

Index Values End of Month

	2000	2001	2002	2003	2004	2005	2006	2007	2008	2009
Dow	10,414	9,852	8,896	9,782	10,428	10,806	12,222	13,372	8,829	10,345
S&P 500	1,315	1,139	936	1,058	1,174	1,249	1,401	1,481	896	1,096
Nasdaq	2,598	1,931	1,479	1,960	2,097	2,233	2,432	2,661	1,536	2,145
TSX	8,820	7,426	6,570	7,859	9,030	10,824	12,752	13,689	9,271	11,447
Russell 1000	1,331	1,152	952	1,093	1,210	1,306	1,464	1,550	925	1,150
Russell 2000	1,108	1,145	1,010	1,358	1,575	1,683	1,954	1,908	1,176	1,441
Russell 3000 Growth	2,547	1,979	1,520	1,776	1,868	2,026	2,180	2,415	1,433	1,903
Russell 3000 Value	2,095	2,018	1,795	2,072	2,429	2,601	3,057	3,046	1,834	2,121

Percent Gain for November

	2000	2001	2002	2003	2004	2005	2006	2007	2008	2009
Dow	-5.1	8.6	5.9	-0.2	4.0	3.5	1.2	-4.0	-5.3	6.5
S&P 500	-8.0	7.5	5.7	0.7	3.9	3.5	1.6	-4.4	-7.5	5.7
Nasdaq	-22.9	14.2	11.2	1.5	6.2	5.3	2.7	-6.9	-10.8	4.9
TSX	-8.5	7.8	5.1	1.1	1.8	4.2	3.3	-6.4	-5.0	4.9
Russell 1000	-9.3	7.5	5.7	1.0	4.1	3.5	1.9	-4.5	-7.9	5.6
Russell 2000	-10.4	7.6	8.8	3.5	8.6	4.7	2.5	-7.3	-12.0	3.0
Russell 3000 Growth	-15.0	9.5	5.6	1.1	3.7	4.3	1.9	-4.1	-8.5	5.7
Russell 3000 Value	-3.8	5.7	6.1	1.3	5.1	3.0	2.0	-5.4	-7.9	5.2

November Market Avg. Performance 2000 to 2009 [1]

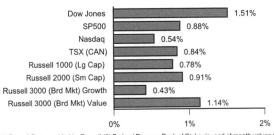

Dow Jones	1.51%
SP500	0.88%
Nasdaq	0.54%
TSX (CAN)	0.84%
Russell 1000 (Lg Cap)	0.78%
Russell 2000 (Sm Cap)	0.91%
Russell 3000 (Brd Mkt) Growth	0.43%
Russell 3000 (Brd Mkt) Value	1.14%

Interest Corner Nov[2]

	Fed Funds % [3]	3 Mo. T-Bill % [4]	10 Yr % [5]	20 Yr % [6]
2009	0.25	0.06	3.21	4.07
2008	1.00	0.01	2.93	3.71
2007	4.50	3.15	3.97	4.44
2006	5.25	5.03	4.46	4.66
2005	4.00	3.95	4.49	4.81

(1) Russell Data provided by Russell (2) Federal Reserve Bank of St. Louis- end of month values (3) Target rate set by FOMC (4)(5)(6) Constant yield maturities

THACKRAY SECTOR THERMOMETER

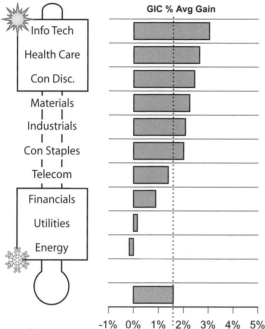

GIC[2] % Avg Gain	Fq % Gain >S&P 500	SP GIC SECTOR 1990-2009[1]
3.0 %	65 %	Information Technology
2.6	60	Health Care
2.4	65	Consumer Discretionary
2.2	55	Materials
2.1	65	Industrials
2.0	45	Consumer Staples
1.4	40	Telecom
0.9	35	Financial
0.2	35	Utilities
-0.2 %	25 %	Energy
1.6 %	N/A %	S&P 500

Thermometer labels (top to bottom): Info Tech, Health Care, Con Disc., Materials, Industrials, Con Staples, Telecom, Financials, Utilities, Energy

Chart axis: -1% 0% 1% 2% 3% 4% 5%

Sector Commentary

♦ From 1990 to 2009, the top two sectors of November, Information Technology and Consumer Discretionary have produced average gains of 3.0% and 2.6% respectively. ♦ The top half of the thermometer is dominated by the non-defensive sectors, and the bottom half by the defensives. The exception to this is the Health Care sector which has been the second best sector. ♦ In 2009 generally the sector distribution was the same as the long term distribution, in that the same sectors were in their respective halves. ♦ Materials, Health Care and Industrials were the top three sectors with returns of 11.3%, 9.0% and 8.7% respectively. ♦ Utilities, Consumer Staples and Energy were the bottom three sectors with returns of 4.2%, 3.8%, and 2.8%, respectively.

Sub-Sector Commentary

♦ In 2009 November was a strong month in the markets with the S&P 500 producing a gain of 5.7% and as a result a lot of the sub-sectors got shuffled. The top three sub-sectors: Auto Components, Gold stocks and Metals & Mining produced gains of 19.8%, 17.3% and 14%, respectively. The Auto & Components sector doesn't typically start its run until the New Year. The gold sector extended its bull run and the Metals and Mining sector started early.

		SELECTED SUB-SECTORS 1990-2009[3]
5.6 %	50 %	Agriculture Products (94-2009)
3.7	53	Semiconductor (SOX) 95-2009
3.4	65	Retail
2.8	70	Software & Services
2.6	60	Pharmaceuticals
2.2	55	Metals & Mining
2.2	47	Biotech (93-2009)
2.1	55	Insurance
2.0	45	Airlines
2.0	40	Transportation
1.2	40	Gold (XAU)
1.2	45	Auto & Components
0.7	40	Banks
0.3	30	Integrated Oil & Gas

(1) Sector data provided by Standard and Poors (2) GIC is short form for Global Industry Classification (3) Sub Sector data provided by Standard and Poors, except where marked by symbol.

MATERIAL STOCKS — MATERIAL GAINS
➔ IN (Oct 28 - Jan 6) ➔ OUT ➔ IN (Jan 23 - May 5)

The materials sector (U.S.) generally does well during the favorable six months of the year, from the end of October to the beginning of May. The sector is economically sensitive and is leveraged to the economic forecasts. Generally, if the economy is expected to slow, the materials sector tends to decline, vice versa.

In the past I have focused my writings on the seasonal strength of the materials sector in the time period between the latter days of January to the first few days of May. Although the materials sector has done very well at this time of year, there is another time period when the materials sector has outperformed the broad markets – from October 28th to January 6th. During this time period the sector has produced an average gain of 8.6% in the years from 1990 to 2010 and has been positive 81% of the time.

Positive 100% of the time

A lot of investors will ask the question: why not stay in the market for the entire October 28th to May 5th period? In fact this is a very viable strategy, especially for investors looking to hold positions for a longer term.

The time period from January 7th to January 22nd has had an average loss of 3.5% and only been positive 29% of the time (1989/90 to 2009/10). The complete materials strategy is in the market from October 28th to January 6th, out of the market from January 7 to the 22nd, and back in on the 23rd to May 5th. This complete strategy has produced an average gain of 16.9% and has been positive 100% of the time.

Materials Sector vs. S&P 500 1989/90 to 2009/10 Positive ☐

	Oct 28 to Jan6		Jan 23 to May 5		Compound Growth	
Year	S&P 500	Ind.	S&P 500	Ind.	S&P 500	Ind.
1989/90	5.1 %	9.1 %	2.4 %	-3.1 %	7.7 %	5.7 %
1990/91	5.4	9.2	16.0	15.3	22.2	26.0
1991/92	8.8	1.5	-0.3	5.5	8.5	7.1
1992/93	3.8	5.6	1.9	4.3	5.8	10.2
1993/94	0.5	9.4	-4.9	-5.3	-4.4	3.6
1994/95	-1.1	-3.5	11.9	6.1	10.7	2.4
1995/96	6.4	7.6	4.6	11.1	11.3	19.5
1996/97	6.7	2.3	5.6	2.3	12.6	4.6
1997/98	10.2	1.4	15.8	20.9	27.7	22.6
1998/99	19.4	6.1	10.0	31.5	31.3	39.6
1999/00	8.2	15.7	-0.6	-7.1	7.6	7.5
2000/01	-5.9	19.2	-5.7	15.1	-11.2	37.2
2001/02	6.2	8.5	-4.1	14.9	1.8	24.7
2002/03	3.5	9.2	5.5	2.7	9.2	12.1
2003/04	9.0	16.6	-2.0	-3.0	6.8	13.1
2004/05	5.6	5.4	0.4	0.3	6.0	5.8
2005/06	9.0	16.3	5.1	14.7	14.6	33.5
2006/07	2.4	3.2	5.8	10.7	8.3	14.2
2007/08	-8.1	-5.1	7.4	16.7	-1.2	10.8
2008/09	10.1	12.0	9.2	23.3	20.3	38.1
2009/10	6.9	13.8	6.8	3.0	14.2	17.2
Avg.	5.3 %	7.8 %	4.3 %	8.6 %	10.0 %	16.9 %

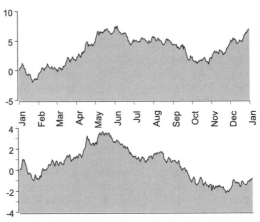

Materials Sector - Avg. Year 1990 to 2009

Materials / S&P 500 Rel. Strength - Avg Yr. 1990 - 2009

Ⓨ *Alternate Strategy—*
Investors can bridge the gap between the two positive seasonal trends for the materials sector by holding from October 28th to May 5th. Longer term investors may prefer this strategy, shorter term investors can use technical tools to determine the appropriate strategy.

ⓘ *The SP GICS Materials Sector encompasses a wide range materials based companies.*
For more information on the information technology sector, see www.standardandpoors.com

7 MONDAY	023 / 054	**8** TUESDAY	022 / 053

Market Indices & Rates
Weekly Values

Stock Markets	2008	2009
Dow	9,145	9,879
S&P500	952	1,054
Nasdaq	1,689	2,076
TSX	9,775	11,081
FTSE	4,450	5,104
DAX	5,045	5,440
Nikkei	9,029	9,789
Hang Seng	14,320	21,557

Commodities	2008	2009
Oil	64.3	79.0
Gold	742.9	1079.8

9 WEDNESDAY	021 / 052	**10** THURSDAY	020 / 051

Bond Yields	2008	2009
USA 5 Yr Treasury	2.56	2.35
USA 10 Yr T	3.82	3.53
USA 20 Yr T	4.58	4.32
Moody's Aaa	6.37	5.27
Moody's Baa	9.33	6.39
CAN 5 Yr T	2.79	2.71
CAN 10 Yr T	3.75	3.48

11 FRIDAY		019 / 050

Money Market	2008	2009
USA Fed Funds	1.00	0.25
USA 3 Mo T-B	0.40	0.05
CAN tgt overnight rate	2.25	0.25
CAN 3 Mo T-B	1.77	0.22

Foreign Exchange	2008	2009
USD/EUR	1.28	1.48
USD/GBP	1.59	1.65
CAN/USD	1.18	1.07
JPY/USD	98.52	90.29

2009-2010 Strategy Performance

Materials Sector 2009-2010

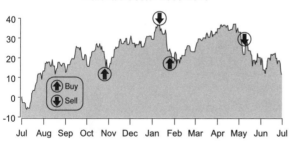

NOVEMBER

M	T	W	T	F	S	S
	1	2	3	4	5	6
7	8	9	10	11	12	13
14	15	16	17	18	19	20
21	22	23	24	25	26	27
28	29	30				

DECEMBER

M	T	W	T	F	S	S
			1	2	3	4
5	6	7	8	9	10	11
12	13	14	15	16	17	18
19	20	21	22	23	24	25
26	27	28	29	30	31	

The complete materials sector strategy worked extremely well in 2009 and 2010. The sector started to rise a few days after the average start date of October 28th, peaked in the beginning of January, fell during the month and started to rise again in the latter part of January and then finally peaked in late April.

This performance in 2009-10 very closely mirrored the average seasonal trend of the sector from 1990 to 2010.

JANUARY

M	T	W	T	F	S	S
						1
2	3	4	5	6	7	8
9	10	11	12	13	14	15
16	17	18	19	20	21	22
23	24	25	26	27	28	29
30	31					

** Weekly avg closing values- except Fed Funds & CAN overnight tgt rate weekly closing values.

INDUSTRIAL STRENGTH — IN-OUT-IN AGAIN
➜ IN (Oct 28 - Dec 31) ➜ OUT ➜ IN (Jan 23 - May 5)

The industrial sector's seasonal trends are largely the same as the broad market, such as the S&P 500. Although the trends are similar, there still exists an opportunity to take advantage of the time period when the industrials tend to outperform.

3.4% extra & and positive 95% of the time

Industrials tend to outperform in the favorable six months, but there is an opportunity to temporarily get out of the sector to avoid a time period when the sector has on average decreased before turning positive again.

The overall strategy is to be invested in the industrial sector from October 28th to December 31st, sell at the end of the day on the 31st and reenter the sector to be invested from January 23rd to May 5th.

Using the IN-OUT-IN AGAIN strategy; from 1989/90 to 2009/10 the industrial sector has produced a total compounded average annual gain of 13.1%.

In addition it has been positive 95% of the time and has outperformed the S&P 500, 81% of the time.

During the OUT time period from January 1st to January 22nd, the industrial sector has on average lost 1.6% and has only been positive 48% of the time.

It should be noted that longer term investors may decide to be invested during the whole time period from October 28th to May5th.

Shorter term investors may decide to use technical analysis to determine if and when they should temporarily sell the industrials sector during its OUT time period.

Industrial Sector vs. S&P 500 1989/90 to 2009/10   Positive ☐

Year	Oct 28 to Dec 31		Jan 23 to May 5		Compound Growth	
	S&P 500	Ind.	S&P 500	Ind.	S&P 500	Ind.
1989/90	5.5 %	6.9 %	2.4 %	5.5 %	8.0 %	12.7 %
1990/91	8.4	10.7	16.0	15.2	25.7	27.5
1991/92	8.6	7.2	-0.3	-1.0	8.2	6.1
1992/93	4.1	6.3	1.9	5.4	6.1	12.0
1993/94	0.4	5.1	-4.9	-6.7	-4.5	-2.0
1994/95	-1.4	-0.5	11.9	12.4	10.3	11.8
1995/96	6.3	10.7	4.6	7.6	11.1	19.1
1996/97	5.7	4.5	5.6	5.2	11.6	9.9
1997/98	10.7	10.5	15.8	11.5	28.2	23.2
1998/99	15.4	10.5	10.0	19.5	26.9	32.1
1999/00	13.3	10.8	-0.6	4.5	12.6	15.8
2000/01	-4.3	1.8	-5.7	4.7	-9.7	6.6
2001/02	3.9	8.1	-4.1	-5.3	-0.3	2.4
2002/03	-2.0	-1.3	5.5	8.6	3.4	7.1
2003/04	7.8	11.6	-2.0	-3.3	5.7	7.9
2004/05	7.7	8.7	0.4	0.2	8.1	8.9
2005/06	5.9	7.6	5.1	14.3	11.3	23.0
2006/07	3.0	3.1	5.8	6.8	9.0	10.1
2007/08	-4.4	-3.4	7.4	9.7	2.7	6.0
2008/09	6.4	7.1	9.2	6.1	16.2	13.7
2009/10	4.9	6.4	6.8	13.4	12.0	20.6
Avg.	5.0 %	6.3 %	4.3 %	6.4 %	9.6 %	13.1 %

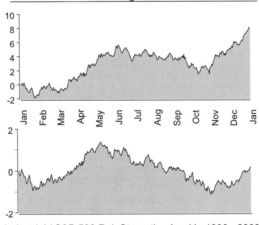

Industrial Sector - Avg. Year 1990 to 2009

Industrial / S&P 500 Rel. Strength - Avg Yr. 1990 - 2009

> ⓨ *Alternate Strategy—*
> *Investors can bridge the gap between the two positive seasonal trends for the industrials sector by holding from October 28th to May 5th. Longer term investors may prefer this strategy, shorter term investors can use technical tools to determine the appropriate strategy.*

> ⓘ The SP GICS Industrial Sector encompasses a wide range industrial based companies.
> For more information on the information technology sector, see www.standardandpoors.com

14 MONDAY	016 / 047	**15** TUESDAY	015 / 046

Market Indices & Rates
Weekly Values**

Stock Markets	2008	2009
Dow	8,636	10,247
S&P500	891	1,093
Nasdaq	1,562	2,158
TSX	9,289	11,424
FTSE	4,247	5,261
DAX	4,754	5,650
Nikkei	8,657	9,825
Hang Seng	13,898	22,411

Commodities	2008	2009
Oil	58.6	78.2
Gold	734.5	1108.5

16 WEDNESDAY	014 / 045	**17** THURSDAY	013 / 044

Bond Yields	2008	2009
USA 5 Yr Treasury	2.41	2.30
USA 10 Yr T	3.78	3.48
USA 20 Yr T	4.49	4.33
Moody's Aaa	6.37	5.28
Moody's Baa	9.26	6.40
CAN 5 Yr T	2.75	2.71
CAN 10 Yr T	3.69	3.50

18 FRIDAY	012 / 043

Money Market	2008	2009
USA Fed Funds	1.00	0.25
USA 3 Mo T-B	0.21	0.07
CAN tgt overnight rate	2.25	0.25
CAN 3 Mo T-B	1.80	0.22

Foreign Exchange	2008	2009
USD/EUR	1.27	1.50
USD/GBP	1.53	1.67
CAN/USD	1.20	1.05
JPY/USD	97.44	89.87

2009-2010 Strategy Performance*

Industrial Sector 2009-2010

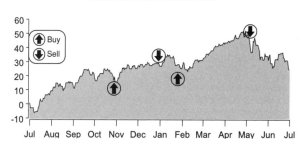

NOVEMBER

M	T	W	T	F	S	S
	1	2	3	4	5	6
7	8	9	10	11	12	13
14	15	16	17	18	19	20
21	22	23	24	25	26	27
28	29	30				

DECEMBER

M	T	W	T	F	S	S
			1	2	3	4
5	6	7	8	9	10	11
12	13	14	15	16	17	18
19	20	21	22	23	24	25
26	27	28	29	30	31	

JANUARY

M	T	W	T	F	S	S
						1
2	3	4	5	6	7	8
9	10	11	12	13	14	15
16	17	18	19	20	21	22
23	24	25	26	27	28	29
30	31					

Both segments of the industrial strategy worked well. In 2009 the first segment (Oct 28th to Dec 31st) produced a return of 6.4% and the second segment (Jan 23rd to May 5th) produced a gain of 13.4% for a compound gain of 20.6%. This compares very favorably to the S&P 500 compound gain during the same time period of 12%.

Note, that the return during the time to be out of the sector (Jan 1st to Jan 22nd) was negative for 2010.

* Buy and Sell dates are approximate representations of strategy dates.
** Weekly avg closing values- except Fed Funds & CAN overnight tgt rate weekly closing values.

At the macro level, the metals and mining (M&M) sector is driven by future economic growth expectations. When worldwide growth expectations are increasing, there is a greater need for raw materials, when they are decreasing, the need is less.

Within the macro trend, the M&M sector has traditionally followed the overall market cycle of performing well from autumn until spring. This is the time of year that investors have a positive outlook on the economy and as a result the cyclical part of the market tends to outperform, including the metals and mining sector.

9.4% extra and positive 76% of the time

The metals and mining sector has two seasonal "sweet spots" – the first from November 19th to January 5th and the second from January 23rd to May 5th. Investors have the option to hold and "bridge the gap" across the two sweet spots, but over the long-term, nimble traders have been able to capture extra value by being out of the sector from January 6th to the 22nd. During this time period, the metals and mining sector has produced an average loss of 3.1% and has only been positive 48% of the time.

From a portfolio perspective, it is important to consider reducing exposure at the beginning of May. The danger of holding on too long is that the sector tends not to do well in the late summer, particularly in September. For more detail on why the metals and mining sector under performs in late summer, see the *September Pair Strategy - Long Gold and Short Metals and Mining Strategy.*

ⓘ *For more information on the metals and mining sector, see www.standardandpoors.com*

Metals & Mining Sector vs. S&P 500 1989/90 to 2009/10

Positive ▢

Year	Nov 19 to Jan 5 S&P 500	Nov 19 to Jan 5 M&M	Jan 23 to May 5 S&P 500	Jan 23 to May 5 M&M	Compound Growth S&P 500	Compound Growth M&M
1989/90	3.1 %	6.3 %	2.4 %	-4.6 %	5.6 %	1.4 %
1990/91	1.2	6.4	16.0	7.1	17.4	13.9
1991/92	8.9	1.0	-0.3	-1.7	8.5	-0.7
1992/93	2.7	12.5	1.9	3.2	4.7	16.1
1993/94	0.9	9.0	-4.9	-11.1	-4.1	-3.1
1994/95	-0.2	-1.2	11.9	-3.0	11.6	-4.1
1995/96	2.8	8.3	4.6	5.8	7.5	14.6
1996/97	1.5	-1.9	5.6	-1.2	7.2	-3.0
1997/98	4.1	-4.5	15.8	19.3	20.6	13.9
1998/99	8.8	-7.9	10.0	31.0	19.6	20.6
1999/00	-1.6	21.7	-0.6	-10.4	-2.2	9.1
2000/01	-5.1	17.0	-5.7	19.6	-10.5	40.0
2001/02	3.0	5.5	-4.1	12.8	-1.3	19.0
2002/03	0.9	9.3	5.5	3.2	6.4	12.8
2003/04	8.5	18.2	-2.0	-12.1	6.4	3.9
2004/05	0.0	-8.4	0.4	-4.0	0.4	-12.0
2005/06	2.0	17.3	5.1	27.3	7.2	49.4
2006/07	0.6	3.0	5.8	17.2	6.5	20.8
2007/08	-3.2	0.9	7.4	27.4	3.9	28.5
2008/09	8.0	43.8	9.2	30.6	17.9	87.8
2009/10	2.4	6.3	6.8	4.8	9.4	11.3
Avg.	2.3 %	7.7 %	4.3 %	7.7 %	6.8 %	16.2 %

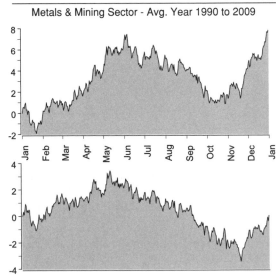

Metals & Mining Sector - Avg. Year 1990 to 2009

Metals & Mining / S&P 500 Rel. Strength- Avg Yr. 1990-2009

NOVEMBER

21 MONDAY	009 / 040	**22** TUESDAY	008 / 039

23 WEDNESDAY 007 / 038 **24** THURSDAY 006 / 037

25 FRIDAY 005 / 036

WEEK 47
Market Indices & Rates
Weekly Values**

Stock Markets	2008	2009
Dow	8,059	10,384
S&P500	814	1,103
Nasdaq	1,410	2,180
TSX	8,400	11,595
FTSE	4,000	5,318
DAX	4,368	5,747
Nikkei	8,148	9,649
Hang Seng	12,844	22,759

Commodities	2008	2009
Oil	52.3	78.4
Gold	749.3	1137.9

Bond Yields	2008	2009
USA 5 Yr Treasury	2.12	2.19
USA 10 Yr T	3.38	3.35
USA 20 Yr T	4.14	4.19
Moody's Aaa	5.99	5.16
Moody's Baa	9.14	6.27
CAN 5 Yr T	2.62	2.60
CAN 10 Yr T	3.49	3.39

Money Market	2008	2009
USA Fed Funds	1.00	0.25
USA 3 Mo T-B	0.07	0.04
CAN tgt overnight rate	2.25	0.25
CAN 3 Mo T-B	1.83	0.22

Foreign Exchange	2008	2009
USD/EUR	1.26	1.49
USD/GBP	1.50	1.67
CAN/USD	1.25	1.06
JPY/USD	96.05	89.10

2009-2010 Strategy Performance*

Metals & Mining June 2009 to May 2010

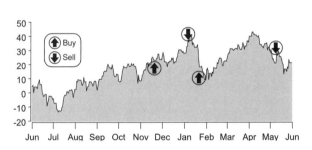

The metals and mining sector did well in 2009. In the first sweet spot from November 19th to January 5th the sector outperformed the S&P 500, and in the second sweet spot under performed the S&P 500. Overall, the sector outperformed the S&P 500.

By getting out of the sector on January 5th and reentering for the second part of the strategy, January 23rd to May 5th, investors avoided a loss of 10.8% .

NOVEMBER

M	T	W	T	F	S	S
	1	2	3	4	5	6
7	8	9	10	11	12	13
14	15	16	17	18	19	20
21	22	23	24	25	26	27
28	29	30				

DECEMBER

M	T	W	T	F	S	S
			1	2	3	4
5	6	7	8	9	10	11
12	13	14	15	16	17	18
19	20	21	22	23	24	25
26	27	28	29	30	31	

JANUARY

M	T	W	T	F	S	S
						1
2	3	4	5	6	7	8
9	10	11	12	13	14	15
16	17	18	19	20	21	22
23	24	25	26	27	28	29
30	31					

* Buy and Sell dates are approximate representations of strategy dates.
** Weekly avg closing values- except Fed Funds & CAN overnight tgt rate weekly closing values.

- 140 -

THANKSGIVING
GIVE THANKS & TAKE RETURNS
Day Before and After – Two of the Best Days

We have a lot to be thankful for on Thanksgiving Day. As a bonus, the day before and the day after Thanksgiving have been two of the best days of the year in the stock market.

Each day by itself has produced spectacular results. From 1950 to 2009, the S&P 500 has had an average gain of 0.4% on the day before Thanksgiving and 0.4% on the day after.

The day before Thanksgiving and the day after have had an average cumulative return of 0.7% and together have been positive 85% of the time

To put the performance of these two days in perspective, the average daily return of the market over the same time period is 0.03%.

The Thanksgiving days are almost ten times better and have a much greater frequency of being positive.

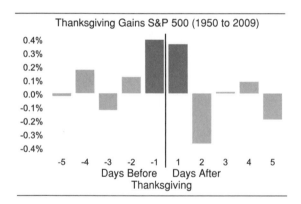

Thanksgiving Gains S&P 500 (1950 to 2009)

Days Before   Days After
Thanksgiving

Ⓨ *Alternate Strategy — Although the focus has been on the performance of two specific days, the day before and the day after Thanksgiving, the holiday occurs at the end of November which tends to be a strong month. December, the next month is also strong. Investors have the good option of expanding their trade out to include the "Santa Arrives Early & Stays Late" Strategy.*

ⓘ *History of Thanksgiving:*
It was originally a "thanksgiving feast" by the pilgrims for surviving their first winter. Initially it was celebrated sporadically and the holiday, when it was granted, had its date changed several times. It was not until 1941 that it was proclaimed to be the 4th Thursday in November.

S&P500	Day Before	Day After
		Positive
1950	1.4	0.8
1951	-0.2	-1.1
1952	0.6	0.5
1953	0.1	0.6
1954	0.6	1.0
1955	0.1	-0.1
1956	-0.5	1.1
1957	2.9	1.1
1958	1.7	1.1
1959	0.2	0.5
1960	0.1	0.6
1961	-0.1	0.2
1962	0.6	1.2
1963	-0.2	1.4
1964	-0.3	-0.3
1965	0.2	0.1
1966	0.7	0.8
1967	0.6	0.3
1968	0.5	0.6
1969	0.4	0.6
1970	0.4	1.0
1971	0.2	1.8
1972	0.6	0.3
1973	1.1	-0.3
1974	0.7	0.0
1975	0.3	0.3
1976	0.4	0.7
1977	0.4	0.2
1978	0.5	0.3
1979	0.2	0.8
1980	0.6	0.2
1981	0.4	0.8
1982	0.7	0.7
1983	0.1	0.1
1984	0.2	1.5
1985	0.9	-0.2
1986	0.2	0.2
1987	-0.9	-1.5
1988	0.7	-0.7
1989	0.7	0.6
1990	0.2	-0.3
1991	-0.4	-0.4
1992	0.4	0.2
1993	0.3	0.2
1994	0.0	0.5
1995	-0.3	0.3
1996	-0.1	0.3
1997	0.1	0.4
1998	0.3	0.5
1999	0.9	0.0
2000	-1.9	1.5
2001	-0.5	1.2
2002	2.8	-0.3
2003	0.4	0.0
2004	0.4	0.1
2005	0.3	0.2
2006	0.2	-0.4
2007	-1.6	1.7
2008	3.5	1.0
2009	0.5	-1.7
Total Avg %	0.4%	0.4%
Fq > 0 %	78%	77%

(Vertical label along right side: THANKSGIVING DAY)

NOVEMBER/DECEMBER

28 MONDAY 002 / 033

29 TUESDAY 001 / 032

30 WEDNESDAY 000 / 031

1 THURSDAY 030 / 030

2 FRIDAY 029 / 029

WEEK 48

Market Indices & Rates
Weekly Values**

Stock Markets	2008	2009
Dow	8,620	10,415
S&P500	873	1,104
Nasdaq	1,501	2,165
TSX	8,710	11,540
FTSE	4,198	5,297
DAX	4,602	5,735
Nikkei	8,356	9,327
Hang Seng	13,229	22,230

Commodities	2008	2009
Oil	53.1	76.1
Gold	816.8	1172.4

Bond Yields	2008	2009
USA 5 Yr Treasury	2.06	2.12
USA 10 Yr T	3.10	3.30
USA 20 Yr T	3.84	4.14
Moody's Aaa	5.75	5.07
Moody's Baa	9.10	6.24
CAN 5 Yr T	2.50	2.43
CAN 10 Yr T	3.39	3.27

Money Market	2008	2009
USA Fed Funds	1.00	0.25
USA 3 Mo T-B	0.07	0.05
CAN tgt overnight rate	2.25	0.25
CAN 3 Mo T-B	1.74	0.22

Foreign Exchange	2008	2009
USD/EUR	1.29	1.50
USD/GBP	1.53	1.66
CAN/USD	1.24	1.06
JPY/USD	95.35	87.72

2009 Strategy Performance

Days Before and After Thanksgiving S&P 500 (2009)

In 2009, the day before Thanksgiving was positive and the day after negative.

Unfortunately, the day after had a much bigger impact on the total strategy, placing it in the red. At the time the market was in a period of consolidation, but shortly afterwards it resumed its rally.

DECEMBER
M	T	W	T	F	S	S
			1	2	3	4
5	6	7	8	9	10	11
12	13	14	15	16	17	18
19	20	21	22	23	24	25
26	27	28	29	30	31	

JANUARY
M	T	W	T	F	S	S
						1
2	3	4	5	6	7	8
9	10	11	12	13	14	15
16	17	18	19	20	21	22
23	24	25	26	27	28	29
30	31					

FEBRUARY
M	T	W	T	F	S	S
	1	2	3	4	5	
6	7	8	9	10	11	12
13	14	15	16	17	18	19
20	21	22	23	24	25	26
27	28	29				

** Weekly avg closing values- except Fed Funds & CAN overnight tgt rate weekly closing values.

- 142 -

DECEMBER

	MONDAY	TUESDAY	WEDNESDAY
WEEK 48	28	29	30
WEEK 49	**5** 26	**6** 25	**7** 24
WEEK 50	**12** 19	**13** 18	**14** 17
WEEK 51	**19** 12	**20** 11	**21** 10
WEEK 52	**26** 5 CAN Market Closed- Christmas Day USA Market Closed- Christmas Day	**27** 4 CAN Market Closed- Boxing Day	**28** 3

THURSDAY	FRIDAY
1 30	**2** 29
8 23	**9** 22
15 16	**16** 15
22 9	**23** 8
29 2	**30**

JANUARY

M	T	W	T	F	S	S
						1
2	3	4	5	6	7	8
9	10	11	12	13	14	15
16	17	18	19	20	21	22
23	24	25	26	27	28	29
30	31					

FEBRUARY

M	T	W	T	F	S	S
		1	2	3	4	5
6	7	8	9	10	11	12
13	14	15	16	17	18	19
20	21	22	23	24	25	26
27	28	29				

MARCH

M	T	W	T	F	S	S
			1	2	3	4
5	6	7	8	9	10	11
12	13	14	15	16	17	18
19	20	21	22	23	24	25
26	27	28	29	30	31	

APRIL

M	T	W	T	F	S	S
						1
2	3	4	5	6	7	8
9	10	11	12	13	14	15
16	17	18	19	20	21	22
23	24	25	26	27	28	29
30						

DECEMBER
S U M M A R Y

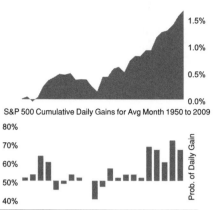

S&P 500 Cumulative Daily Gains for Avg Month 1950 to 2009

♦ December is one of the best months of the year. Make sure your Christmas shopping includes stocks. ♦ The best method of participating in the Christmas rally has been to enter the stock market on December 15th (see *Santa Arrives Early & Stays Late* strategy). ♦ The Nasdaq tends to outperform the S&P 500 from December 15th to January 23rd. ♦ The US dollar has a habit of weakening in December for a rally in January.

BEST / WORST DECEMBER BROAD MKTS. 2000-2009

BEST DECEMBER MARKETS
♦ Russell 2000 (2000) 8.4%
♦ Russell 2000 (2009) 7.9%
♦ Dow (2003) 6.9%

WORST DECEMBER MARKETS
♦ Nasdaq (2002) -9.7%
♦ Russell 3000 Gr (2002) -7.0%
♦ Dow (2002) -6.2%

Index Values End of Month

	2000	2001	2002	2003	2004	2005	2006	2007	2008	2009
Dow	10,787	10,022	8,342	10,454	10,783	10,718	12,463	13,265	8,776	10,428
S&P 500	1,320	1,148	880	1,112	1,212	1,248	1,418	1,468	903	1,115
Nasdaq	2,471	1,950	1,336	2,003	2,175	2,205	2,415	2,652	1,577	2,269
TSX	8,934	7,688	6,615	8,221	9,247	11,272	12,908	13,833	8,988	11,746
Russell 1000	1,346	1,163	896	1,143	1,251	1,306	1,480	1,538	938	1,176
Russell 2000	1,202	1,214	952	1,384	1,619	1,673	1,958	1,904	1,241	1,554
Russell 3000 Growth	2,481	1,982	1,413	1,831	1,939	2,018	2,184	2,406	1,460	1,966
Russell 3000 Value	2,204	2,068	1,713	2,191	2,502	2,610	3,116	3,009	1,860	2,164

Percent Gain for December

	2000	2001	2002	2003	2004	2005	2006	2007	2008	2009
Dow	3.6	1.7	-6.2	6.9	3.4	-0.8	2.0	-0.8	-0.6	0.8
S&P 500	0.4	0.8	-6.0	5.1	3.2	-0.1	1.3	-0.9	0.8	1.8
Nasdaq	-4.9	1.0	-9.7	2.2	3.7	-1.2	-0.7	-0.3	2.7	5.8
TSX	1.3	3.5	0.7	4.6	2.4	4.1	1.2	1.1	-3.1	2.6
Russell 1000	1.1	0.9	-5.8	4.6	3.5	0.0	1.1	-0.8	1.3	2.3
Russell 2000	8.4	6.0	-5.7	1.9	2.8	-0.6	0.2	-0.2	5.6	7.9
Russell 3000 Growth	-2.6	0.1	-7.0	3.1	3.8	-0.4	0.2	-0.4	1.9	3.3
Russell 3000 Value	5.2	2.4	-4.5	5.7	3.0	0.3	1.9	-1.2	1.4	2.0

December Market Avg. Performance 2000 to 2009[1]

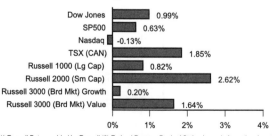

Dow Jones 0.99%
SP500 0.63%
Nasdaq -0.13%
TSX (CAN) 1.85%
Russell 1000 (Lg Cap) 0.82%
Russell 2000 (Sm Cap) 2.62%
Russell 3000 (Brd Mkt) Growth 0.20%
Russell 3000 (Brd Mkt) Value 1.64%

Interest Corner Dec[2]

	Fed Funds %[3]	3 Mo. T-Bill %[4]	10 Yr %[5]	20 Yr %[6]
2009	0.25	0.06	3.85	4.58
2008	0.25	0.11	2.25	3.05
2007	4.25	3.36	4.04	4.50
2006	5.25	5.02	4.71	4.91
2005	4.25	4.08	4.39	4.61

(1) Russell Data provided by Russell (2) Federal Reserve Bank of St. Louis- end of month values (3) Target rate set by FOMC (4)(5)(6) Constant yield maturities

THACKRAY SECTOR THERMOMETER

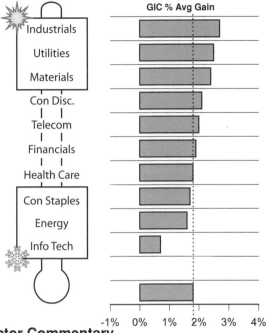

GIC[2] % Avg Gain	Fq % Gain >S&P 500	
SP GIC SECTOR 1990-2009[1]		
2.7 %	60 %	Industrials
2.5	55	Utilities
2.4	45	Materials
2.1	55	Consumer Discretionary
2.0	55	Telecom
1.9	55	Financials
1.8	55	Health Care
1.7	45	Consumer Staples
1.6	40	Energy
0.7 %	40 %	Information Technology
1.8 %	N/A %	S&P 500

Sector Commentary

♦ In 2009, after a "hot" November the market cooled somewhat with December producing an acceptable 1.8% gain. In fact, the month's 2009 gain was the same as the long-term average. ♦ Typically Information Technology takes a break in December, but in 2009 it led the pack with a 5.6% gain. ♦ The Utilities sector is typically at the top of the thermometer (Utilities has a strong seasonal period from mid-December to the end of the month). In 2009 it was the second best sector with a gain of 5.2%. ♦ At the bottom of the pack for 2009 were the Consumer Staples, Energy and Financial sectors producing losses of 0.6%, 0.9% and 1.6%, respectively. On average these three sectors have been at the bottom part of the thermometer (1990 to 2009). ♦ The 2009 ranking for the other sectors generally mirrored the long-term ranking of the TST.

Sub-Sector Commentary

♦ In December 2009 the sub-sectors were disperse compared to their placement with the long-term average. From a long-term average basis the Airline sector has been on the bottom of the list and Gold stocks have been near the top. In 2009 these sectors reversed their placement: Airlines was the top sector and Gold stocks the worst.

		SELECTED SUB-SECTORS 1990-2009[3]
5.4 %	59 %	Biotech (93-2009)
3.9	55	Gold (XAU)
3.7	60	Metals & Mining
2.7	50	Insurance
2.4	56	Agriculture Products (94-2009)
1.7	45	Software & Services
1.4	40	Integrated Oil & Gas
1.3	45	Pharmaceuticals
1.2	50	Banks
1.2	35	Retail
1.1	40	Auto & Components
1.0	35	Transportation
0.8	40	Semiconductor (SOX) 95-2009
0.4	35	Airlines

(1) Sector data provided by Standard and Poors (2) GIC is short form for Global Industry Classification (3) Sub Sector data provided by Standard and Poors, except where marked by symbol.

U.S. DOLLAR — SHORT & LONG
➔ SELL SHORT December ➔ LONG January

From 1973 to 2010 the U.S. dollar (USD) has had a seasonal trend of decreasing in December and increasing in January. This "v" shape trend provides an opportunity for a nimble trader to sell the USD at the beginning of December and buy it back at the end of the month, in the expectation of making a profit.

The second half of the opportunity is in January when the dollar tends to reverse its downward trend. An investor would have reaped a double benefit from 1973 to 2010 with the combined strategy of going "short" the dollar in December and "long" in January.

*1.7% extra &
positive 60% of the time*

Why does the dollar, on average, produce this "v" shape pattern?

Typically, firms in other countries tend to settle their foreign exchange books at end of year in their domestic currency. The conversion to non-USD currencies tends to push the USD down.

USD vs Trade Weighted Currencies
1973/74 to 2009/10

	Negative		Positive	
Year	DEC	JAN	Growth
1973/74	0.9 %	2.7 %	1.8 %
1974/75	-1.1	-1.0	0.1
1975/76	0.2	-0.3	-0.5
1976/77	-1.9	0.5	2.4
1977/78	-2.9	0.4	3.3
1978/79	-2.5	2.5	5.1
1979/80	-1.3	-0.2	1.1
1980/81	-0.9	3.0	3.9
1981/82	1.6	2.7	1.0
1982/83	-2.7	2.4	5.2
1983/84	0.5	1.8	1.2
1984/85	1.3	0.9	-0.3
1985/86	-0.4	-1.3	-1.0
1986/87	-1.8	-3.2	-1.4
1987/88	-4.4	3.9	8.4
1988/89	1.8	3.0	1.1
1989/90	-1.7	0.2	1.9
1990/91	0.5	-1.6	-2.1
1991/92	-3.4	2.8	6.3
1992/93	0.6	0.2	-0.3
1993/94	0.6	-1.3	-1.8
1994/95	0.5	-0.3	-0.8
1995/96	0.1	2.6	2.5
1996/97	0.8	3.6	2.7
1997/98	1.7	0.6	-1.1
1998/99	-2.3	1.0	3.3
1999/00	-0.7	2.5	3.2
2000/01	-3.3	1.0	4.2
2001/02	1.7	2.1	0.3
2002/03	-2.8	-2.0	0.8
2003/04	-2.8	0.9	3.7
2004/05	-0.5	2.8	3.3
2005/06	-0.4	-2.2	-1.8
2006/07	1.5	1.4	-0.1
2007/08	0.3	-1.2	-1.5
2008/09	-4.6	4.0	8.8
2009/10	3.0	1.5	-1.6
Avg.	-0.7 %	1.0 %	1.7 %

USD vs. Trade Weighted Currencies- Avg. Year 1973 to 2009

The USD tends to reverse its decline in January. Foreign firms increase their net dollar holdings to pay for purchases that require USD. This upward bounce has taken place on a fairly consistent basis with the dollar rising 70% of the time.

Although the USD has only been negative 54% of the time in December, it has produced an average loss of 0.7%. The longest period when the short trade did not work was from 1992 to 1997.

This is consistent with the strong USD in the 1990's that was the result of a rapidly growing economy based upon technology advances.

> (i) *The U.S. dollar is measured against the Trade Weighted Major World Currencies. The Euro is becoming a substantial benchmark, but at the current time there is not enough data to establish long-term trends.*

5 MONDAY	026 / 026		**6** TUESDAY	025 / 025

7 WEDNESDAY	024 / 024		**8** THURSDAY	023 / 023

9 FRIDAY 022 / 022

WEEK 49

Market Indices & Rates
Weekly Values**

Stock Markets	2008	2009
Dow	8,434	10,405
S&P500	851	1,104
Nasdaq	1,459	2,175
TSX	8,241	11,616
FTSE	4,114	5,293
DAX	4,488	5,754
Nikkei	8,021	9,705
Hang Seng	13,692	22,255

Commodities	2008	2009
Oil	45.5	76.8
Gold	769.3	1196.0

Bond Yields	2008	2009
USA 5 Yr Treasury	1.63	2.10
USA 10 Yr T	2.66	3.34
USA 20 Yr T	3.44	4.18
Moody's Aaa	5.31	5.11
Moody's Baa	8.78	6.29
CAN 5 Yr T	2.25	2.41
CAN 10 Yr T	3.12	3.26

Money Market	2008	2009
USA Fed Funds	1.00	0.25
USA 3 Mo T-B	0.04	0.06
CAN tgt overnight rate	2.25	0.25
CAN 3 Mo T-B	1.49	0.21

Foreign Exchange	2008	2009
USD/EUR	1.27	1.50
USD/GBP	1.48	1.66
CAN/USD	1.26	1.05
JPY/USD	93.09	87.78

2009-2010 Strategy Performance

USD vs Trade Weighted Currencies June 2009 - July 2010

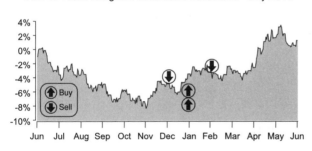

The USD fell for most of the second part of the year up until November, where it started to rise and then once again fell in December. It had an uptick towards the end of the month creating a loss for the first part of the strategy.

The USD started to rise in January, but then fell in the second half of the month. In the end the second half of the strategy was positive.

DECEMBER

M	T	W	T	F	S	S
			1	2	3	4
5	6	7	8	9	10	11
12	13	14	15	16	17	18
19	20	21	22	23	24	25
26	27	28	29	30	31	

JANUARY

M	T	W	T	F	S	S
						1
2	3	4	5	6	7	8
9	10	11	12	13	14	15
16	17	18	19	20	21	22
23	24	25	26	27	28	29
30	31					

FEBRUARY

M	T	W	T	F	S	S
		1	2	3	4	5
6	7	8	9	10	11	12
13	14	15	16	17	18	19
20	21	22	23	24	25	26
27	28	29				

** Weekly avg closing values- except Fed Funds & CAN overnight tgt rate weekly closing values.

SMALL CAP (SMALL COMPANY) EFFECT
January Effect Starts Early - Ends Late
Small Companies Outperform - Dec 19th to Mar 7th

At different stages of the business cycle, small capitalization companies (small caps represented by the Russell 2000), perform better than the large capitalization companies (large caps represented by the Russell 1000).

Evidence shows that the small caps relative outperformance also has a seasonal component as they typically outperform large caps from December 19th to March 7th.

3.5% extra & 22 times out of 31 better than the S&P 500

Russell 2000 - Avg. Year 1979 to 2009

Russell 2000 / Russell 1000 - Avg Yr. 1979 - 2009

The core part of the small cap seasonal strategy occurs in January and includes what has been described as the January Effect (Wachtel 1942, 184).

This well documented anomaly of superior performance of stocks in the month of January is based upon the tenet that investors sell stocks in December for tax loss reasons, artificially driving down prices, and creating a great opportunity for astute investors.

In recent times, the January Effect starts mid-December and is more pronounced for small caps as their prices are more volatile than large caps.

Wachtel, S.B. 1942. Certain observations on seasonal movements in stock prices. The Journal of Business and Economics (Winter): 184.

Russell 2000 vs. Russell 1000 Gains
Dec 19th to Mar 7th 1979 to 2010
Positive

Dec 19 - Mar7	Russell 2000	Russell 1000	Diff
79 / 80	-0.4	-1.3	0.9
80 / 81	4.0	-2.	6.8
81 / 82	-12.1	-12.4	0.3
82 / 83	19.8	11.8	8.0
83 / 84	-7.5	-6.4	-1.1
84 / 85	17.1	7.7	9.4
85 / 86	11.7	8.2	3.5
86 / 87	21.5	17.2	4.3
87 / 88	16.8	8.3	8.5
88 / 89	9.1	6.9	2.2
89 / 90	-1.8	-2.0	0.2
90 / 91	28.8	14.7	14.2
91 / 92	16.8	6.0	10.8
92 / 93	5.1	1.5	3.7
93 / 94	5.6	0.6	5.1
94 / 95	5.5	5.3	0.1
95 / 96	7.9	8.3	-0.4
96 / 97	3.5	9.5	-6.0
97 / 98	10.1	10.2	-0.2
98 / 99	0.1	7.3	-7.2
99 / 00	27.7	-1.7	29.4
00 / 01	4.7	-5.2	9.8
01 / 02	1.9	1.6	0.3
02 / 03	-7.8	-6.7	-1.0
03 / 04	9.6	6.4	3.3
04 / 05	0.3	2.8	-2.5
05 / 06	5.6	0.8	4.7
06 / 07	-0.8	-1.6	0.9
07 / 08	-12.5	-10.9	-1.5
08 / 09	-26.7	-22.2	-4.5
09 / 10	9.1	3.6	5.5
Avg.	5.6 %	2.1 %	3.5 %

(i) *Russell 2000 (small cap index): The 2000 smallest companies in the Russell 3000 stock index (a broad market index). Russell 1000 (large cap index): The 1000 largest companies in the Russell 3000 stock index*

For more information on the Russell indexes, see www.Russell.com

12 MONDAY	019 / 019	**13** TUESDAY	018 / 018

14 WEDNESDAY	017 / 017	**15** THURSDAY	016 / 016

16 FRIDAY 015 / 015

WEEK 50

Market Indices & Rates
Weekly Values**

Stock Markets	2008	2009
Dow	8,716	10,378
S&P500	890	1,100
Nasdaq	1,547	2,186
TSX	8,501	11,425
FTSE	4,344	5,249
DAX	4,746	5,717
Nikkei	8,468	10,057
Hang Seng	15,150	21,946

Commodities	2008	2009
Oil	44.7	71.5
Gold	798.3	1136.6

Bond Yields	2008	2009
USA 5 Yr Treasury	1.62	2.18
USA 10 Yr T	2.67	3.47
USA 20 Yr T	3.38	4.33
Moody's Aaa	5.35	5.25
Moody's Baa	8.72	6.37
CAN 5 Yr T	2.18	2.50
CAN 10 Yr T	3.08	3.33

Money Market	2008	2009
USA Fed Funds	1.00	0.25
USA 3 Mo T-B	0.02	0.03
CAN tgt overnight rate	1.50	0.25
CAN 3 Mo T-B	1.21	0.21

Foreign Exchange	2008	2009
USD/EUR	1.30	1.48
USD/GBP	1.49	1.63
CAN/USD	1.25	1.06
JPY/USD	92.41	88.78

2009-2010 Strategy Performance

Russell 2000 vs Russell 1000 Dec 19th to Mar 7th (2009-2010)

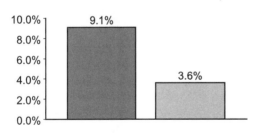

In 2009 small caps took off almost right at the start of their seasonal time period. By the end of the period, small caps had almost tripled the outperformance of large caps.

Although small caps continued their outperformance into April, they corrected much harder when the market started to fall apart at the end of April and into May.

DECEMBER

M	T	W	T	F	S	S
			1	2	3	4
5	6	7	8	9	10	11
12	13	14	15	16	17	18
19	20	21	22	23	24	25
26	27	28	29	30	31	

JANUARY

M	T	W	T	F	S	S
						1
2	3	4	5	6	7	8
9	10	11	12	13	14	15
16	17	18	19	20	21	22
23	24	25	26	27	28	29
30	31					

FEBRUARY

M	T	W	T	F	S	S
		1	2	3	4	5
6	7	8	9	10	11	12
13	14	15	16	17	18	19
20	21	22	23	24	25	26
27	28	29				

** Weekly avg closing values- except Fed Funds & CAN overnight tgt rate weekly closing values.

DO THE "NAZ" WITH SANTA
Nasdaq gives more at Christmas – Dec 15th to Jan 23rd

One of the best times to invest in the major markets is Christmas time. What few investors know is that this seasonally strong time favors the Nasdaq market.

From December 15th to January 23rd, starting in 1972 and ending in 2010, the Nasdaq has outperformed the S&P 500 by an average 2.4% per year.

This rate of return is considered to be very high given that the length of favorable time is just over one month.

2.4% extra & 85% of time better than S&P 500

Looking for reasons that the Nasdaq outperforms? Interestingly, the Nasdaq starts to outperform at the same time as small companies in December (see *Small Company Effect* strategy).

As investors move into the market to scoop up bargains that have been sold for tax losses, smaller companies and stocks with greater volatility tend to outperform.

Compared with the S&P 500 and Dow Jones, the Nasdaq market, given its composition, tends to be a much greater recipient of the upward move created by investors picking up cheap stocks at this time of the year.

Nasdaq vs. S&P 500 Dec 15th to Jan 23rd 1971/72 To 2009/10

Dec 15 to Jan 23	Nasdaq	S&P 500	Diff
	Positive		
1971/72	7.5 %	6.1 %	1.3 %
1972/73	-0.7	0.0	-0.7
1973/74	6.8	4.1	2.8
1974/75	8.9	7.5	1.4
1975/76	13.8	13.0	0.9
1976/77	2.8	-1.7	4.5
1977/78	-3.5	-5.1	1.6
1978/79	6.2	4.7	1.4
1979/80	5.6	4.1	1.5
1980/81	3.3	0.8	2.5
1981/82	-5.0	-6.0	1.0
1982/83	5.5	4.7	0.8
1983/84	1.4	0.9	0.4
1984/85	13.3	9.0	4.3
1985/86	0.8	-2.7	3.5
1986/87	10.2	9.2	1.0
1987/88	9.1	1.8	7.3
1988/89	4.6	3.3	1.3
1989/90	-3.8	-5.5	1.7
1990/91	4.1	1.0	3.1
1991/92	15.2	7.9	7.2
1992/93	7.2	0.8	6.4
1993/94	5.7	2.5	3.2
1994/95	4.7	2.4	2.3
1995/96	-1.0	-0.7	-0.3
1996/97	7.3	6.7	0.6
1997/98	2.6	0.4	2.1
1998/99	18.9	7.4	11.6
1999/00	18.6	2.7	15.9
2000/01	4.1	1.5	2.6
2001/02	-1.6	0.5	-2.0
2002/03	1.9	-0.2	2.1
2003/04	9.0	6.3	2.7
2004/05	-5.8	-3.0	-2.9
2005/06	-0.6	-0.7	0.1
2006/07	-0.9	0.2	-1.1
2007/08	-12.1	-8.8	-3.3
2008/09	-4.1	-5.4	1.3
2009/10	-0.3	-2.0	1.7
Avg	4.1 %	1.7 %	2.4 %

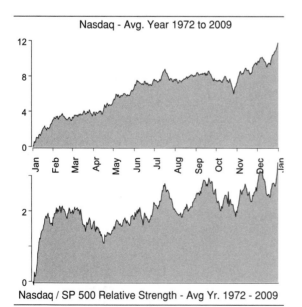

Nasdaq - Avg. Year 1972 to 2009

Nasdaq / SP 500 Relative Strength - Avg Yr. 1972 - 2009

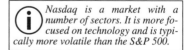

Alternate Strategy — For those investors who favor the Nasdaq, an alternative strategy is to invest in the Nasdaq at an earlier date: October 28th. Historically, on average the Nasdaq has started its out performance at this time. The "Do the Naz with Santa" strategy focuses on the sweet spot of the Nasdaq's outperformance.

Nasdaq is a market with a number of sectors. It is more focused on technology and is typically more volatile than the S&P 500.

DECEMBER

19 MONDAY	012 / 012

20 TUESDAY	011 / 011

21 WEDNESDAY	010 / 010

22 THURSDAY	009 / 009

23 FRIDAY	008 / 008

WEEK 51

Market Indices & Rates
Weekly Values**

Stock Markets	2008	2009
Dow	8,699	10,406
S&P500	892	1,106
Nasdaq	1,559	2,202
TSX	8,577	11,532
FTSE	4,306	5,267
DAX	4,709	5,839
Nikkei	8,620	10,134
Hang Seng	15,253	21,607

Commodities	2008	2009
Oil	39.7	71.8
Gold	845.1	1121.0

Bond Yields	2008	2009
USA 5 Yr Treasury	1.36	2.31
USA 10 Yr T	2.26	3.56
USA 20 Yr T	3.04	4.38
Moody's Aaa	4.95	5.26
Moody's Baa	8.30	6.33
CAN 5 Yr T	1.92	2.57
CAN 10 Yr T	2.90	3.40

Money Market	2008	2009
USA Fed Funds	0.25	0.25
USA 3 Mo T-B	0.03	0.04
CAN tgt overnight rate	1.50	0.25
CAN 3 Mo T-B	0.82	0.19

Foreign Exchange	2008	2009
USD/EUR	1.40	1.45
USD/GBP	1.52	1.62
CAN/USD	1.22	1.07
JPY/USD	89.40	89.61

DECEMBER

M	T	W	T	F	S	S
			1	2	3	4
5	6	7	8	9	10	11
12	13	14	15	16	17	18
19	20	21	22	23	24	25
26	27	28	29	30	31	

JANUARY

M	T	W	T	F	S	S
						1
2	3	4	5	6	7	8
9	10	11	12	13	14	15
16	17	18	19	20	21	22
23	24	25	26	27	28	29
30	31					

FEBRUARY

M	T	W	T	F	S	S
		1	2	3	4	5
6	7	8	9	10	11	12
13	14	15	16	17	18	19
20	21	22	23	24	25	26
27	28	29				

2009-2010 Strategy Performance*

Nasdaq % Gain September 2009 to June 2010

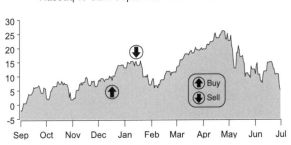

In 2009, the Nasdaq started its outperformance right on the start day for the strategy. The market started to turn down just before the end of the strategy. Regardless, the Nasdaq was able to maintain its outperformance over the S&P 500 at the end of its seasonal period.

After the 2010 January/February correction, the Nasdaq once again outperformed until the next correction that started in April.

** Weekly avg closing values- except Fed Funds & CAN overnight tgt rate weekly closing values.

- 152 -

SANTA ARRIVES EARLY & STAYS LATE
Dec 15th to Jan 6th

Every year investors wait for Santa Claus to come to town. They often get rewarded, but many leave with small returns because they focus on one or two days of outperformance. The best way to get the gift of Christmas is to get in early and stay late. The market typically makes a move up about halfway through December and continues through to the first week in January.

The first part of this move can be attributed to investors taking advantage of the *"January Effect,"* buying stocks that have been beaten down because of tax-loss selling (see *Small Company Effect* strategy).

The second part of the move, the start of January, benefits from the beginning of the month effect (see *Super Seven* strategy). The first few days in January are also boosted by money managers locking in their selections for the New Year.

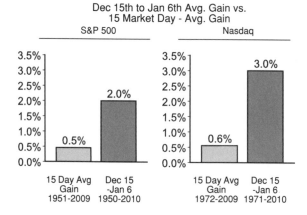

Dec 15th to Jan 6th Avg. Gain vs.
15 Market Day - Avg. Gain

The *Santa Arrives Early & Stays Late* strategy starts on December 15th and ends January 6th. This Christmas strategy with the S&P 500 from 1950 to 2010 has on average lasted fifteen days and produced a return of 2.0%.

This compares to the 0.5% return for the average fifteen day period (taken from any time period) from 1951 to 2009 (year adjustment is used to more closely align strategy with benchmark years). The net result is that this Christmas strategy has been four times better than the average fifteen day period.

Ⓨ *Alternate Strategy—The Extended Santa Rally:*
The focus of the "Santa Arrives Early Stays Late" is around the Christmas days, but on average, after January 6th, the market tends to tread water for only a few days before rallying until the beginning of February (February 3rd).

% Change Dec 15th to Jan 6th		
Date	S&P 500 Change	Nasdaq Change
50 / 51	7.5%	N/A %
51 / 52	2.4	"
52 / 53	1.7	"
53 / 54	1.8	"
54 / 55	2.0	"
55 / 56	0.2	"
56 / 57	0.3	"
57 / 58	-0.1	"
58 / 59	4.5	"
59 / 60	1.8	"
60 / 61	2.7	"
61 / 62	-3.2	"
62 / 63	2.5	"
63 / 64	2.2	"
64 / 65	1.7	"
65 / 66	1.3	"
66 / 67	-0.6	"
67 / 68	0.5	"
68 / 69	-4.7	"
69 / 70	2.2	"
70 / 71	2.8	"
71 / 72	6.0	6.1
72 / 73	1.4	1.9
73 / 74	6.0	5.0
74 / 75	6.0	4.3
75 / 76	6.5	7.2
76 / 77	0.0	2.8
77 / 78	-2.6	-2.2
78 / 79	3.2	3.3
79 / 80	-2.2	-1.3
80 / 81	6.9	6.7
81 / 82	-2.9	-2.3
82 / 83	5.7	2.3
83 / 84	3.6	4.2
84 / 85	0.6	3.0
85 / 86	0.3	0.6
86 / 87	2.2	2.8
87 / 88	6.9	12.1
88 / 89	1.9	3.2
89 / 90	0.4	2.4
90 / 91	-1.8	-0.4
91 / 92	8.7	10.5
92 / 93	0.4	4.1
93 / 94	0.9	3.9
94 / 95	1.3	3.3
95 / 96	0.0	-0.5
96 / 97	2.6	2.5
97 / 98	1.4	2.8
98 / 99	11.5	18.0
99 / 00	0.0	4.4
00 / 01	-3.2	-11.8
01 / 02	4.4	5.4
02 / 03	4.4	4.3
03 / 04	4.6	5.6
04 / 05	-1.3	-3.2
05 / 06	1.0	1.9
06 / 07	-1.1	-0.8
07 / 08	-3.8	-5.0
08 / 09	6.2	7.2
09 / 10	2.1	4.0
AVG.	2.0%	3.0%

26 MONDAY	005 / 005	**27** TUESDAY	004 / 004

Market Indices & Rates
Weekly Values**

Stock Markets	2008	2009
Dow	8,481	10,466
S&P500	869	1,120
Nasdaq	1,527	2,261
TSX	8,291	11,649
FTSE	4,241	5,349
DAX	4,634	5,945
Nikkei	8,645	10,398
Hang Seng	14,342	21,221

Commodities	2008	2009
Oil	32.4	74.8
Gold	846.3	1091.6

28 WEDNESDAY	003 / 003	**29** THURSDAY	002 / 002

Bond Yields	2008	2009
USA 5 Yr Treasury	1.50	2.50
USA 10 Yr T	2.18	3.76
USA 20 Yr T	2.93	4.53
Moody's Aaa	4.72	5.32
Moody's Baa	8.09	6.42
CAN 5 Yr T	1.83	2.72
CAN 10 Yr T	2.80	3.57

Money Market	2008	2009
USA Fed Funds	0.25	0.25
USA 3 Mo T-B	0.02	0.07
CAN tgt overnight rate	1.50	0.25
CAN 3 Mo T-B	0.84	0.19

30 FRIDAY	001 / 001

Foreign Exchange	2008	2009
USD/EUR	1.40	1.43
USD/GBP	1.47	1.60
CAN/USD	1.21	1.05
JPY/USD	90.35	91.22

2009-2010 Strategy Performance

Nasdaq & S&P 500 Santa Trade 2009-2010

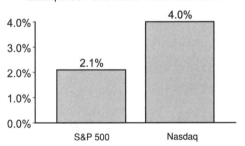

In 2009 Santa came early and stayed late. He treated both the Nasdaq and the S&P 500, but he gave more to the Nasdaq.

The media tends to focus on the S&P 500 when looking at stock market returns at the end of the year. Investors can typically increase their returns by using the Nasdaq instead. This was true in 2009-2010.

DECEMBER

M	T	W	T	F	S	S
			1	2	3	4
5	6	7	8	9	10	11
12	13	14	15	16	17	18
19	20	21	22	23	24	25
26	27	28	29	30	31	

JANUARY

M	T	W	T	F	S	S
						1
2	3	4	5	6	7	8
9	10	11	12	13	14	15
16	17	18	19	20	21	22
23	24	25	26	27	28	29
30	31					

FEBRUARY

M	T	W	T	F	S	S
		1	2	3	4	5
6	7	8	9	10	11	12
13	14	15	16	17	18	19
20	21	22	23	24	25	26
27	28	29				

** Weekly avg closing values- except Fed Funds & CAN overnight tgt rate weekly closing values.

FINANCIALS (U.S.) YEAR END CLEAN UP
Outperform January 19th to April 13th

The U.S. financial sector often starts its strong performance in October and then steps up its performance in mid-December and then really outperforms starting in mid-January.

If fundamental and technical indicators are favorable then a justification to enter the market early can exist, otherwise a mid-January date represents the start of the seasonal sweet spot.

Financials Sector vs. S&P 500
1989/90 to 2009/10

Jan 19 to Apr 13	Financials	Positive S&P 500	Diff
1989/90	-4.3 %	1.8 %	-6.1 %
1990/91	27.7	14.5	13.2
1991/92	-2.8	-3.1	0.2
1992/93	11.3	2.8	8.5
1993/94	-2.7	-5.9	3.2
1994/95	10.4	8.4	1.9
1995/96	5.6	4.7	1.0
1996/97	-2.6	-5.0	2.4
1997/98	22.3	15.4	6.9
1998/99	13.2	8.6	4.6
1999/00	5.9	-1.0	6.9
2000/01	-6.3	-12.2	5.9
2001/02	2.6	-1.5	4.1
2002/03	-5.2	-3.7	-1.5
2003/04	0.6	-0.9	1.5
2004/05	-6.2	-1.9	-4.4
2005/06	1.1	0.9	0.2
2006/07	-3.1	1.9	-5.0
2007/08	-1.4	0.6	-2.0
2008/09	15.4	1.0	14.4
2009/10	11.2	5.4	5.8
Avg.	4.4 %	1.5 %	2.9 %

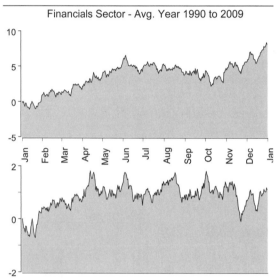

Financials Sector - Avg. Year 1990 to 2009

Financials / S&P 500 Relative Strength - Avg Yr. 1990-2009

Extra 2.9% &
15 out of 21 times better than the S&P 500

In the 1990s and early 2000s, financial stocks benefited from the tailwind of falling interest rates. During this period, with a few exceptions, this sector has participated in both the rallies and the declines.

The real sweet spot on average each year, from 1989/90 to 2009/10, has been from mid-January to mid-April.

The main driver for the strong seasonal performance of the financial sector has been the year-end earnings of the banks that start to report in mid-January. A strong performance from mid-December has been the result of investors getting into the market early to take advantage of positive year-end earnings.

Interest rates are at historic lows and although they may move lower over the next few years, it is not possible for them to have the same decline that they have had since the 1980s.

Given this situation investors should concentrate their financial investments during the strong seasonal period.

It should be noted that Canadian banks have their year-ends at the end of October (reporting in November) and as such their seasonally strong period starts in October.

Financial SP GIC Sector # 40:
An index that contains companies involved in activities such as banking, mortgage finance, consumer finance, specialized finance, investment banking and brokerage, asset management and custody, corporate lending, insurance, financial investment, and real estate, including REITs.

2 MONDAY

3 TUESDAY

4 WEDNESDAY

5 THURSDAY

6 FRIDAY

2010 Strategy Performance

Financials (U.S.) September 2009 to June 2010

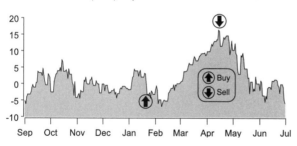

The big question over the last few years has been the strength of the financial sector. It was the financial sector that lead the market down in 2007 so investors still focus on the strength of the sector to determine the direction of the market. Over the last year the financial sector has been showing strength which has been good for the market. Even though there has been debate around the real strength of the numbers, investing during the sector's sweet spot worked very well. The sector started its outperformance on schedule and finished its run just days before the market started to collapse in April.

** Weekly avg closing values- except Fed Funds & CAN overnight tgt rate weekly closing values.

JANUARY

M	T	W	T	F	S	S
						1
2	3	4	5	6	7	8
9	10	11	12	13	14	15
16	17	18	19	20	21	22
23	24	25	26	27	28	29
30	31					

FEBRUARY

M	T	W	T	F	S	S
		1	2	3	4	5
6	7	8	9	10	11	12
13	14	15	16	17	18	19
20	21	22	23	24	25	26
27	28	29				

MARCH

M	T	W	T	F	S	S
			1	2	3	4
5	6	7	8	9	10	11
12	13	14	15	16	17	18
19	20	21	22	23	24	25
26	27	28	29	30	31	

APPENDIX

STOCK MARKET RETURNS

S&P 500 PERCENT CHANGES

	JAN	FEB	MAR	APR	MAY	JUN
1950	1.7 %	1.0 %	0.4 %	4.5 %	3.9 %	— 5.8 %
1951	6.1	0.6	— 1.8	4.8	— 4.1	— 2.6
1952	1.6	— 3.6	4.8	— 4.3	2.3	4.6
1953	— 0.7	— 1.8	— 2.4	— 2.6	— 0.3	— 1.6
1954	5.1	0.3	3.0	4.9	3.3	0.1
1955	1.8	0.4	— 0.5	3.8	— 0.1	8.2
1956	— 3.6	3.5	6.9	— 0.2	— 6.6	3.9
1957	— 4.2	— 3.3	2.0	3.7	3.7	— 0.1
1958	4.3	2.1	3.1	3.2	1.5	2.6
1959	0.4	— 0.1	0.1	3.9	1.9	— 0.4
1960	— 7.1	0.9	— 1.4	— 1.8	2.7	2.0
1961	6.3	2.7	2.6	0.4	1.9	— 2.9
1962	— 3.8	1.6	— 0.6	— 6.2	— 8.6	— 8.2
1963	4.9	— 2.9	3.5	4.9	1.4	— 2.0
1964	2.7	1.0	1.5	0.6	1.1	1.6
1965	3.3	— 0.1	— 1.5	3.4	— 0.8	— 4.9
1966	0.5	— 1.8	— 2.2	2.1	— 5.4	— 1.6
1967	7.8	0.2	3.9	4.2	— 5.2	1.8
1968	— 4.4	— 3.1	0.9	8.0	1.3	0.9
1969	— 0.8	— 4.7	3.4	2.1	— 0.2	— 5.6
1970	— 7.6	5.3	0.1	— 9.0	— 6.1	— 5.0
1971	4.0	0.9	3.7	3.6	— 4.2	— 0.9
1972	1.8	2.5	0.6	0.4	1.7	— 2.2
1973	— 1.7	— 3.7	— 0.1	— 4.1	— 1.9	— 0.7
1974	— 1.0	— 0.4	— 2.3	— 3.9	— 3.4	— 1.5
1975	12.3	6.0	2.2	4.7	4.4	4.4
1976	11.8	— 1.1	3.1	— 1.1	— 1.4	4.1
1977	— 5.1	— 2.2	— 1.4	0.0	— 2.4	4.5
1978	— 6.2	— 2.5	2.5	8.5	0.4	— 1.8
1979	4.0	— 3.7	5.5	0.2	— 2.6	3.9
1980	5.8	— 0.4	— 10.2	4.1	4.7	2.7
1981	— 4.6	1.3	3.6	— 2.3	— 0.2	— 1.0
1982	— 1.8	— 6.1	— 1.0	4.0	— 3.9	— 2.0
1983	3.3	1.9	3.3	7.5	— 1.2	3.2
1984	— 0.9	— 3.9	1.3	0.5	— 5.9	1.7
1985	7.4	0.9	— 0.3	— 0.5	5.4	1.2
1986	0.2	7.1	5.3	— 1.4	5.0	1.4
1987	13.2	3.7	2.6	— 1.1	0.6	4.8
1988	4.0	4.2	— 3.3	0.9	0.3	4.3
1989	7.1	— 2.9	2.1	5.0	3.5	— 0.8
1990	— 6.9	0.9	2.4	— 2.7	9.2	— 0.9
1991	4.2	6.7	2.2	0.0	3.9	— 4.8
1992	— 2.0	1.0	— 2.2	2.8	0.1	— 1.7
1993	0.7	1.0	1.9	— 2.5	2.3	0.1
1994	3.3	— 3.0	— 4.6	1.2	1.2	— 2.7
1995	2.4	3.6	2.7	2.8	3.6	2.1
1996	3.3	0.7	0.8	1.3	2.3	0.2
1997	6.1	0.6	— 4.3	5.8	5.9	4.3
1998	1.0	7.0	5.0	0.9	— 1.9	3.9
1999	4.1	— 3.2	3.9	3.8	— 2.5	5.4
2000	— 5.1	— 2.0	9.7	— 3.1	— 2.2	2.4
2001	3.5	— 9.2	— 6.4	7.7	0.5	— 2.5
2002	— 1.6	— 2.1	3.7	— 6.1	— 0.9	— 7.2
2003	— 2.7	— 1.7	0.8	8.1	5.1	1.1
2004	1.7	1.2	— 1.6	— 1.7	1.2	1.8
2005	— 2.5	1.9	— 1.9	— 2.0	3.0	0.0
2006	2.5	0.0	1.1	1.2	— 3.1	0.0
2007	1.4	— 2.2	1.0	4.3	3.3	— 1.8
2008	— 6.1	— 3.5	— 0.6	4.8	1.1	— 8.6
2009	— 8.6	— 11.0	8.5	9.4	5.3	0.0
FQ POS*	37 / 60	31 / 60	39 / 60	41 / 60	35 / 60	31 / 60
% FQ POS*	62 %	52 %	65 %	68 %	58 %	52 %
AVG GAIN*	1.1 %	-0.3 %	1.1 %	1.5 %	0.4 %	0.0 %
RANK GAIN*	4	11	5	3	8	10

S&P 500 PERCENT CHANGES — STOCK MKT

JUL	AUG	SEP	OCT	NOV	DEC		YEAR
0.8 %	3.3 %	5.6 %	0.4 %	− 0.1 %	4.6 %	1950	21.8 %
6.9	3.9	− 0.1	− 1.4	− 0.3	3.9	1951	16.5
1.8	− 1.5	− 2.0	− 0.1	4.6	3.5	1952	11.8
2.5	− 5.8	0.1	5.1	0.9	0.2	1953	− 6.6
5.7	− 3.4	8.3	− 1.9	8.1	5.1	1954	45.0
6.1	− 0.8	1.1	− 3.0	7.5	− 0.1	1955	26.4
5.2	− 3.8	− 4.5	0.5	− 1.1	3.5	1956	2.6
1.1	− 5.6	− 6.2	− 3.2	1.6	− 4.1	1957	− 14.3
4.3	1.2	4.8	2.5	2.2	5.2	1958	38.1
3.5	− 1.5	− 4.6	1.1	1.3	2.8	1959	8.5
− 2.5	2.6	− 6.0	− 0.2	4.0	4.6	1960	− 3.0
3.3	2.0	− 2.0	2.8	3.9	0.3	1961	23.1
6.4	1.5	− 4.8	0.4	10.2	1.3	1962	− 11.8
− 0.3	4.9	− 1.1	3.2	− 1.1	2.4	1963	18.9
1.8	− 1.6	2.9	0.8	− 0.5	0.4	1964	13.0
1.3	2.3	3.2	2.7	− 0.9	0.9	1965	9.1
− 1.3	− 7.8	− 0.7	4.8	0.3	− 0.1	1966	− 13.1
4.5	− 1.2	3.3	− 3.5	0.8	2.6	1967	20.1
− 1.8	1.1	3.9	0.7	4.8	− 4.2	1968	7.7
− 6.0	4.0	− 2.5	4.3	− 3.4	− 1.9	1969	− 11.4
7.3	4.4	3.4	− 1.2	4.7	5.7	1970	0.1
− 3.2	3.6	− 0.7	− 4.2	− 0.3	8.6	1971	10.8
0.2	3.4	− 0.5	0.9	4.6	1.2	1972	15.6
3.8	− 3.7	4.0	− 0.1	− 11.4	1.7	1973	− 17.4
− 7.8	− 9.0	− 11.9	16.3	− 5.3	− 2.0	1974	− 29.7
− 6.8	− 2.1	− 3.5	6.2	2.5	− 1.2	1975	31.5
− 0.8	− 0.5	2.3	− 2.2	− 0.8	5.2	1976	19.1
− 1.6	− 2.1	− 0.2	− 4.3	2.7	0.3	1977	− 11.5
5.4	2.6	− 0.7	− 9.2	1.7	1.5	1978	1.1
0.9	5.3	0.0	− 6.9	4.3	1.7	1979	12.3
6.5	0.6	2.5	1.6	10.2	− 3.4	1980	25.8
− 0.2	− 6.2	− 5.4	4.9	3.7	− 3.0	1981	− 9.7
− 2.3	11.6	0.8	11.0	3.6	1.5	1982	14.8
− 3.0	1.1	1.0	− 1.5	1.7	− 0.9	1983	17.3
− 1.6	10.6	− 0.3	0.0	− 1.5	2.2	1984	1.4
− 0.5	− 1.2	− 3.5	4.3	6.5	4.5	1985	26.3
− 5.9	7.1	− 8.5	5.5	2.1	− 2.8	1986	14.6
4.8	3.5	− 2.4	− 21.8	− 8.5	7.3	1987	2.0
− 0.5	− 3.9	4.0	2.6	− 1.9	1.5	1988	12.4
8.8	1.6	− 0.7	− 2.5	1.7	2.1	1989	27.3
− 0.5	− 9.4	− 5.1	− 0.7	6.0	2.5	1990	− 6.6
4.5	2.0	− 1.9	1.2	− 4.4	11.2	1991	26.3
3.9	− 2.4	0.9	0.2	3.0	1.0	1992	4.5
− 0.5	3.4	− 1.0	1.9	− 1.3	1.0	1993	7.1
3.1	3.8	− 2.7	2.1	− 4.0	1.2	1994	− 1.5
3.2	0.0	4.0	− 0.5	4.1	1.7	1995	34.1
− 4.6	1.9	5.4	2.6	7.3	− 2.2	1996	20.3
7.8	− 5.7	5.3	− 3.4	4.5	1.6	1997	31.0
− 1.2	− 14.6	6.2	8.0	5.9	5.6	1998	26.7
− 3.2	− 0.6	− 2.9	6.3	1.9	5.8	1999	19.5
− 1.6	6.1	− 5.3	− 0.5	− 8.0	0.4	2000	− 10.1
− 1.1	− 6.4	− 8.2	1.8	7.5	0.8	2001	− 13.0
− 7.9	0.5	− 11.0	8.6	5.7	− 6.0	2002	− 23.4
1.6	1.8	− 1.2	5.5	0.7	5.1	2003	26.4
-3.4	0.2	0.9	1.4	3.9	3.2	2004	9.0
3.6	− 1.1	0.7	− 1.8	3.5	− 0.1	2005	3.0
0.5	2.1	2.5	3.2	1.6	1.3	2006	13.6
− 3.2	1.3	3.6	1.5	− 4.4	− 0.9	2007	3.5
− 1.0	1.2	− 9.2	− 16.8	− 7.5	0.8	2008	-38.5
7.4	3.4	3.6	− 2.0	5.7	1.8	2009	23.5
32 / 60	34 / 60	26 / 60	35 / 60	40 / 60	46 / 60		44 / 60
53 %	57 %	43 %	58 %	67 %	77 %		73 %
0.9 %	0.1 %	− 0.6 %	0.6 %	1.6 %	1.7 %		8.7 %
6	9	12	7	2	1		

S&P 500 MONTH CLOSING VALUES

	JAN	FEB	MAR	APR	MAY	JUN
1950	17	17	17	18	19	18
1951	22	22	21	22	22	21
1952	24	23	24	23	24	25
1953	26	26	25	25	25	24
1954	26	26	27	28	29	29
1955	37	37	37	38	38	41
1956	44	45	48	48	45	47
1957	45	43	44	46	47	47
1958	42	41	42	43	44	45
1959	55	55	55	58	59	58
1960	56	56	55	54	56	57
1961	62	63	65	65	67	65
1962	69	70	70	65	60	55
1963	66	64	67	70	71	69
1964	77	78	79	79	80	82
1965	88	87	86	89	88	84
1966	93	91	89	91	86	85
1967	87	87	90	94	89	91
1968	92	89	90	97	99	100
1969	103	98	102	104	103	98
1970	85	90	90	82	77	73
1971	96	97	100	104	100	99
1972	104	107	107	108	110	107
1973	116	112	112	107	105	104
1974	97	96	94	90	87	86
1975	77	82	83	87	91	95
1976	101	100	103	102	100	104
1977	102	100	98	98	96	100
1978	89	87	89	97	97	96
1979	100	96	102	102	99	103
1980	114	114	102	106	111	114
1981	130	131	136	133	133	131
1982	120	113	112	116	112	110
1983	145	148	153	164	162	168
1984	163	157	159	160	151	153
1985	180	181	181	180	190	192
1986	212	227	239	236	247	251
1987	274	284	292	288	290	304
1988	257	268	259	261	262	274
1989	297	289	295	310	321	318
1990	329	332	340	331	361	358
1991	344	367	375	375	390	371
1992	409	413	404	415	415	408
1993	439	443	452	440	450	451
1994	482	467	446	451	457	444
1995	470	487	501	515	533	545
1996	636	640	646	654	669	671
1997	786	791	757	801	848	885
1998	980	1049	1102	1112	1091	1134
1999	1280	1238	1286	1335	1302	1373
2000	1394	1366	1499	1452	1421	1455
2001	1366	1240	1160	1249	1256	1224
2002	1130	1107	1147	1077	1067	990
2003	856	841	848	917	964	975
2004	1131	1145	1126	1107	1121	1141
2005	1181	1204	1181	1157	1192	1191
2006	1280	1281	1295	1311	1270	1270
2007	1438	1407	1421	1482	1531	1503
2008	1379	1331	1323	1386	1400	1280
2009	826	735	798	873	919	919

S&P 500 MONTH CLOSING VALUES

STOCK MKT

JUL	AUG	SEP	OCT	NOV	DEC	
18	18	19	20	20	20	**1950**
22	23	23	23	23	24	**1951**
25	25	25	25	26	27	**1952**
25	23	23	25	25	25	**1953**
31	30	32	32	34	36	**1954**
44	43	44	42	46	45	**1955**
49	48	45	46	45	47	**1956**
48	45	42	41	42	40	**1957**
47	48	50	51	52	55	**1958**
61	60	57	58	58	60	**1959**
56	57	54	53	56	58	**1960**
67	68	67	69	71	72	**1961**
58	59	56	57	62	63	**1962**
69	73	72	74	73	75	**1963**
83	82	84	85	84	85	**1964**
85	87	90	92	92	92	**1965**
84	77	77	80	80	80	**1966**
95	94	97	93	94	96	**1967**
98	99	103	103	108	104	**1968**
92	96	93	97	94	92	**1969**
78	82	84	83	87	92	**1970**
96	99	98	94	94	102	**1971**
107	111	111	112	117	118	**1972**
108	104	108	108	96	98	**1973**
79	72	64	74	70	69	**1974**
89	87	84	89	91	90	**1975**
103	103	105	103	102	107	**1976**
99	97	97	92	95	95	**1977**
101	103	103	93	95	96	**1978**
104	109	109	102	106	108	**1979**
122	122	125	127	141	136	**1980**
131	123	116	122	126	123	**1981**
107	120	120	134	139	141	**1982**
163	164	166	164	166	165	**1983**
151	167	166	166	164	167	**1984**
191	189	182	190	202	211	**1985**
236	253	231	244	249	242	**1986**
319	330	322	252	230	247	**1987**
272	262	272	279	274	278	**1988**
346	351	349	340	346	353	**1989**
356	323	306	304	322	330	**1990**
388	395	388	392	375	417	**1991**
424	414	418	419	431	436	**1992**
448	464	459	468	462	466	**1993**
458	475	463	472	454	459	**1994**
562	562	584	582	605	616	**1995**
640	652	687	705	757	741	**1996**
954	899	947	915	955	970	**1997**
1121	957	1017	1099	1164	1229	**1998**
1329	1320	1283	1363	1389	1469	**1999**
1431	1518	1437	1429	1315	1320	**2000**
1211	1134	1041	1060	1139	1148	**2001**
912	916	815	886	936	880	**2002**
990	1008	996	1051	1058	1112	**2003**
1102	1104	1115	1130	1174	1212	**2004**
1234	1220	1229	1207	1249	1248	**2005**
1277	1304	1336	1378	1401	1418	**2006**
1455	1474	1527	1549	1481	1468	**2007**
1267	1283	1165	969	896	903	**2008**
987	1021	1057	1036	1096	1115	**2009**

DOW JONES PERCENT MONTH CHANGES

	JAN	FEB	MAR	APR	MAY	JUN
1950	0.8 %	0.8 %	1.3 %	4.0 %	4.2 %	− 6.4 %
1951	5.7	1.3	− 1.7	4.5	− 3.6	− 2.8
1952	0.6	− 3.9	3.6	− 4.4	2.1	4.3
1953	− 0.7	− 2.0	− 1.5	− 1.8	− 0.9	− 1.5
1954	4.1	0.7	3.1	5.2	2.6	1.8
1955	1.1	0.8	− 0.5	3.9	− 0.2	6.2
1956	− 3.6	2.8	5.8	0.8	− 7.4	3.1
1957	− 4.1	− 3.0	2.2	4.1	2.1	− 0.3
1958	3.3	− 2.2	1.6	2.0	1.5	3.3
1959	1.8	1.6	− 0.3	3.7	3.2	0.0
1960	− 8.4	1.2	− 2.1	− 2.4	4.0	2.4
1961	5.2	2.1	2.2	0.3	2.7	− 1.8
1962	− 4.3	1.2	− 0.2	− 5.9	− 7.8	− 8.5
1963	4.7	− 2.9	3.0	5.2	1.3	− 2.8
1964	2.9	1.9	1.6	− 0.3	1.2	1.3
1965	3.3	0.1	− 1.6	3.7	− 0.5	− 5.4
1966	1.5	− 3.2	− 2.8	1.0	− 5.3	− 1.6
1967	8.2	− 1.2	3.2	3.6	− 5.0	0.9
1968	− 5.5	− 1.8	0.0	8.5	− 1.4	− 0.1
1969	0.2	− 4.3	3.3	1.6	− 1.3	− 6.9
1970	− 7.0	4.5	1.0	− 6.3	− 4.8	− 2.4
1971	3.5	1.2	2.9	4.1	− 3.6	− 1.8
1972	1.3	2.9	1.4	1.4	0.7	− 3.3
1973	− 2.1	− 4.4	− 0.4	− 3.1	− 2.2	− 1.1
1974	0.6	0.6	− 1.6	− 1.2	− 4.1	0.0
1975	14.2	5.0	3.9	6.9	1.3	5.6
1976	14.4	− 0.3	2.8	− 0.3	− 2.2	2.8
1977	− 5.0	− 1.9	− 1.8	0.8	− 3.0	2.0
1978	− 7.4	− 3.6	2.1	10.5	0.4	− 2.6
1979	4.2	− 3.6	6.6	− 0.8	− 3.8	2.4
1980	4.4	− 1.5	− 9.0	4.0	4.1	2.0
1981	− 1.7	2.9	3.0	− 0.6	− 0.6	− 1.5
1982	− 0.4	− 5.4	− 0.2	3.1	− 3.4	− 0.9
1983	2.8	3.4	1.6	8.5	− 2.1	1.8
1984	− 3.0	− 5.4	0.9	0.5	− 5.6	2.5
1985	6.2	− 0.2	− 1.3	− 0.7	4.6	1.5
1986	1.6	8.8	6.4	− 1.9	5.2	0.9
1987	13.8	3.1	3.6	− 0.8	0.2	5.5
1988	1.0	5.8	− 4.0	2.2	− 0.1	5.4
1989	8.0	− 3.6	1.6	5.5	2.5	− 1.6
1990	− 5.9	1.4	3.0	− 1.9	8.3	0.1
1991	3.9	5.3	1.1	− 0.9	4.8	− 4.0
1992	1.7	1.4	− 1.0	3.8	1.1	− 2.3
1993	0.3	1.8	1.9	− 0.2	2.9	− 0.3
1994	6.0	− 3.7	− 5.1	1.3	2.1	− 3.5
1995	0.2	4.3	3.7	3.9	3.3	2.0
1996	5.4	1.7	1.9	− 0.3	1.3	0.2
1997	5.7	0.9	− 4.3	6.5	4.6	4.7
1998	0.0	8.1	3.0	3.0	− 1.8	0.6
1999	1.9	− 0.6	5.2	10.2	− 2.1	3.9
2000	− 4.5	− 7.4	7.8	− 1.7	− 2.0	− 0.7
2001	0.9	− 3.6	− 5.9	8.7	1.6	− 3.8
2002	− 1.0	1.9	2.9	− 4.4	− 0.2	− 6.9
2003	− 3.5	− 2.0	1.3	6.1	4.4	1.5
2004	0.3	0.9	− 2.1	− 1.3	− 0.4	2.4
2005	− 2.7	2.6	− 2.4	− 3.0	2.7	− 1.8
2006	1.4	1.2	1.1	2.3	− 1.7	− 0.2
2007	1.3	− 2.8	0.7	5.7	4.3	− 1.6
2008	− 4.6	− 3.0	0.0	4.5	− 1.4	− 10.2
2009	− 8.8	− 11.7	7.7	7.3	4.1	− 0.6
FQ POS	39 / 60	33 / 60	38 / 60	38 / 60	31 / 60	28 / 60
% FQ POS	65 %	55 %	63 %	63 %	52 %	47 %
AVG GAIN	1.1 %	− 0.1 %	1.0 %	2.0 %	0.2 %	− 0.3 %
RANK GAIN	5	10	6	1	8	11

DOW JONES PERCENT MONTH CHANGES 🇺🇸 STOCK MKT

JUL	AUG	SEP	OCT	NOV	DEC		YEAR
0.1 %	3.6 %	4.4 %	− 0.6 %	1.2 %	3.4 %	1950	17.6 %
6.3	4.8	0.3	− 3.2	− 0.4	3.0	1951	14.4
1.9	− 1.6	− 1.6	− 0.5	5.4	2.9	1952	8.4
2.6	− 5.2	1.1	4.5	2.0	− 0.2	1953	− 3.8
4.3	− 3.5	7.4	− 2.3	9.9	4.6	1954	44.0
3.2	0.5	− 0.3	− 2.5	6.2	1.1	1955	20.8
5.1	− 3.1	− 5.3	1.0	− 1.5	5.6	1956	2.3
1.0	− 4.7	− 5.8	− 3.4	2.0	− 3.2	1957	− 12.8
5.2	1.1	4.6	2.1	2.6	4.7	1958	34.0
4.9	− 1.6	− 4.9	2.4	1.9	3.1	1959	16.4
− 3.7	1.5	− 7.3	0.1	2.9	3.1	1960	− 9.3
3.1	2.1	− 2.6	0.4	2.5	1.3	1961	18.7
6.5	1.9	− 5.0	1.9	10.1	0.4	1962	− 10.8
− 1.6	4.9	0.5	3.1	− 0.6	1.7	1963	17.0
1.2	− 0.3	4.4	− 0.3	0.3	− 0.1	1964	14.6
1.6	1.3	4.2	3.2	− 1.5	2.4	1965	10.9
− 2.6	− 7.0	− 1.8	4.2	− 1.9	− 0.7	1966	− 18.9
5.1	− 0.3	2.8	− 5.1	− 0.4	3.3	1967	15.2
− 1.6	1.5	4.4	1.8	3.4	− 4.2	1968	4.3
− 6.6	2.6	− 2.8	5.3	− 5.1	− 1.5	1969	− 15.2
7.4	4.2	− 0.5	− 0.7	5.1	5.6	1970	4.8
− 3.7	4.6	− 1.2	− 5.4	− 0.9	7.1	1971	6.1
0.5	4.2	− 1.1	0.2	6.6	0.2	1972	14.6
3.9	− 4.2	6.7	1.0	− 14.0	3.5	1973	− 16.6
− 5.6	− 10.4	− 10.4	9.5	− 7.0	− 0.4	1974	− 27.6
− 5.4	0.5	− 5.0	5.3	3.0	− 1.0	1975	38.3
− 1.8	− 1.1	1.7	− 2.6	− 1.8	6.1	1976	17.9
− 2.9	− 3.2	− 1.7	− 3.4	1.4	0.2	1977	− 17.3
5.3	1.7	− 1.3	− 8.5	0.8	0.8	1978	− 3.2
0.5	4.9	− 1.0	− 7.2	0.8	2.0	1979	4.2
7.8	− 0.3	0.0	− 0.8	7.4	− 2.9	1980	14.9
− 2.5	− 7.4	− 3.6	0.3	4.3	− 1.6	1981	− 9.2
− 0.4	11.5	− 0.6	10.6	4.8	0.7	1982	19.6
− 1.9	1.4	1.4	− 0.6	4.1	− 1.4	1983	20.3
− 1.5	9.8	− 1.4	0.1	− 1.5	1.9	1984	− 3.7
0.9	− 1.0	− 0.4	3.4	7.1	5.1	1985	27.7
− 6.2	6.9	− 6.9	6.2	1.9	− 1.0	1986	22.6
6.4	3.5	− 2.5	− 23.2	− 8.0	5.7	1987	2.3
− 0.6	− 4.6	4.0	1.7	− 1.6	2.6	1988	11.9
9.0	2.9	− 1.6	− 1.8	2.3	1.7	1989	27.0
0.9	− 10.0	− 6.2	− 0.4	4.8	2.9	1990	− 4.3
4.1	0.6	− 0.9	1.7	− 5.7	9.5	1991	20.3
2.3	− 4.0	0.4	− 1.4	2.4	− 0.1	1992	4.2
0.7	3.2	− 2.6	3.5	0.1	1.9	1993	13.7
3.8	4.0	− 1.8	1.7	− 4.3	2.5	1994	2.1
3.3	− 2.1	3.9	− 0.7	6.7	0.8	1995	33.5
− 2.2	1.6	4.7	2.5	8.2	− 1.1	1996	26.0
7.2	− 7.3	4.2	− 6.3	5.1	1.1	1997	22.6
− 0.8	− 15.1	4.0	9.6	6.1	0.7	1998	16.1
− 2.9	1.6	− 4.5	3.8	1.4	5.3	1999	24.7
0.7	6.6	− 5.0	3.0	− 5.1	3.6	2000	− 5.8
0.2	− 5.4	− 11.1	2.6	8.6	1.7	2001	− 7.1
− 5.5	− 0.8	− 12.4	10.6	5.9	− 6.2	2002	− 16.8
2.8	2.0	− 1.5	5.7	− 0.2	6.9	2003	25.3
− 2.8	0.3	− 0.9	− 0.5	4.0	3.4	2004	3.1
3.6	− 1.5	0.8	− 1.2	3.5	− 0.8	2005	− 0.6
0.3	1.7	2.6	3.4	1.2	2.0	2006	16.3
− 1.5	1.1	4.0	0.2	− 4.0	− 0.8	2007	6.4
0.2	1.5	− 6.0	− 14.1	− 5.3	− 0.6	2008	− 33.8
8.6	3.5	2.3	0.0	6.5	0.8	2009	18.8
37 / 60	35 / 60	23 / 60	35 / 60	40 / 60	42 / 60		42 / 60
62 %	58 %	38 %	58 %	67 %	70 %		70 %
1.1 %	0.1 %	− 0.9 %	0.3 %	1.6 %	1.7 %		8.1 %
4	9	12	7	3	2		

DOW JONES
MONTH CLOSING VALUES

	JAN	FEB	MAR	APR	MAY	JUN
1950	202	203	206	214	223	209
1951	249	252	248	259	250	243
1952	271	260	270	258	263	274
1953	290	284	280	275	272	268
1954	292	295	304	319	328	334
1955	409	412	410	426	425	451
1956	471	484	512	516	478	493
1957	479	465	475	494	505	503
1958	450	440	447	456	463	478
1959	594	604	602	624	644	644
1960	623	630	617	602	626	641
1961	648	662	677	679	697	684
1962	700	708	707	665	613	561
1963	683	663	683	718	727	707
1964	785	800	813	811	821	832
1965	903	904	889	922	918	868
1966	984	952	925	934	884	870
1967	850	839	866	897	853	860
1968	856	841	841	912	899	898
1969	946	905	936	950	938	873
1970	744	778	786	736	700	684
1971	869	879	904	942	908	891
1972	902	928	941	954	961	929
1973	999	955	951	921	901	892
1974	856	861	847	837	802	802
1975	704	739	768	821	832	879
1976	975	973	1000	997	975	1003
1977	954	936	919	927	899	916
1978	770	742	757	837	841	819
1979	839	809	862	855	822	842
1980	876	863	786	817	851	868
1981	947	975	1004	998	992	977
1982	871	824	823	848	820	812
1983	1076	1113	1130	1226	1200	1222
1984	1221	1155	1165	1171	1105	1132
1985	1287	1284	1267	1258	1315	1336
1986	1571	1709	1819	1784	1877	1893
1987	2158	2224	2305	2286	2292	2419
1988	1958	2072	1988	2032	2031	2142
1989	2342	2258	2294	2419	2480	2440
1990	2591	2627	2707	2657	2877	2881
1991	2736	2882	2914	2888	3028	2907
1992	3223	3268	3236	3359	3397	3319
1993	3310	3371	3435	3428	3527	3516
1994	3978	3832	3636	3682	3758	3625
1995	3844	4011	4158	4321	4465	4556
1996	5395	5486	5587	5569	5643	5655
1997	6813	6878	6584	7009	7331	7673
1998	7907	8546	8800	9063	8900	8952
1999	9359	9307	9786	10789	10560	10971
2000	10941	10128	10922	10734	10522	10448
2001	10887	10495	9879	10735	10912	10502
2002	9920	10106	10404	9946	9925	9243
2003	8054	7891	7992	8480	8850	8985
2004	10488	10584	10358	10226	10188	10435
2005	10490	10766	10504	10193	10467	10275
2006	10865	10993	11109	11367	11168	11150
2007	12622	12269	12354	13063	13628	13409
2008	12650	12266	12263	12820	12638	11350
2009	8001	7063	7609	8168	8500	8447

JUL	AUG	SEP	OCT	NOV	DEC	
209	217	226	225	228	235	**1950**
258	270	271	262	261	269	**1951**
280	275	271	269	284	292	**1952**
275	261	264	276	281	281	**1953**
348	336	361	352	387	404	**1954**
466	468	467	455	483	488	**1955**
518	502	475	480	473	500	**1956**
509	484	456	441	450	436	**1957**
503	509	532	543	558	584	**1958**
675	664	632	647	659	679	**1959**
617	626	580	580	597	616	**1960**
705	720	701	704	722	731	**1961**
598	609	579	590	649	652	**1962**
695	729	733	755	751	763	**1963**
841	839	875	873	875	874	**1964**
882	893	931	961	947	969	**1965**
847	788	774	807	792	786	**1966**
904	901	927	880	876	905	**1967**
883	896	936	952	985	944	**1968**
816	837	813	856	812	800	**1969**
734	765	761	756	794	839	**1970**
858	898	887	839	831	890	**1971**
925	964	953	956	1018	1020	**1972**
926	888	947	957	822	851	**1973**
757	679	608	666	619	616	**1974**
832	835	794	836	861	852	**1975**
985	974	990	965	947	1005	**1976**
890	862	847	818	830	831	**1977**
862	877	866	793	799	805	**1978**
846	888	879	816	822	839	**1979**
935	933	932	925	993	964	**1980**
952	882	850	853	889	875	**1981**
809	901	896	992	1039	1047	**1982**
1199	1216	1233	1225	1276	1259	**1983**
1115	1224	1207	1207	1189	1212	**1984**
1348	1334	1329	1374	1472	1547	**1985**
1775	1898	1768	1878	1914	1896	**1986**
2572	2663	2596	1994	1834	1939	**1987**
2129	2032	2113	2149	2115	2169	**1988**
2661	2737	2693	2645	2706	2753	**1989**
2905	2614	2453	2442	2560	2634	**1990**
3025	3044	3017	3069	2895	3169	**1991**
3394	3257	3272	3226	3305	3301	**1992**
3540	3651	3555	3681	3684	3754	**1993**
3765	3913	3843	3908	3739	3834	**1994**
4709	4611	4789	4756	5075	5117	**1995**
5529	5616	5882	6029	6522	6448	**1996**
8223	7622	7945	7442	7823	7908	**1997**
8883	7539	7843	8592	9117	9181	**1998**
10655	10829	10337	10730	10878	11453	**1999**
10522	11215	10651	10971	10415	10788	**2000**
10523	9950	8848	9075	9852	10022	**2001**
8737	8664	7592	8397	8896	8342	**2002**
9234	9416	9275	9801	9782	10454	**2003**
10140	10174	10080	10027	10428	10783	**2004**
10641	10482	10569	10440	10806	10718	**2005**
11186	11381	11679	12801	12222	12463	**2006**
13212	13358	13896	13930	13372	13265	**2007**
11378	11544	10851	9325	8829	8776	**2008**
9172	9496	9712	9713	10345	10428	**2009**

NASDAQ PERCENT MONTH CHANGES

	JAN	FEB	MAR	APR	MAY	JUN
1972	4.2	5.5	2.2	2.5	0.9	— 1.8
1973	— 4.0	— 6.2	— 2.4	— 8.2	— 4.8	— 1.6
1974	3.0	— 0.6	— 2.2	— 5.9	— 7.7	— 5.3
1975	16.6	4.6	3.6	3.8	5.8	4.7
1976	12.1	3.7	0.4	— 0.6	— 2.3	2.6
1977	— 2.4	— 1.0	— 0.5	1.4	0.1	4.3
1978	— 4.0	0.6	4.7	8.5	4.4	0.0
1979	6.6	— 2.6	7.5	1.6	— 1.8	5.1
1980	7.0	— 2.3	— 17.1	6.9	7.5	4.9
1981	— 2.2	0.1	6.1	3.1	3.1	— 3.5
1982	— 3.8	— 4.8	— 2.1	5.2	— 3.3	— 4.1
1983	6.9	5.0	3.9	8.2	5.3	3.2
1984	— 3.7	— 5.9	— 0.7	— 1.3	— 5.9	2.9
1985	12.8	2.0	— 1.8	0.5	3.6	1.9
1986	3.4	7.1	4.2	2.3	4.4	1.3
1987	12.4	8.4	1.2	— 2.9	— 0.3	2.0
1988	4.3	6.5	2.1	1.2	— 2.3	6.6
1989	5.2	— 0.4	1.8	5.1	4.3	— 2.4
1990	— 8.6	2.4	2.3	— 3.5	9.3	0.7
1991	10.8	9.4	6.4	0.5	4.4	— 6.0
1992	5.8	2.1	— 4.7	— 4.2	1.1	— 3.7
1993	2.9	— 3.7	2.9	— 4.2	5.9	0.5
1994	3.0	— 1.0	— 6.2	— 1.3	0.2	— 4.0
1995	0.4	5.1	3.0	3.3	2.4	8.0
1996	0.7	3.8	0.1	8.1	4.4	— 4.7
1997	6.9	— 5.1	— 6.7	3.2	11.1	3.0
1998	3.1	9.3	3.7	1.8	— 4.8	6.5
1999	14.3	— 8.7	7.6	3.3	— 2.8	8.7
2000	— 3.2	19.2	— 2.6	— 15.6	— 11.9	16.6
2001	12.2	— 22.4	— 14.5	15.0	— 0.3	2.4
2002	— 0.8	— 10.5	6.6	— 8.5	— 4.3	— 9.4
2003	— 1.1	1.3	0.3	9.2	9.0	1.7
2004	3.1	— 1.8	— 1.8	— 3.7	3.5	3.1
2005	— 5.2	— 0.5	— 2.6	— 3.9	7.6	— 0.5
2006	4.6	— 1.1	2.6	— 0.7	— 6.2	— 0.3
2007	2.0	— 1.9	0.2	4.3	3.1	0.0
2008	— 9.9	— 5.0	0.3	5.9	4.6	— 9.1
2009	— 6.4	— 6.7	10.9	12.3	3.3	3.4
FQ POS	25/38	18/38	24/38	24/38	24/38	23/38
% FQ POS	66 %	47 %	63 %	63 %	63 %	61 %
AVG GAIN	2.9 %	0.1 %	0.5 %	1.4 %	1.3 %	1.0 %
RANK GAIN	1	10	7	4	5	6

JUL	AUG	SEP	OCT	NOV	DEC		YEAR
− 1.8	1.7	− 0.3	0.5	2.1	0.6	**1972**	17.2
7.6	− 3.5	6.0	− 0.9	− 15.1	− 1.4	**1973**	− 31.1
− 7.9	− 10.9	− 10.7	17.2	− 3.5	− 5.0	**1974**	− 35.1
− 4.4	− 5.0	− 5.9	3.6	2.4	− 1.5	**1975**	29.8
1.1	− 1.7	1.7	− 1.0	0.9	7.4	**1976**	26.1
0.9	− 0.5	0.7	− 3.3	5.8	1.8	**1977**	7.3
5.0	6.9	− 1.6	− 16.4	3.2	2.9	**1978**	12.3
2.3	6.4	− 0.3	− 9.6	6.4	4.8	**1979**	28.1
8.9	5.7	3.4	2.7	8.0	− 2.8	**1980**	33.9
− 1.9	− 7.5	− 8.0	8.4	3.1	− 2.7	**1981**	− 3.2
− 2.3	6.2	5.6	13.3	9.3	0.0	**1982**	18.7
− 4.6	− 3.8	1.4	− 7.4	4.1	− 2.5	**1983**	19.9
− 4.2	10.9	− 1.8	− 1.2	− 1.9	1.9	**1984**	− 11.3
1.7	− 1.2	− 5.8	4.4	7.4	3.5	**1985**	31.5
− 8.4	3.1	− 8.4	2.9	− 0.3	− 3.0	**1986**	7.4
2.4	4.6	− 2.4	− 27.2	− 5.6	8.3	**1987**	− 5.2
− 1.9	− 2.8	2.9	− 1.3	− 2.9	2.7	**1988**	15.4
4.2	3.4	0.8	− 3.7	0.1	− 0.3	**1989**	19.2
− 5.2	− 13.0	− 9.6	− 4.3	8.9	4.1	**1990**	− 17.8
5.5	4.7	0.2	3.1	− 3.5	11.9	**1991**	56.9
3.1	− 3.0	3.6	3.8	7.9	3.7	**1992**	15.5
0.1	5.4	2.7	2.2	− 3.2	3.0	**1993**	14.7
2.3	6.0	− 0.2	1.7	− 3.5	0.2	**1994**	− 3.2
7.3	1.9	2.3	− 0.7	2.2	− 0.7	**1995**	39.9
− 8.8	5.6	7.5	− 0.4	5.8	− 0.1	**1996**	22.7
10.5	− 0.4	6.2	− -5.5	0.4	− 1.9	**1997**	21.6
− 1.2	− 19.9	13.0	4.6	10.1	12.5	**1998**	39.6
− 1.8	3.8	0.2	8.0	12.5	22.0	**1999**	85.6
− 5.0	11.7	− 12.7	− 8.3	− 22.9	− 4.9	**2000**	− 39.3
− 6.2	− 10.9	− 17.0	12.8	14.2	1.0	**2001**	− 21.1
− 9.2	− 1.0	− 10.9	13.5	11.2	− 9.7	**2002**	− 31.5
6.9	4.3	− 1.3	8.1	1.5	2.2	**2003**	50.0
− 7.8	− 2.6	3.2	4.1	6.2	3.7	**2004**	8.6
6.2	− 1.5	0.0	− 1.5	5.3	− 1.2	**2005**	1.4
− 3.7	4.4	3.4	4.8	2.7	− 0.7	**2006**	9.5
− 2.2	2.0	4.0	5.8	− 6.9	− 0.3	**2007**	9.8
1.4	1.8	− 11.6	− 17.7	− 10.8	2.7	**2008**	− 40.5
7.8	1.5	5.6	− 3.6	4.9	5.8	**2009**	43.9
19/38	21/38	20/38	20/38	26/38	22/38		27/38
50 %	55 %	53 %	53 %	68 %	58 %		71 %
− 0.1 %	0.3 %	− 0.9 %	0.3 %	1.7 %	1.8 %		11.8 %
11	8	12	9	3	2		

NASDAQ MONTH
CLOSING VALUES

	JAN	FEB	MAR	APR	MAY	JUN
1972	119	125	128	131	133	130
1973	128	120	117	108	103	101
1974	95	94	92	87	80	76
1975	70	73	76	79	83	87
1976	87	90	91	90	88	90
1977	96	95	94	95	96	100
1978	101	101	106	115	120	120
1979	126	123	132	134	131	138
1980	162	158	131	140	150	158
1981	198	198	210	217	223	216
1982	188	179	176	185	179	171
1983	248	261	271	293	309	319
1984	268	253	251	247	233	240
1985	279	284	279	281	291	296
1986	336	360	375	383	400	406
1987	392	425	430	418	417	425
1988	345	367	375	379	370	395
1989	401	400	407	428	446	435
1990	416	426	436	420	459	462
1991	414	453	482	485	506	476
1992	620	633	604	579	585	564
1993	696	671	690	661	701	704
1994	800	793	743	734	735	706
1995	755	794	817	844	865	933
1996	1060	1100	1101	1191	1243	1185
1997	1380	1309	1222	1261	1400	1442
1998	1619	1771	1836	1868	1779	1895
1999	2506	2288	2461	2543	2471	2686
2000	3940	4697	4573	3861	3401	3966
2001	2773	2152	1840	2116	2110	2161
2002	1934	1731	1845	1688	1616	1463
2003	1321	1338	1341	1464	1596	1623
2004	2066	2030	1994	1920	1987	2048
2005	2062	2052	1999	1922	2068	2057
2006	2306	2281	2340	2323	2179	2172
2007	2464	2416	2422	2525	2605	2603
2008	2390	2271	2279	2413	2523	2293
2009	1476	1378	1529	1717	1774	1835

NASDAQ MONTH CLOSING VALUES 📶 STOCK MKT

JUL	AUG	SEP	OCT	NOV	DEC	
128	130	130	130	133	134	1972
109	105	111	110	94	92	1973
70	62	56	65	63	60	1974
83	79	74	77	79	78	1975
91	90	91	90	91	98	1976
101	100	101	98	103	105	1977
126	135	133	111	115	118	1978
141	150	150	136	144	151	1979
172	182	188	193	208	202	1980
212	196	180	195	201	196	1981
167	178	188	213	232	232	1982
304	292	297	275	286	279	1983
230	255	250	247	242	247	1984
301	298	280	293	314	325	1985
371	383	351	361	360	349	1986
435	455	444	323	305	331	1987
387	377	388	383	372	381	1988
454	469	473	456	456	455	1989
438	381	345	330	359	374	1990
502	526	527	543	524	586	1991
581	563	583	605	653	677	1992
705	743	763	779	754	777	1993
722	766	764	777	750	752	1994
1001	1020	1044	1036	1059	1052	1995
1081	1142	1227	1222	1293	1291	1996
1594	1587	1686	1594	1601	1570	1997
1872	1499	1694	1771	1950	2193	1998
2638	2739	2746	2966	3336	4069	1999
3767	4206	3673	3370	2598	2471	2000
2027	1805	1499	1690	1931	1950	2001
1328	1315	1172	1330	1479	1336	2002
1735	1810	1787	1932	1960	2003	2003
1887	1838	1897	1975	2097	2175	2004
2185	2152	2152	2120	2233	2205	2005
2091	2184	2258	2367	2432	2415	2006
2546	2596	2702	2859	2661	2652	2007
2326	2368	2092	1721	1536	1577	2008
1979	2009	2122	2045	2145	2269	2009

S&P/TSX MONTH PERCENT CHANGES

	JAN	FEB	MAR	APR	MAY	JUN
1985	8.1	0.0	0.7	0.8	3.8	— 0.8
1986	— 1.7	0.5	6.7	1.1	1.4	— 1.2
1987	9.2	4.5	6.9	— 0.6	— 0.9	1.5
1988	— 3.3	4.8	3.4	0.8	— 2.7	5.9
1989	6.7	— 1.2	0.2	1.4	2.2	1.5
1990	— 6.7	— 0.5	— 1.3	— 8.2	6.7	— 0.6
1991	0.5	5.8	1.0	-0.8	2.2	— 2.3
1992	2.4	— 0.4	— 4.7	— 1.7	1.0	0.0
1993	— 1.3	4.4	4.4	5.2	2.5	2.2
1994	5.4	— 2.9	— 2.1	— 1.4	1.4	— 7.0
1995	— 4.7	2.7	4.6	— -0.8	4.0	1.8
1996	5.4	— 0.7	0.8	3.5	1.9	— 3.9
1997	3.1	0.8	— 5.0	2.2	6.8	0.9
1998	0.0	5.9	6.6	1.4	— 1.0	— 2.9
1999	3.8	— 6.2	4.5	6.3	— 2.5	2.5
2000	0.8	7.6	3.7	— 1.2	— 1.0	10.2
2001	4.3	— 13.3	— 5.8	4.5	2.7	— 5.2
2002	— 0.5	— 0.1	2.8	— 2.4	— 0.1	— 6.7
2003	— 0.7	— 0.2	— 3.2	3.8	4.2	1.8
2004	3.7	3.1	— 2.3	— 4.0	2.1	1.5
2005	— 0.5	5.0	— 0.6	— 3.5	3.6	3.1
2006	6.0	— 2.2	3.6	0.8	— 3.8	— 1.1
2007	1.0	0.1	0.9	1.9	4.8	— 1.1
2008	— 4.9	3.3	— 1.7	4.4	5.6	— 1.7
2009	— 3.3	— 6.6	7.4	6.9	11.2	0.0
FQ POS	15/25	13/25	16/25	15/25	18/25	12/25
% FQ POS	60 %	52 %	64 %	60 %	72 %	48 %
AVG GAIN	1.3 %	0.6 %	1.2 %	0.8 %	2.2 %	-0.1 %
RANK GAIN	3	8	4	5	2	9

JUL	AUG	SEP	OCT	NOV	DEC		YEAR
2.4	1.5	— 6.7	1.6	6.8	1.3	1985	20.5
— 4.9	3.2	— 1.6	1.6	0.7	0.6	1986	6.0
7.8	— 0.9	— 2.3	— 22.6	— 1.4	6.1	1987	3.1
— 1.9	— 2.7	— 0.1	3.4	— 3.0	2.9	1988	7.3
5.6	1.0	— 1.7	— 0.6	0.6	0.7	1989	17.1
0.5	— 6.0	— 5.6	— 2.5	2.3	3.4	1990	— 18.0
2.1	— 0.6	— 3.7	3.8	— 1.9	1.9	1991	7.8
1.6	— 1.2	— 3.1	1.2	— 1.6	2.1	1992	— 4.6
0.0	4.3	— 3.6	6.6	— 1.8	3.4	1993	29.0
3.8	4.1	0.1	— 1.4	— 4.6	2.9	1994	— 2.5
1.9	— 2.1	0.3	— 1.6	4.5	1.1	1995	11.9
— 2.3	4.3	2.9	5.8	7.5	— 1.5	1996	25.7
6.8	— 3.9	6.5	— 2.8	— 4.8	2.9	1997	13.0
— 5.9	— 20.2	1.5	10.6	2.2	2.2	1998	— 3.2
1.0	— 1.6	— 0.2	4.3	3.6	11.9	1999	29.7
2.1	8.1	— 7.7	— 7.1	— 8.5	1.3	2000	6.2
— 0.6	— 3.8	— 7.6	0.7	7.8	3.5	2001	— 13.9
— 7.6	0.1	— 6.5	1.1	5.1	0.7	2002	— 14.0
3.9	3.6	— 1.3	4.7	1.1	4.6	2003	24.3
— 1.0	— 1.0	3.5	2.3	1.8	2.4	2004	12.5
5.3	2.4	3.2	— 5.7	4.2	4.1	2005	21.9
1.9	2.1	— 2.6	5.0	3.3	1.2	2006	14.5
— 0.3	— 1.5	3.2	3.7	— 6.4	1.1	2007	7.2
— 6.0	1.3	— 14.7	— 16.9	— 5.0	— 3.1	2008	— 35.0
4.0	0.8	4.8	— 4.2	4.9	2.6	2009	30.7
16/25	13/25	9/25	15/25	15/25	23/25		18/25
64 %	52 %	36 %	60 %	60 %	92 %		72 %
0.8 %	— 0.4 %	— 1.7 %	— 0.4 %	0.7 %	2.4 %		7.9 %
6	10	12	11	8	1		

S&P/TSX MONTH CLOSING VALUES

	JAN	FEB	MAR	APR	MAY	JUN
1985	2595	2595	2613	2635	2736	2713
1986	2843	2856	3047	3079	3122	3086
1987	3349	3499	3739	3717	3685	3740
1988	3057	3205	3314	3340	3249	3441
1989	3617	3572	3578	3628	3707	3761
1990	3704	3687	3640	3341	3565	3544
1991	3273	3462	3496	3469	3546	3466
1992	3596	3582	3412	3356	3388	3388
1993	3305	3452	3602	3789	3883	3966
1994	4555	4424	4330	4267	4327	4025
1995	4018	4125	4314	4280	4449	4527
1996	4968	4934	4971	5147	5246	5044
1997	6110	6158	5850	5977	6382	6438
1998	6700	7093	7559	7665	7590	7367
1999	6730	6313	6598	7015	6842	7010
2000	8481	9129	9462	9348	9252	10196
2001	9322	8079	7608	7947	8162	7736
2002	7649	7638	7852	7663	7656	7146
2003	6570	6555	6343	6586	6860	6983
2004	8521	8789	8586	8244	8417	8546
2005	9204	9668	9612	9275	9607	9903
2006	11946	11688	12111	12204	11745	11613
2007	13034	13045	13166	13417	14057	13907
2008	13155	13583	13350	13937	14715	14467
2009	8695	8123	8720	9325	10370	10375

S&P/TSX PERCENT CLOSING VALUES ★ STOCK MKT

JUL	AUG	SEP	OCT	NOV	DEC	
2779	2820	2632	2675	2857	2893	1985
2935	3028	2979	3027	3047	3066	1986
4030	3994	3902	3019	2978	3160	1987
3377	3286	3284	3396	3295	3390	1988
3971	4010	3943	3919	3943	3970	1989
3561	3346	3159	3081	3151	3257	1990
3540	3518	3388	3516	3449	3512	1991
3443	3403	3298	3336	3283	3350	1992
3967	4138	3991	4256	4180	4321	1993
4179	4350	4354	4292	4093	4214	1994
4615	4517	4530	4459	4661	4714	1995
4929	5143	5291	5599	6017	5927	1996
6878	6612	7040	6842	6513	6699	1997
6931	5531	5614	6208	6344	6486	1998
7081	6971	6958	7256	7520	8414	1999
10406	11248	10378	9640	8820	8934	2000
7690	7399	6839	6886	7426	7688	2001
6605	6612	6180	6249	6570	6615	2002
7258	7517	7421	7773	7859	8221	2003
8458	8377	8668	8871	9030	9247	2004
10423	10669	11012	10383	10824	11272	2005
11831	12074	11761	12345	12752	12908	2006
13869	13660	14099	14625	13689	13833	2007
13593	13771	11753	9763	9271	8988	2008
10787	10868	11935	10911	11447	11746	2009

S&P 500 1950 - 2009
BEST - WORST

10 BEST   ## 10 WORST

YEARS

	Close	Change	Change
1954	36	11 pt	45.0 %
1958	55	15	38.1
1995	616	157	34.1
1975	90	22	31.5
1997	970	230	31.0
1989	353	76	27.3
1998	1229	259	26.7
1955	45	10	26.4
2003	1112	232	26.4
1985	211	44	26.3

YEARS

	Close	Change	Change
2008	903	− 566 pt	− 38.5 %
1974	69	− 29	− 29.7
2002	880	− 268	− 23.4
1973	98	− 21	− 17.4
1957	40	− 7	− 14.3
1966	80	− 12	− 13.1
2001	1148	− 172	− 13.0
1962	63	− 8	− 11.8
1977	95	− 12	− 11.5
1969	92	− 12	− 11.4

MONTHS

	Close	Change	Change
Oct 1974	74	10 pt	16.3 %
Aug 1982	120	12	11.6
Dec 1991	417	42	11.2
Oct 1982	134	13	11.0
Aug 1984	167	16	10.6
Nov 1980	141	13	10.2
Nov 1962	62	6	10.2
Mar 2000	1499	132	9.7
Apr 2009	798	75	9.4
May 1990	361	30	9.2

MONTHS

	Close	Change	Change
Oct 1987	252	− 70 pt	− 21.8 %
Oct 2008	969	− 196	− 16.8
Aug 1998	957	− 163	− 14.6
Sep 1974	64	− 9	− 11.9
Nov 1973	96	− 12	− 11.4
Sep 2002	815	− 101	− 11.0
Feb 2009	735	− 91	− 11.0
Mar 1980	102	− 12	− 10.2
Aug 1990	323	− 34	− 9.4
Feb 2001	1240	− 126	− 9.2

DAYS

		Close	Change	Change
Mon	2008 Oct 13	1003	104 pt	11.6 %
Tue	2008 Oct 28	941	92	10.8
Wed	1987 Oct 21	258	22	9.1
Mon	2009 Mar 23	883	54	7.1
Thu	2008 Nov 13	911	59	6.9
Mon	2008 Nov 24	852	52	6.5
Tues	2009 Mar 10	720	43	6.4
Fri	2008 Nov 21	800	48	6.3
Wed	2002 Jul 24	843	46	5.7
Tue	2008 Sep 30	1166	60	5.4

DAYS

		Close	Change	Change
Mon	1987 Oct 19	225	− 58 pt	− 20.5 %
Wed	2008 Oct 15	908	− 90	− 9.0
Mon	2008 Dec 01	816	− 80	− 8.9
Mon	2008 Sep 29	1106	− 107	− 8.8
Mon	1987 Oct 26	228	− 21	− 8.3
Thu	2008 Oct 09	910	− 75	− 7.6
Mon	1997 Oct 27	877	− 65	− 6.9
Mon	1998 Aug 31	957	− 70	− 6.8
Fri	1988 Jan 8	243	− 18	− 6.8
Thu	2008 Nov 20	752	− 54	− 6.7

10 BEST

10 WORST

YEARS

	Close	Change	Change
1954	404	124 pt	44 %
1975	852	236	38.3
1958	584	148	34.0
1995	5117	1283	33.5
1985	1547	335	27.7
1989	2753	585	27.0
1996	6448	1331	26.0
2003	10454	2112	25.3
1999	11453	2272	25.2
1997	7908	1460	22.6

YEARS

	Close	Change	Change
2008	8776	− 4488 pt	− 33.8 %
1974	616	− 235	− 27.6
1966	786	− 184	− 18.9
1977	831	− 174	− 17.3
2002	8342	− 1680	− 16.8
1973	851	− 169	− 16.6
1969	800	− 143	− 15.2
1957	436	− 64	− 12.8
1962	652	− 79	− 10.8
1960	616	− 64	− 9.3

MONTHS

	Close	Change	Change
Aug 1982	901	93 pt	11.5 %
Oct 1982	992	95	10.6
Oct 2002	8397	805	10.6
Apr 1978	837	80	10.5
Apr 1999	10789	1003	10.2
Nov 1962	649	60	10.1
Nov 1954	387	35	9.9
Aug 1984	1224	109	9.8
Oct 1998	8592	750	9.6
Oct 1974	666	58	9.5

MONTHS

	Close	Change	Change
Oct 1987	1994	− 603 pt	− 23.2 %
Aug 1998	7539	− 1344	− 15.1
Oct 2008	9325	− 1526	− 14.1
Nov 1973	822	− 134	− 14.0
Sep 2002	7592	− 1072	− 12.4
Feb 2009	7063	− 938	− 11.7
Sep 2001	8848	− 1102	− 11.1
Sep 1974	608	− 71	− 10.4
Aug 1974	679	− 79	− 10.4
Jun 2008	11350	− 1288	− 10.2

DAYS

		Close	Change	Change
Mon	2008 Oct 13	9388	936 pt	11.1 %
Tue	2008 Oct 28	9065	889	10.9
Wed	1987 Oct 21	2028	187	10.2
Mon	2009 Mar 23	7776	497	6.8
Thu	2008 Nov 13	8835	553	6.7
Fri	2008 Nov 21	8046	494	6.5
Wed	2002 Jul 24	8191	489	6.3
Tue	1987 Oct 20	1841	102	5.9
Tue	2009 Mar 10	6926	379	5.8
Mon	2002 Jul 29	8712	448	5.4

DAYS

		Close	Change	Change
Mon	1987 Oct 19	1739	− 508 pt	− 22.6 %
Mon	1987 Oct 26	1794	− 157	− 8.0
Wed	2008 Oct 15	8578	− 733	− 7.9
Mon	2008 Dec 01	8149	− 680	− 7.7
Thu	2008 Oct 09	8579	− 679	− 7.3
Mon	1997 Oct 27	8366	− 554	− 7.2
Mon	2001 Sep 17	8921	− 685	− 7.1
Mon	2008 Sep 29	10365	− 778	− 7.0
Fri	1989 Oct 13	2569	− 191	− 6.9
Fri	1988 Jan 8	1911	− 141	− 6.9

NASDAQ 1972- 2009
BEST - WORST

10 BEST

10 WORST

YEARS

	Close	Change	Change
1999	4069	1877 pt	85.6 %
1991	586	213	56.9
2003	2003	668	50.0
2009	2269	692	43.9
1995	1052	300	39.9
1998	2193	622	39.6
1980	202	51	33.9
1985	325	78	31.5
1975	78	18	29.8
1979	151	33	28.1

YEARS

	Close	Change	Change
2008	1577	− 1075 pt	− 40.5 %
2000	2471	− 1599	− 39.3
1974	60	− 32	− 35.1
2002	1336	− 615	− 31.5
1973	92	− 42	− 31.1
2001	1950	− 520	− 21.1
1990	374	− 81	− 17.8
1984	247	− 32	− 11.3
1987	331	− 18	− 5.2
1981	196	− 7	− 3.2

MONTHS

	Close	Change	Change
Dec 1999	4069	733 pt	22.0 %
Feb 2000	4697	756	19.2
Oct 1974	65	10	17.2
Jun 2000	3966	565	16.6
Apr 2001	2116	276	15.0
Nov 2001	1931	240	14.2
Oct 2002	1330	158	13.5
Oct 1982	1771	25	13.3
Sep 1998	1694	195	13.0
Oct 2001	1690	191	12.8

MONTHS

	Close	Change	Change
Oct 1987	323	− 121 pt	− 27.2 %
Nov 2000	2598	− 772	− 22.9
Feb 2001	2152	− 621	− 22.4
Aug 1998	1499	− 373	− 19.9
Oct 2008	1721	− 371	− 17.7
Mar 1980	131	− 27	− 17.1
Sep 2001	1499	− 307	− 17.0
Oct 1978	111	− 22	− 16.4
Apr 2000	3861	− 712	− 15.6
Nov 1973	94	− 17	− 15.1

DAYS

		Close	Change	Change
Wed	2001 Jan 3	2617	325 pt	14.2 %
Mon	2008 Oct 13	1844	195	11.8
Tue	2000 Dec 5	2890	274	10.5
Tue	2008 Oct 28	1649	144	9.5
Thu	2001 Apr 5	1785	146	8.9
Wed	2001 Apr 18	2079	156	8.1
Tue	2000 May 30	3459	254	7.9
Fri	2000 Oct 13	3317	242	7.9
Thu	2000 Oct 19	3419	247	7.8
Wed	2002 May 8	1696	122	7.8

DAYS

		Close	Change	Change
Mon	1987 Oct 19	360	− 46 pt	− 11.3 %
Fri	2000 Apr 14	3321	− 355	− 9.7
Mon	2008 Sep 29	1984	− 200	− 9.1
Mon	1987 Oct 26	299	− 30	− 9.0
Tue	1987 Oct 20	328	− 32	− 9.0
Mon	2008 Dec 01	1398	− 138	− 9.0
Mon	1998 Aug 31	1499	− 140	− 8.6
Wed	2008 Oct 15	1628	− 151	− 8.5
Mon	2000 Apr 03	4224	− 349	− 7.6
Tue	2001 Jan 02	2292	− 179	− 7.2

10 BEST

10 WORST

YEARS

	Close	Change	Change
2009	8414	2758 pt	30.7 %
1999	4321	1928	29.7
1993	5927	971	29.0
1996	8221	1213	25.7
2003	11272	1606	24.3
2005	2893	2026	21.9
1985	3970	500	20.8
1989	12908	580	17.1
2006	6699	1636	14.5
1997	9247	772	13.0

YEARS

	Close	Change	Change
2008	8988	– 4845 pt	35.0 %
1990	3257	– 713	– 18.0
2002	6615	– 1074	– 14.0
2001	7688	– 1245	– 13.9
1992	3350	– 162	– 4.6
1998	6486	– 214	– 3.2
1994	4214	– 108	– 2.5
1987	3160	94	3.1
1986	3066	173	6.0
2000	8934	520	6.2

MONTHS

	Close	Change	Change
Dec 1999	8414	891 pt	11.8 %
May 2009	8500	1045	11.2
Oct 1998	6208	594	10.6
Jun 2000	10196	943	10.2
Jan 1985	2595	195	8.1
Aug 2000	11248	842	8.1
Nov 2001	7426	540	7.8
Jul 1987	4030	290	7.8
Feb 2000	9129	648	7.6
Nov 1996	6017	418	7.5

MONTHS

	Close	Change	Change
Oct 1987	3019	– 883 pt	– 22.6 %
Aug 1998	5531	– 1401	– 20.2
Oct 2008	9763	– 1990	– 16.9
Sep 2008	11753	– 2018	– 14.7
Feb 2001	8079	– 1243	– 13.3
Nov 2000	8820	– 820	– 8.5
Apr 1990	3341	– 299	– 8.2
Sep 2000	10378	– 870	– 7.7
Sep 2001	6839	– 561	– 7.6
Jul 2002	6605	– 540	– 7.6

DAYS

		Close	Change	Change
Tue	2008 Oct 14	9956	891 pt	9.8 %
Wed	1987 Oct 21	3246	269	9.0
Mon	2008 Oct 20	10251	689	7.2
Tue	2008 Oct 28	9152	614	7.2
Fri	2008 Sep 19	12913	848	7.0
Fri	2008 Nov 28	9271	517	5.9
Fri	2008 Nov 21	8155	431	5.6
Mon	2008 Dec 08	8567	450	5.5
Mon	2009 Mar 23	8959	452	5.3
Fri	1987 Oct 30	3019	147	5.1

DAYS

		Close	Change	Change
Mon	1987 Oct 19	3192	– 407 pt	– 11.3 %
Mon	2008 Dec 01	8406	– 864	– 9.3
Thu	2008 Nov 20	7725	– 766	– 9.0
Mon	2008 Oct 27	8537	– 757	– 8.1
Wed	2000 Oct 25	9512	– 840	– 8.1
Mon	1987 Oct 26	2846	– 233	– 7.6
Thu	2008 Oct 02	10901	– 814	– 6.9
Mon	2008 Sep 29	11285	– 841	– 6.9
Tue	1987 Oct 20	2977	– 215	– 6.7
Fri	2001 Feb 16	8393	– 574	– 6.4

BOND YIELDS

BOND YIELDS 10 YEAR TREASURY*

	JAN	FEB	MAR	APR	MAY	JUN
1954	2.48	2.47	2.37	2.29	2.37	2.38
1955	2.61	2.65	2.68	2.75	2.76	2.78
1956	2.9	2.84	2.96	3.18	3.07	3
1957	3.46	3.34	3.41	3.48	3.6	3.8
1958	3.09	3.05	2.98	2.88	2.92	2.97
1959	4.02	3.96	3.99	4.12	4.31	4.34
1960	4.72	4.49	4.25	4.28	4.35	4.15
1961	3.84	3.78	3.74	3.78	3.71	3.88
1962	4.08	4.04	3.93	3.84	3.87	3.91
1963	3.83	3.92	3.93	3.97	3.93	3.99
1964	4.17	4.15	4.22	4.23	4.2	4.17
1965	4.19	4.21	4.21	4.2	4.21	4.21
1966	4.61	4.83	4.87	4.75	4.78	4.81
1967	4.58	4.63	4.54	4.59	4.85	5.02
1968	5.53	5.56	5.74	5.64	5.87	5.72
1969	6.04	6.19	6.3	6.17	6.32	6.57
1970	7.79	7.24	7.07	7.39	7.91	7.84
1971	6.24	6.11	5.7	5.83	6.39	6.52
1972	5.95	6.08	6.07	6.19	6.13	6.11
1973	6.46	6.64	6.71	6.67	6.85	6.9
1974	6.99	6.96	7.21	7.51	7.58	7.54
1975	7.5	7.39	7.73	8.23	8.06	7.86
1976	7.74	7.79	7.73	7.56	7.9	7.86
1977	7.21	7.39	7.46	7.37	7.46	7.28
1978	7.96	8.03	8.04	8.15	8.35	8.46
1979	9.1	9.1	9.12	9.18	9.25	8.91
1980	10.8	12.41	12.75	11.47	10.18	9.78
1981	12.57	13.19	13.12	13.68	14.1	13.47
1982	14.59	14.43	13.86	13.87	13.62	14.3
1983	10.46	10.72	10.51	10.4	10.38	10.85
1984	11.67	11.84	12.32	12.63	13.41	13.56
1985	11.38	11.51	11.86	11.43	10.85	10.16
1986	9.19	8.7	7.78	7.3	7.71	7.8
1987	7.08	7.25	7.25	8.02	8.61	8.4
1988	8.67	8.21	8.37	8.72	9.09	8.92
1989	9.09	9.17	9.36	9.18	8.86	8.28
1990	8.21	8.47	8.59	8.79	8.76	8.48
1991	8.09	7.85	8.11	8.04	8.07	8.28
1992	7.03	7.34	7.54	7.48	7.39	7.26
1993	6.6	6.26	5.98	5.97	6.04	5.96
1994	5.75	5.97	6.48	6.97	7.18	7.1
1995	7.78	7.47	7.2	7.06	6.63	6.17
1996	5.65	5.81	6.27	6.51	6.74	6.91
1997	6.58	6.42	6.69	6.89	6.71	6.49
1998	5.54	5.57	5.65	5.64	5.65	5.5
1999	4.72	5	5.23	5.18	5.54	5.9
2000	6.66	6.52	6.26	5.99	6.44	6.1
2001	5.16	5.1	4.89	5.14	5.39	5.28
2002	5.04	4.91	5.28	5.21	5.16	4.93
2003	4.05	3.9	3.81	3.96	3.57	3.33
2004	4.15	4.08	3.83	4.35	4.72	4.73
2005	4.22	4.17	4.5	4.34	4.14	4.00
2006	4.42	4.57	4.72	4.99	5.11	5.11
2007	4.76	4.72	4.56	4.69	4.75	5.10
2008	3.74	3.74	3.51	3.68	3.88	4.10
2009	2.52	2.87	2.82	2.93	3.29	3.72

* Source: Federal Reserve Bank of St. Louis, monthly data calculated as average of business days

10 YEAR TREASURY  BOND YIELDS

JUL	AUG	SEP	OCT	NOV	DEC	
2.3	2.36	2.38	2.43	2.48	2.51	1954
2.9	2.97	2.97	2.88	2.89	2.96	1955
3.11	3.33	3.38	3.34	3.49	3.59	1956
3.93	3.93	3.92	3.97	3.72	3.21	1957
3.2	3.54	3.76	3.8	3.74	3.86	1958
4.4	4.43	4.68	4.53	4.53	4.69	1959
3.9	3.8	3.8	3.89	3.93	3.84	1960
3.92	4.04	3.98	3.92	3.94	4.06	1961
4.01	3.98	3.98	3.93	3.92	3.86	1962
4.02	4	4.08	4.11	4.12	4.13	1963
4.19	4.19	4.2	4.19	4.15	4.18	1964
4.2	4.25	4.29	4.35	4.45	4.62	1965
5.02	5.22	5.18	5.01	5.16	4.84	1966
5.16	5.28	5.3	5.48	5.75	5.7	1967
5.5	5.42	5.46	5.58	5.7	6.03	1968
6.72	6.69	7.16	7.1	7.14	7.65	1969
7.46	7.53	7.39	7.33	6.84	6.39	1970
6.73	6.58	6.14	5.93	5.81	5.93	1971
6.11	6.21	6.55	6.48	6.28	6.36	1972
7.13	7.4	7.09	6.79	6.73	6.74	1973
7.81	8.04	8.04	7.9	7.68	7.43	1974
8.06	8.4	8.43	8.14	8.05	8	1975
7.83	7.77	7.59	7.41	7.29	6.87	1976
7.33	7.4	7.34	7.52	7.58	7.69	1977
8.64	8.41	8.42	8.64	8.81	9.01	1978
8.95	9.03	9.33	10.3	10.65	10.39	1979
10.25	11.1	11.51	11.75	12.68	12.84	1980
14.28	14.94	15.32	15.15	13.39	13.72	1981
13.95	13.06	12.34	10.91	10.55	10.54	1982
11.38	11.85	11.65	11.54	11.69	11.83	1983
13.36	12.72	12.52	12.16	11.57	11.5	1984
10.31	10.33	10.37	10.24	9.78	9.26	1985
7.3	7.17	7.45	7.43	7.25	7.11	1986
8.45	8.76	9.42	9.52	8.86	8.99	1987
9.06	9.26	8.98	8.8	8.96	9.11	1988
8.02	8.11	8.19	8.01	7.87	7.84	1989
8.47	8.75	8.89	8.72	8.39	8.08	1990
8.27	7.9	7.65	7.53	7.42	7.09	1991
6.84	6.59	6.42	6.59	6.87	6.77	1992
5.81	5.68	5.36	5.33	5.72	5.77	1993
7.3	7.24	7.46	7.74	7.96	7.81	1994
6.28	6.49	6.2	6.04	5.93	5.71	1995
6.87	6.64	6.83	6.53	6.2	6.3	1996
6.22	6.3	6.21	6.03	5.88	5.81	1997
5.46	5.34	4.81	4.53	4.83	4.65	1998
5.79	5.94	5.92	6.11	6.03	6.28	1999
6.05	5.83	5.8	5.74	5.72	5.24	2000
5.24	4.97	4.73	4.57	4.65	5.09	2001
4.65	4.26	3.87	3.94	4.05	4.03	2002
3.98	4.45	4.27	4.29	4.3	4.27	2003
4.5	4.28	4.13	4.1	4.19	4.23	2004
4.18	4.26	4.20	4.46	4.54	4.47	2005
5.09	4.88	4.72	4.73	4.60	4.56	2006
5.00	4.67	4.52	4.53	4.15	4.10	2007
4.01	3.89	3.69	3.81	3.53	2.42	2008
3.56	3.59	3.40	3.39	3.40	3.59	2009

BOND YIELDS 5 YEAR TREASURY*

	JAN	FEB	MAR	APR	MAY	JUN
1954	2.17	2.04	1.93	1.87	1.92	1.92
1955	2.32	2.38	2.48	2.55	2.56	2.59
1956	2.84	2.74	2.93	3.20	3.08	2.97
1957	3.47	3.39	3.46	3.53	3.64	3.83
1958	2.88	2.78	2.64	2.46	2.41	2.46
1959	4.01	3.96	3.99	4.12	4.35	4.50
1960	4.92	4.69	4.31	4.29	4.49	4.12
1961	3.67	3.66	3.60	3.57	3.47	3.81
1962	3.94	3.89	3.68	3.60	3.66	3.64
1963	3.58	3.66	3.68	3.74	3.72	3.81
1964	4.07	4.03	4.14	4.15	4.05	4.02
1965	4.10	4.15	4.15	4.15	4.15	4.15
1966	4.86	4.98	4.92	4.83	4.89	4.97
1967	4.70	4.74	4.54	4.51	4.75	5.01
1968	5.54	5.59	5.76	5.69	6.04	5.85
1969	6.25	6.34	6.41	6.30	6.54	6.75
1970	8.17	7.82	7.21	7.50	7.97	7.85
1971	5.89	5.56	5.00	5.65	6.28	6.53
1972	5.59	5.69	5.87	6.17	5.85	5.91
1973	6.34	6.60	6.80	6.67	6.80	6.69
1974	6.95	6.82	7.31	7.92	8.18	8.10
1975	7.41	7.11	7.30	7.99	7.72	7.51
1976	7.46	7.45	7.49	7.25	7.59	7.61
1977	6.58	6.83	6.93	6.79	6.94	6.76
1978	7.77	7.83	7.86	7.98	8.18	8.36
1979	9.20	9.13	9.20	9.25	9.24	8.85
1980	10.74	12.60	13.47	11.84	9.95	9.21
1981	12.77	13.41	13.41	13.99	14.63	13.95
1982	14.65	14.54	13.98	14.00	13.75	14.43
1983	10.03	10.26	10.08	10.02	10.03	10.63
1984	11.37	11.54	12.02	12.37	13.17	13.48
1985	10.93	11.13	11.52	11.01	10.34	9.60
1986	8.68	8.34	7.46	7.05	7.52	7.64
1987	6.64	6.79	6.79	7.57	8.26	8.02
1988	8.18	7.71	7.83	8.19	8.58	8.49
1989	9.15	9.27	9.51	9.30	8.91	8.29
1990	8.12	8.42	8.60	8.77	8.74	8.43
1991	7.70	7.47	7.77	7.70	7.70	7.94
1992	6.24	6.58	6.95	6.78	6.69	6.48
1993	5.83	5.43	5.19	5.13	5.20	5.22
1994	5.09	5.40	5.94	6.52	6.78	6.70
1995	7.76	7.37	7.05	6.86	6.41	5.93
1996	5.36	5.38	5.97	6.30	6.48	6.69
1997	6.33	6.20	6.54	6.76	6.57	6.38
1998	5.42	5.49	5.61	5.61	5.63	5.52
1999	4.60	4.91	5.14	5.08	5.44	5.81
2000	6.58	6.68	6.50	6.26	6.69	6.30
2001	4.86	4.89	4.64	4.76	4.93	4.81
2002	4.34	4.30	4.74	4.65	4.49	4.19
2003	3.05	2.90	2.78	2.93	2.52	2.27
2004	3.12	3.07	2.79	3.39	3.85	3.93
2005	3.71	3.77	4.17	4.00	3.85	3.77
2006	4.35	4.57	4.72	4.90	5.00	5.07
2007	4.75	4.71	4.48	4.59	4.67	5.03
2008	2.98	2.78	2.48	2.84	3.15	3.49
2009	1.60	1.87	1.82	1.86	2.13	2.71

* Source: Federal Reserve Bank of St. Louis, monthly data calculated as average of business days

5 YEAR TREASURY BOND YIELDS

JUL	AUG	SEP	OCT	NOV	DEC	
1.85	1.90	1.96	2.02	2.09	2.16	1954
2.72	2.86	2.85	2.76	2.81	2.93	1955
3.12	3.41	3.47	3.40	3.56	3.70	1956
4.00	4.00	4.03	4.08	3.72	3.08	1957
2.77	3.29	3.69	3.78	3.70	3.82	1958
4.58	4.57	4.90	4.72	4.75	5.01	1959
3.79	3.62	3.61	3.76	3.81	3.67	1960
3.84	3.96	3.90	3.80	3.82	3.91	1961
3.80	3.71	3.70	3.64	3.60	3.56	1962
3.89	3.89	3.96	3.97	4.01	4.04	1963
4.03	4.05	4.08	4.07	4.04	4.09	1964
4.15	4.20	4.25	4.34	4.46	4.72	1965
5.17	5.50	5.50	5.27	5.36	5.00	1966
5.23	5.31	5.40	5.57	5.78	5.75	1967
5.60	5.50	5.48	5.55	5.66	6.12	1968
7.01	7.03	7.57	7.51	7.53	7.96	1969
7.59	7.57	7.29	7.12	6.47	5.95	1970
6.85	6.55	6.14	5.93	5.78	5.69	1971
5.97	6.02	6.25	6.18	6.12	6.16	1972
7.33	7.63	7.05	6.77	6.92	6.80	1973
8.38	8.63	8.37	7.97	7.68	7.31	1974
7.92	8.33	8.37	7.97	7.80	7.76	1975
7.49	7.31	7.13	6.75	6.52	6.10	1976
6.84	7.03	7.04	7.32	7.34	7.48	1977
8.54	8.33	8.43	8.61	8.84	9.08	1978
8.90	9.06	9.41	10.63	10.93	10.42	1979
9.53	10.84	11.62	11.86	12.83	13.25	1980
14.79	15.56	15.93	15.41	13.38	13.60	1981
14.07	13.00	12.25	10.80	10.38	10.22	1982
11.21	11.63	11.43	11.28	11.41	11.54	1983
13.27	12.68	12.53	12.06	11.33	11.07	1984
9.70	9.81	9.81	9.69	9.28	8.73	1985
7.06	6.80	6.92	6.83	6.76	6.67	1986
8.01	8.32	8.94	9.08	8.35	8.45	1987
8.66	8.94	8.69	8.51	8.79	9.09	1988
7.83	8.09	8.17	7.97	7.81	7.75	1989
8.33	8.44	8.51	8.33	8.02	7.73	1990
7.91	7.43	7.14	6.87	6.62	6.19	1991
5.84	5.60	5.38	5.60	6.04	6.08	1992
5.09	5.03	4.73	4.71	5.06	5.15	1993
6.91	6.88	7.08	7.40	7.72	7.78	1994
6.01	6.24	6.00	5.86	5.69	5.51	1995
6.64	6.39	6.60	6.27	5.97	6.07	1996
6.12	6.16	6.11	5.93	5.80	5.77	1997
5.46	5.27	4.62	4.18	4.54	4.45	1998
5.68	5.84	5.80	6.03	5.97	6.19	1999
6.18	6.06	5.93	5.78	5.70	5.17	2000
4.76	4.57	4.12	3.91	3.97	4.39	2001
3.81	3.29	2.94	2.95	3.05	3.03	2002
2.87	3.37	3.18	3.19	3.29	3.27	2003
3.69	3.47	3.36	3.35	3.53	3.60	2004
3.98	4.12	4.01	4.33	4.45	4.39	2005
5.04	4.82	4.67	4.69	4.58	4.53	2006
4.88	4.43	4.20	4.20	3.67	3.49	2007
3.30	3.14	2.88	2.73	2.29	1.52	2008
2.46	2.57	2.37	2.33	2.23	2.34	2009

BOND YIELDS 🇺🇸 3 MONTH TREASURY

	JAN	FEB	MAR	APR	MAY	JUN
1982	12.92	14.28	13.31	13.34	12.71	13.08
1983	8.12	8.39	8.66	8.51	8.50	9.14
1984	9.26	9.46	9.89	10.07	10.22	10.26
1985	8.02	8.56	8.83	8.22	7.73	7.18
1986	7.30	7.29	6.76	6.24	6.33	6.40
1987	5.58	5.75	5.77	5.82	5.85	5.85
1988	6.00	5.84	5.87	6.08	6.45	6.66
1999	8.56	8.84	9.14	8.96	8.74	8.43
1990	7.90	8.00	8.17	8.04	8.01	7.99
1991	6.41	6.12	6.09	5.83	5.63	5.75
1992	3.91	3.95	4.14	3.84	3.72	3.75
1993	3.07	2.99	3.01	2.93	3.03	3.14
1994	3.04	3.33	3.59	3.78	4.27	4.25
1995	5.90	5.94	5.91	5.84	5.85	5.64
1996	5.15	4.96	5.10	5.09	5.15	5.23
1997	5.17	5.14	5.28	5.30	5.20	5.07
1998	5.18	5.23	5.16	5.08	5.14	5.12
1999	4.45	4.56	4.57	4.41	4.63	4.72
2000	5.50	5.73	5.86	5.82	5.99	5.86
2001	5.29	5.01	4.54	3.97	3.70	3.57
2002	1.68	1.76	1.83	1.75	1.76	1.73
2003	1.19	1.19	1.15	1.15	1.09	0.94
2004	0.90	0.94	0.95	0.96	1.04	1.29
2005	2.37	2.58	2.80	2.84	2.90	3.04
2006	4.34	4.54	4.63	4.72	4.84	4.92
2007	5.11	5.16	5.08	5.01	4.87	4.74
2008	2.82	2.17	1.28	1.31	1.76	1.89
2009	0.13	0.30	0.22	0.16	0.18	0.18

* Source: Federal Reserve Bank of St. Louis, monthly data calculated as average of business days

3 MONTH TREASURY BOND YIELDS

JUL	AUG	SEP	OCT	NOV	DEC	
11.86	9.00	8.19	7.97	8.35	8.20	**1982**
9.45	9.74	9.36	8.99	9.11	9.36	**1983**
10.53	10.90	10.80	10.12	8.92	8.34	**1984**
7.32	7.37	7.33	7.40	7.48	7.33	**1985**
6.00	5.69	5.35	5.32	5.50	5.68	**1986**
5.88	6.23	6.62	6.35	5.89	5.96	**1987**
6.95	7.30	7.48	7.60	8.03	8.35	**1988**
8.15	8.17	8.01	7.90	7.94	7.88	**1999**
7.87	7.69	7.60	7.40	7.29	6.95	**1990**
5.75	5.50	5.37	5.14	4.69	4.18	**1991**
3.28	3.20	2.97	2.93	3.21	3.29	**1992**
3.11	3.09	3.01	3.09	3.18	3.13	**1993**
4.46	4.61	4.75	5.10	5.45	5.76	**1994**
5.59	5.57	5.43	5.44	5.52	5.29	**1995**
5.30	5.19	5.24	5.12	5.17	5.04	**1996**
5.19	5.28	5.08	5.11	5.28	5.30	**1997**
5.09	5.04	4.74	4.07	4.53	4.50	**1998**
4.69	4.87	4.82	5.02	5.23	5.36	**1999**
6.14	6.28	6.18	6.29	6.36	5.94	**2000**
3.59	3.44	2.69	2.20	1.91	1.72	**2001**
1.71	1.65	1.66	1.61	1.25	1.21	**2002**
0.92	0.97	0.96	0.94	0.95	0.91	**2003**
1.36	1.50	1.68	1.79	2.11	2.22	**2004**
3.29	3.52	3.49	3.79	3.97	3.97	**2005**
5.08	5.09	4.93	5.05	5.07	4.97	**2006**
4.96	4.32	3.99	4.00	3.35	3.07	**2007**
1.66	1.75	1.15	0.69	0.19	0.03	**2008**
0.18	0.17	0.12	0.07	0.05	0.05	**2009**

MOODY'S SEASONED CORPORATE Aaa*

	JAN	FEB	MAR	APR	MAY	JUN
1950	2.57	2.58	2.58	2.60	2.61	2.62
1951	2.66	2.66	2.78	2.87	2.89	2.94
1952	2.98	2.93	2.96	2.93	2.93	2.94
1953	3.02	3.07	3.12	3.23	3.34	3.40
1954	3.06	2.95	2.86	2.85	2.88	2.90
1955	2.93	2.93	3.02	3.01	3.04	3.05
1956	3.11	3.08	3.10	3.24	3.28	3.26
1957	3.77	3.67	3.66	3.67	3.74	3.91
1958	3.60	3.59	3.63	3.60	3.57	3.57
1959	4.12	4.14	4.13	4.23	4.37	4.46
1960	4.61	4.56	4.49	4.45	4.46	4.45
1961	4.32	4.27	4.22	4.25	4.27	4.33
1962	4.42	4.42	4.39	4.33	4.28	4.28
1963	4.21	4.19	4.19	4.21	4.22	4.23
1964	4.39	4.36	4.38	4.40	4.41	4.41
1965	4.43	4.41	4.42	4.43	4.44	4.46
1966	4.74	4.78	4.92	4.96	4.98	5.07
1967	5.20	5.03	5.13	5.11	5.24	5.44
1968	6.17	6.10	6.11	6.21	6.27	6.28
1969	6.59	6.66	6.85	6.89	6.79	6.98
1970	7.91	7.93	7.84	7.83	8.11	8.48
1971	7.36	7.08	7.21	7.25	7.53	7.64
1972	7.19	7.27	7.24	7.30	7.30	7.23
1973	7.15	7.22	7.29	7.26	7.29	7.37
1974	7.83	7.85	8.01	8.25	8.37	8.47
1975	8.83	8.62	8.67	8.95	8.90	8.77
1976	8.60	8.55	8.52	8.40	8.58	8.62
1977	7.96	8.04	8.10	8.04	8.05	7.95
1978	8.41	8.47	8.47	8.56	8.69	8.76
1979	9.25	9.26	9.37	9.38	9.50	9.29
1980	11.09	12.38	12.96	12.04	10.99	10.58
1981	12.81	13.35	13.33	13.88	14.32	13.75
1982	15.18	15.27	14.58	14.46	14.26	14.81
1983	11.79	12.01	11.73	11.51	11.46	11.74
1984	12.20	12.08	12.57	12.81	13.28	13.55
1985	12.08	12.13	12.56	12.23	11.72	10.94
1986	10.05	9.67	9.00	8.79	9.09	9.13
1987	8.36	8.38	8.36	8.85	9.33	9.32
1988	9.88	9.40	9.39	9.67	9.90	9.86
1989	9.62	9.64	9.80	9.79	9.57	9.10
1990	8.99	9.22	9.37	9.46	9.47	9.26
1991	9.04	8.83	8.93	8.86	8.86	9.01
1992	8.20	8.29	8.35	8.33	8.28	8.22
1993	7.91	7.71	7.58	7.46	7.43	7.33
1994	6.92	7.08	7.48	7.88	7.99	7.97
1995	8.46	8.26	8.12	8.03	7.65	7.30
1996	6.81	6.99	7.35	7.50	7.62	7.71
1997	7.42	7.31	7.55	7.73	7.58	7.41
1998	6.61	6.67	6.72	6.69	6.69	6.53
1999	6.24	6.40	6.62	6.64	6.93	7.23
2000	7.78	7.68	7.68	7.64	7.99	7.67
2001	7.15	7.10	6.98	7.20	7.29	7.18
2002	6.55	6.51	6.81	6.76	6.75	6.63
2003	6.17	5.95	5.89	5.74	5.22	4.97
2004	5.54	5.50	5.33	5.73	6.04	6.01
2005	5.36	5.20	5.40	5.33	5.15	4.96
2006	5.29	5.35	5.53	5.84	5.95	5.89
2007	5.40	5.39	5.30	5.47	5.47	5.79
2008	5.33	5.53	5.51	5.55	5.57	5.68
2009	5.05	5.27	5.50	5.39	5.54	5.61

* Source: Federal Reserve Bank of St. Louis, monthly data calculated as average of business days

MOODY'S SEASONED CORPORATE Aaa — BOND YIELDS

JUL	AUG	SEP	OCT	NOV	DEC	
2.65	2.61	2.64	2.67	2.67	2.67	1950
2.94	2.88	2.84	2.89	2.96	3.01	1951
2.95	2.94	2.95	3.01	2.98	2.97	1952
3.28	3.24	3.29	3.16	3.11	3.13	1953
2.89	2.87	2.89	2.87	2.89	2.90	1954
3.06	3.11	3.13	3.10	3.10	3.15	1955
3.28	3.43	3.56	3.59	3.69	3.75	1956
3.99	4.10	4.12	4.10	4.08	3.81	1957
3.67	3.85	4.09	4.11	4.09	4.08	1958
4.47	4.43	4.52	4.57	4.56	4.58	1959
4.41	4.28	4.25	4.30	4.31	4.35	1960
4.41	4.45	4.45	4.42	4.39	4.42	1961
4.34	4.35	4.32	4.28	4.25	4.24	1962
4.26	4.29	4.31	4.32	4.33	4.35	1963
4.40	4.41	4.42	4.42	4.43	4.44	1964
4.48	4.49	4.52	4.56	4.60	4.68	1965
5.16	5.31	5.49	5.41	5.35	5.39	1966
5.58	5.62	5.65	5.82	6.07	6.19	1967
6.24	6.02	5.97	6.09	6.19	6.45	1968
7.08	6.97	7.14	7.33	7.35	7.72	1969
8.44	8.13	8.09	8.03	8.05	7.64	1970
7.64	7.59	7.44	7.39	7.26	7.25	1971
7.21	7.19	7.22	7.21	7.12	7.08	1972
7.45	7.68	7.63	7.60	7.67	7.68	1973
8.72	9.00	9.24	9.27	8.89	8.89	1974
8.84	8.95	8.95	8.86	8.78	8.79	1975
8.56	8.45	8.38	8.32	8.25	7.98	1976
7.94	7.98	7.92	8.04	8.08	8.19	1977
8.88	8.69	8.69	8.89	9.03	9.16	1978
9.20	9.23	9.44	10.13	10.76	10.74	1979
11.07	11.64	12.02	12.31	12.97	13.21	1980
14.38	14.89	15.49	15.40	14.22	14.23	1981
14.61	13.71	12.94	12.12	11.68	11.83	1982
12.15	12.51	12.37	12.25	12.41	12.57	1983
13.44	12.87	12.66	12.63	12.29	12.13	1984
10.97	11.05	11.07	11.02	10.55	10.16	1985
8.88	8.72	8.89	8.86	8.68	8.49	1986
9.42	9.67	10.18	10.52	10.01	10.11	1987
9.96	10.11	9.82	9.51	9.45	9.57	1988
8.93	8.96	9.01	8.92	8.89	8.86	1989
9.24	9.41	9.56	9.53	9.30	9.05	1990
9.00	8.75	8.61	8.55	8.48	8.31	1991
8.07	7.95	7.92	7.99	8.10	7.98	1992
7.17	6.85	6.66	6.67	6.93	6.93	1993
8.11	8.07	8.34	8.57	8.68	8.46	1994
7.41	7.57	7.32	7.12	7.02	6.82	1995
7.65	7.46	7.66	7.39	7.10	7.20	1996
7.14	7.22	7.15	7.00	6.87	6.76	1997
6.55	6.52	6.40	6.37	6.41	6.22	1998
7.19	7.40	7.39	7.55	7.36	7.55	1999
7.65	7.55	7.62	7.55	7.45	7.21	2000
7.13	7.02	7.17	7.03	6.97	6.77	2001
6.53	6.37	6.15	6.32	6.31	6.21	2002
5.49	5.88	5.72	5.70	5.65	5.62	2003
5.82	5.65	5.46	5.47	5.52	5.47	2004
5.06	5.09	5.13	5.35	5.42	5.37	2005
5.85	5.68	5.51	5.51	5.33	5.32	2006
5.73	5.79	5.74	5.66	5.44	5.49	2007
5.67	5.64	5.65	6.28	6.12	5.05	2008
5.41	5.26	5.13	5.15	5.19	5.26	2009

MOODY'S SEASONED CORPORATE Baa*

	JAN	FEB	MAR	APR	MAY	JUN
1950	3.24	3.24	3.24	3.23	3.25	3.28
1951	3.17	3.16	3.23	3.35	3.40	3.49
1952	3.59	3.53	3.51	3.50	3.49	3.50
1953	3.51	3.53	3.57	3.65	3.78	3.86
1954	3.71	3.61	3.51	3.47	3.47	3.49
1955	3.45	3.47	3.48	3.49	3.50	3.51
1956	3.60	3.58	3.60	3.68	3.73	3.76
1957	4.49	4.47	4.43	4.44	4.52	4.63
1958	4.83	4.66	4.68	4.67	4.62	4.55
1959	4.87	4.89	4.85	4.86	4.96	5.04
1960	5.34	5.34	5.25	5.20	5.28	5.26
1961	5.10	5.07	5.02	5.01	5.01	5.03
1962	5.08	5.07	5.04	5.02	5.00	5.02
1963	4.91	4.89	4.88	4.87	4.85	4.84
1964	4.83	4.83	4.83	4.85	4.85	4.85
1965	4.80	4.78	4.78	4.80	4.81	4.85
1966	5.06	5.12	5.32	5.41	5.48	5.58
1967	5.97	5.82	5.85	5.83	5.96	6.15
1968	6.84	6.80	6.85	6.97	7.03	7.07
1969	7.32	7.30	7.51	7.54	7.52	7.70
1970	8.86	8.78	8.63	8.70	8.98	9.25
1971	8.74	8.39	8.46	8.45	8.62	8.75
1972	8.23	8.23	8.24	8.24	8.23	8.20
1973	7.90	7.97	8.03	8.09	8.06	8.13
1974	8.48	8.53	8.62	8.87	9.05	9.27
1975	10.81	10.65	10.48	10.58	10.69	10.62
1976	10.41	10.24	10.12	9.94	9.86	9.89
1977	9.08	9.12	9.12	9.07	9.01	8.91
1978	9.17	9.20	9.22	9.32	9.49	9.60
1979	10.13	10.08	10.26	10.33	10.47	10.38
1980	12.42	13.57	14.45	14.19	13.17	12.71
1981	15.03	15.37	15.34	15.56	15.95	15.80
1982	17.10	17.18	16.82	16.78	16.64	16.92
1983	13.94	13.95	13.61	13.29	13.09	13.37
1984	13.65	13.59	13.99	14.31	14.74	15.05
1985	13.26	13.23	13.69	13.51	13.15	12.40
1986	11.44	11.11	10.50	10.19	10.29	10.34
1987	9.72	9.65	9.61	10.04	10.51	10.52
1988	11.07	10.62	10.57	10.90	11.04	11.00
1989	10.65	10.61	10.67	10.61	10.46	10.03
1990	9.94	10.14	10.21	10.30	10.41	10.22
1991	10.45	10.07	10.09	9.94	9.86	9.96
1992	9.13	9.23	9.25	9.21	9.13	9.05
1993	8.67	8.39	8.15	8.14	8.21	8.07
1994	7.65	7.76	8.13	8.52	8.62	8.65
1995	9.08	8.85	8.70	8.60	8.20	7.90
1996	7.47	7.63	8.03	8.19	8.30	8.40
1997	8.09	7.94	8.18	8.34	8.20	8.02
1998	7.19	7.25	7.32	7.33	7.30	7.13
1999	7.29	7.39	7.53	7.48	7.72	8.02
2000	8.33	8.29	8.37	8.40	8.90	8.48
2001	7.93	7.87	7.84	8.07	8.07	7.97
2002	7.87	7.89	8.11	8.03	8.09	7.95
2003	7.35	7.06	6.95	6.85	6.38	6.19
2004	6.44	6.27	6.11	6.46	6.75	6.78
2005	6.02	5.82	6.06	6.05	6.01	5.86
2006	6.24	6.27	6.41	6.68	6.75	6.78
2007	6.34	6.28	6.27	6.39	6.39	6.70
2008	6.54	6.82	6.89	6.97	6.93	7.07
2009	8.14	8.08	8.42	8.39	8.06	7.50

* Source: Federal Reserve Bank of St. Louis, monthly data calculated as average of business days

MOODY'S SEASONED CORPORATE Baa* BOND YIELDS

JUL	AUG	SEP	OCT	NOV	DEC	
3.32	3.23	3.21	3.22	3.22	3.20	**1950**
3.53	3.50	3.46	3.50	3.56	3.61	**1951**
3.50	3.51	3.52	3.54	3.53	3.51	**1952**
3.86	3.85	3.88	3.82	3.75	3.74	**1953**
3.50	3.49	3.47	3.46	3.45	3.45	**1954**
3.52	3.56	3.59	3.59	3.58	3.62	**1955**
3.80	3.93	4.07	4.17	4.24	4.37	**1956**
4.73	4.82	4.93	4.99	5.09	5.03	**1957**
4.53	4.67	4.87	4.92	4.87	4.85	**1958**
5.08	5.09	5.18	5.28	5.26	5.28	**1959**
5.22	5.08	5.01	5.11	5.08	5.10	**1960**
5.09	5.11	5.12	5.13	5.11	5.10	**1961**
5.05	5.06	5.03	4.99	4.96	4.92	**1962**
4.84	4.83	4.84	4.83	4.84	4.85	**1963**
4.83	4.82	4.82	4.81	4.81	4.81	**1964**
4.88	4.88	4.91	4.93	4.95	5.02	**1965**
5.68	5.83	6.09	6.10	6.13	6.18	**1966**
6.26	6.33	6.40	6.52	6.72	6.93	**1967**
6.98	6.82	6.79	6.84	7.01	7.23	**1968**
7.84	7.86	8.05	8.22	8.25	8.65	**1969**
9.40	9.44	9.39	9.33	9.38	9.12	**1970**
8.76	8.76	8.59	8.48	8.38	8.38	**1971**
8.23	8.19	8.09	8.06	7.99	7.93	**1972**
8.24	8.53	8.63	8.41	8.42	8.48	**1973**
9.48	9.77	10.18	10.48	10.60	10.63	**1974**
10.55	10.59	10.61	10.62	10.56	10.56	**1975**
9.82	9.64	9.40	9.29	9.23	9.12	**1976**
8.87	8.82	8.80	8.89	8.95	8.99	**1977**
9.60	9.48	9.42	9.59	9.83	9.94	**1978**
10.29	10.35	10.54	11.40	11.99	12.06	**1979**
12.65	13.15	13.70	14.23	14.64	15.14	**1980**
16.17	16.34	16.92	17.11	16.39	16.55	**1981**
16.80	16.32	15.63	14.73	14.30	14.14	**1982**
13.39	13.64	13.55	13.46	13.61	13.75	**1983**
15.15	14.63	14.35	13.94	13.48	13.40	**1984**
12.43	12.50	12.48	12.36	11.99	11.58	**1985**
10.16	10.18	10.20	10.24	10.07	9.97	**1986**
10.61	10.80	11.31	11.62	11.23	11.29	**1987**
11.11	11.21	10.90	10.41	10.48	10.65	**1988**
9.87	9.88	9.91	9.81	9.81	9.82	**1989**
10.20	10.41	10.64	10.74	10.62	10.43	**1990**
9.89	9.65	9.51	9.49	9.45	9.26	**1991**
8.84	8.65	8.62	8.84	8.96	8.81	**1992**
7.93	7.60	7.34	7.31	7.66	7.69	**1993**
8.80	8.74	8.98	9.20	9.32	9.10	**1994**
8.04	8.19	7.93	7.75	7.68	7.49	**1995**
8.35	8.18	8.35	8.07	7.79	7.89	**1996**
7.75	7.82	7.70	7.57	7.42	7.32	**1997**
7.15	7.14	7.09	7.18	7.34	7.23	**1998**
7.95	8.15	8.20	8.38	8.15	8.19	**1999**
8.35	8.26	8.35	8.34	8.28	8.02	**2000**
7.97	7.85	8.03	7.91	7.81	8.05	**2001**
7.90	7.58	7.40	7.73	7.62	7.45	**2002**
6.62	7.01	6.79	6.73	6.66	6.60	**2003**
6.62	6.46	6.27	6.21	6.20	6.15	**2004**
5.95	5.96	6.03	6.30	6.39	6.32	**2005**
6.76	6.59	6.43	6.42	6.20	6.22	**2006**
6.65	6.65	6.59	6.48	6.40	6.65	**2007**
7.16	7.15	7.31	8.88	9.21	8.43	**2008**
7.09	6.58	6.31	6.29	6.32	6.37	**2009**

COMMODITIES

OIL - WEST TEXAS INTERMEDIATE
CLOSING VALUES $ / bbl

	JAN	FEB	MAR	APR	MAY	JUN
1950	2.6	2.6	2.6	2.6	2.6	2.6
1951	2.6	2.6	2.6	2.6	2.6	2.6
1952	2.6	2.6	2.6	2.6	2.6	2.6
1953	2.6	2.6	2.6	2.6	2.6	2.8
1954	2.8	2.8	2.8	2.8	2.8	2.8
1955	2.8	2.8	2.8	2.8	2.8	2.8
1956	2.8	2.8	2.8	2.8	2.8	2.8
1957	2.8	3.1	3.1	3.1	3.1	3.1
1958	3.1	3.1	3.1	3.1	3.1	3.1
1959	3.0	3.0	3.0	3.0	3.0	3.0
1960	3.0	3.0	3.0	3.0	3.0	3.0
1961	3.0	3.0	3.0	3.0	3.0	3.0
1962	3.0	3.0	3.0	3.0	3.0	3.0
1963	3.0	3.0	3.0	3.0	3.0	3.0
1964	3.0	3.0	3.0	3.0	3.0	3.0
1965	2.9	2.9	2.9	2.9	2.9	2.9
1966	2.9	2.9	2.9	2.9	2.9	2.9
1967	3.0	3.0	3.0	3.0	3.0	3.0
1968	3.1	3.1	3.1	3.1	3.1	3.1
1969	3.1	3.1	3.3	3.4	3.4	3.4
1970	3.4	3.4	3.4	3.4	3.4	3.4
1971	3.6	3.6	3.6	3.6	3.6	3.6
1972	3.6	3.6	3.6	3.6	3.6	3.6
1973	3.6	3.6	3.6	3.6	3.6	3.6
1974	10.1	10.1	10.1	10.1	10.1	10.1
1975	11.2	11.2	11.2	11.2	11.2	11.2
1976	11.2	12.0	12.1	12.2	12.2	12.2
1977	13.9	13.9	13.9	13.9	13.9	13.9
1978	14.9	14.9	14.9	14.9	14.9	14.9
1979	14.9	15.9	15.9	15.9	18.1	19.1
1980	32.5	37.0	38.0	39.5	39.5	39.5
1981	38.0	38.0	38.0	38.0	38.0	36.0
1982	33.9	31.6	28.5	33.5	35.9	35.1
1983	31.2	29.0	28.8	30.6	30.0	31.0
1984	29.7	30.1	30.8	30.6	30.5	30.0
1985	25.6	27.3	28.2	28.8	27.6	27.1
1986	22.9	15.4	12.6	12.8	15.4	13.5
1987	18.7	17.7	18.3	18.6	19.4	20.0
1988	17.2	16.8	16.2	17.9	17.4	16.5
1989	18.0	17.8	19.4	21.0	20.0	20.0
1990	22.6	22.1	20.4	18.6	18.2	16.9
1991	25.0	20.5	19.9	20.8	21.2	20.2
1992	18.8	19.0	18.9	20.2	20.9	22.4
1993	19.1	20.1	20.3	20.3	19.9	19.1
1994	15.0	14.8	14.7	16.4	17.9	19.1
1995	18.0	18.5	18.6	19.9	19.7	18.4
1996	18.9	19.1	21.4	23.6	21.3	20.5
1997	25.2	22.2	21.0	19.7	20.8	19.2
1998	16.7	16.1	15.0	15.4	14.9	13.7
1999	12.5	12.0	14.7	17.3	17.8	17.9
2000	27.2	29.4	29.9	25.7	28.8	31.8
2001	29.6	29.6	27.2	27.4	28.6	27.6
2002	19.7	20.7	24.4	26.3	27.0	25.5
2003	32.9	35.9	33.6	28.3	28.1	30.7
2004	34.3	34.7	36.8	36.7	40.3	38.0
2005	46.8	48.0	54.3	53.0	49.8	56.3
2006	65.5	61.6	62.9	69.7	70.9	71.0
2007	54.6	59.3	60.6	64.0	63.5	67.5
2008	93.0	95.4	105.6	112.6	125.4	133.9
2009	41.7	44.8	49.7	51.1	66.3	69.9

* Source: Federal Reserve

OIL - WEST TEXAS INTERMEDIATE
CLOSING VALUES $ / bbl

COMMODITIES

JUL	AUG	SEP	OCT	NOV	DEC	
2.6	2.6	2.6	2.6	2.6	2.6	1950
2.6	2.6	2.6	2.6	2.6	2.6	1951
2.6	2.6	2.6	2.6	2.6	2.6	1952
2.8	2.8	2.8	2.8	2.8	2.8	1953
2.8	2.8	2.8	2.8	2.8	2.8	1954
2.8	2.8	2.8	2.8	2.8	2.8	1955
2.8	2.8	2.8	2.8	2.8	2.8	1956
3.1	3.1	3.1	3.1	3.1	3.0	1957
3.1	3.1	3.1	3.1	3.0	3.0	1958
3.0	3.0	3.0	3.0	3.0	3.0	1959
3.0	3.0	3.0	3.0	3.0	3.0	1960
3.0	3.0	3.0	3.0	3.0	3.0	1961
3.0	3.0	3.0	3.0	3.0	3.0	1962
3.0	3.0	3.0	3.0	3.0	3.0	1963
2.9	2.9	2.9	2.9	2.9	2.9	1964
2.9	2.9	2.9	2.9	2.9	2.9	1965
2.9	2.9	3.0	3.0	3.0	3.0	1966
3.0	3.1	3.1	3.1	3.1	3.1	1967
3.1	3.1	3.1	3.1	3.1	3.1	1968
3.4	3.4	3.4	3.4	3.4	3.4	1969
3.3	3.3	3.3	3.3	3.3	3.6	1970
3.6	3.6	3.6	3.6	3.6	3.6	1971
3.6	3.6	3.6	3.6	3.6	3.6	1972
3.6	4.3	4.3	4.3	4.3	4.3	1973
10.1	10.1	10.1	11.2	11.2	11.2	1974
11.2	11.2	11.2	11.2	11.2	11.2	1975
12.2	12.2	13.9	13.9	13.9	13.9	1976
13.9	14.9	14.9	14.9	14.9	14.9	1977
14.9	14.9	14.9	14.9	14.9	14.9	1978
21.8	26.5	28.5	29.0	31.0	32.5	1979
39.5	38.0	36.0	36.0	36.0	37.0	1980
36.0	36.0	36.0	35.0	36.0	35.0	1981
34.2	34.0	35.6	35.7	34.2	31.7	1982
31.7	31.9	31.1	30.4	29.8	29.2	1983
28.8	29.3	29.3	28.8	28.1	25.4	1984
27.3	27.8	28.3	29.5	30.8	27.2	1985
11.6	15.1	14.9	14.9	15.2	16.1	1986
21.4	20.3	19.5	19.8	18.9	17.2	1987
15.5	15.5	14.5	13.8	14.0	16.3	1988
19.6	18.5	19.6	20.1	19.8	21.1	1989
18.6	27.2	33.7	35.9	32.3	27.3	1990
21.4	21.7	21.9	23.2	22.5	19.5	1991
21.8	21.4	21.9	21.7	20.3	19.4	1992
17.9	18.0	17.5	18.1	16.7	14.5	1993
19.7	18.4	17.5	17.7	18.1	17.2	1994
17.3	18.0	18.2	17.4	18.0	19.0	1995
21.3	22.0	24.0	24.9	23.7	25.4	1996
19.6	19.9	19.8	21.3	20.2	18.3	1997
14.1	13.4	15.0	14.4	12.9	11.3	1998
20.1	21.3	23.9	22.6	25.0	26.1	1999
29.8	31.2	33.9	33.1	34.4	28.5	2000
26.5	27.5	25.9	22.2	19.7	19.3	2001
26.9	28.4	29.7	28.9	26.3	29.4	2002
30.8	31.6	28.3	30.3	31.1	32.2	2003
40.7	44.9	46.0	53.1	48.5	43.3	2004
58.7	65.0	65.6	62.4	58.3	59.4	2005
74.4	73.1	63.9	58.9	59.4	62.0	2006
74.2	72.4	79.9	86.2	94.6	91.7	2007
133.4	116.6	103.9	76.7	57.4	41.0	2008
69.5	70.0	70.6	77.0	77.3	79.4	2009

COMMODITIES 🇺🇸 GOLD $US/OZ LONDON PM MONTH CLOSE

	JAN	FEB	MAR	APR	MAY	JUN
1970	34.9	35.0	35.1	35.6	36.0	35.4
1971	37.9	38.7	38.9	39.0	40.5	40.1
1972	45.8	48.3	48.3	49.0	54.6	62.1
1973	65.1	74.2	84.4	90.5	102.0	120.1
1974	129.2	150.2	168.4	172.2	163.3	154.1
1975	175.8	181.8	178.2	167.0	167.0	166.3
1976	128.2	132.3	129.6	128.4	125.5	123.8
1977	132.3	142.8	148.9	147.3	143.0	143.0
1978	175.8	182.3	181.6	170.9	184.2	183.1
1979	233.7	251.3	240.1	245.3	274.6	277.5
1980	653.0	637.0	494.5	518.0	535.5	653.5
1981	506.5	489.0	513.8	482.8	479.3	426.0
1982	387.0	362.6	320.0	361.3	325.3	317.5
1983	499.5	408.5	414.8	429.3	437.5	416.0
1984	373.8	394.3	388.5	375.8	384.3	373.1
1985	306.7	287.8	329.3	321.4	314.0	317.8
1986	350.5	338.2	344.0	345.8	343.2	345.5
1987	400.5	405.9	405.9	453.3	451.0	447.3
1988	458.0	426.2	457.0	449.0	455.5	436.6
1989	394.0	387.0	383.2	377.6	361.8	373.0
1990	415.1	407.7	368.5	367.8	363.1	352.2
1991	366.0	362.7	355.7	357.8	360.4	368.4
1992	354.1	353.1	341.7	336.4	337.5	343.4
1993	330.5	327.6	337.8	354.3	374.8	378.5
1994	377.9	381.6	389.2	376.5	387.6	388.3
1995	374.9	376.4	392.0	389.8	384.3	387.1
1996	405.6	400.7	396.4	391.3	390.6	382.0
1997	345.5	358.6	348.2	340.2	345.6	334.6
1998	304.9	297.4	301.0	310.7	293.6	296.3
1999	285.4	287.1	279.5	286.6	268.6	261.0
2000	283.3	293.7	276.8	275.1	272.3	288.2
2001	264.5	266.7	257.7	263.2	267.5	270.6
2002	282.3	296.9	301.4	308.2	326.6	318.5
2003	367.5	347.5	334.9	336.8	361.4	346.0
2004	399.8	395.9	423.7	388.5	393.3	395.8
2005	422.2	435.5	427.5	435.7	414.5	437.1
2006	568.8	556.0	582.0	644.0	653.0	613.5
2007	650.5	664.2	661.8	677.0	659.1	650.5
2008	923.3	971.5	933.5	871.0	885.8	930.3
2009	919.5	952.0	916.5	883.3	975.5	934.5

* Source: Bank of England

GOLD $US/OZ LONDON PM MONTH CLOSE — COMMODITIES

JUL	AUG	SEP	OCT	NOV	DEC	
35.3	35.4	36.2	37.5	37.4	37.4	**1970**
41.0	42.7	42.0	42.5	42.9	43.5	**1971**
65.7	67.0	65.5	64.9	62.9	63.9	**1972**
120.2	106.8	103.0	100.1	94.8	106.7	**1973**
143.0	154.6	151.8	158.8	181.7	183.9	**1974**
166.7	159.8	141.3	142.9	138.2	140.3	**1975**
112.5	104.0	116.0	123.2	130.3	134.5	**1976**
144.1	146.0	154.1	161.5	160.1	165.0	**1977**
200.3	208.7	217.1	242.6	193.4	226.0	**1978**
296.5	315.1	397.3	382.0	415.7	512.0	**1979**
614.3	631.3	666.8	629.0	619.8	589.8	**1980**
406.0	425.5	428.8	427.0	414.5	397.5	**1981**
342.9	411.5	397.0	423.3	436.0	456.9	**1982**
422.0	414.3	405.0	382.0	405.0	382.4	**1983**
342.4	348.3	343.8	333.5	329.0	309.0	**1984**
327.5	333.3	326.5	325.1	325.3	326.8	**1985**
357.5	384.7	423.2	401.0	383.5	388.8	**1986**
462.5	453.4	459.5	468.8	492.5	484.1	**1987**
436.8	427.8	397.7	412.4	422.6	410.3	**1988**
368.3	359.8	366.5	375.3	408.2	398.6	**1989**
372.3	387.8	408.4	379.5	384.9	386.2	**1990**
362.9	347.4	354.9	357.5	366.3	353.2	**1991**
357.9	340.0	349.0	339.3	334.2	332.9	**1992**
401.8	371.6	355.5	369.6	370.9	391.8	**1993**
384.0	385.8	394.9	383.9	383.1	383.3	**1994**
383.4	382.4	384.0	382.7	387.8	387.0	**1995**
385.3	386.5	379.0	379.5	371.3	369.3	**1996**
326.4	325.4	332.1	311.4	296.8	290.2	**1997**
288.9	273.4	293.9	292.3	294.7	287.8	**1998**
255.6	254.8	299.0	299.1	291.4	290.3	**1999**
276.8	277.0	273.7	264.5	269.1	274.5	**2000**
265.9	273.0	293.1	278.8	275.5	276.5	**2001**
304.7	312.8	323.7	316.9	319.1	347.2	**2002**
354.8	375.6	388.0	386.3	398.4	416.3	**2003**
391.4	407.3	415.7	425.6	453.4	435.6	**2004**
429.0	433.3	473.3	470.8	495.7	513.0	**2005**
632.5	623.5	599.3	603.8	646.7	632.0	**2006**
665.5	672.0	743.0	789.5	783.5	833.8	**2007**
918.0	833.0	884.5	730.8	814.5	869.8	**2008**
939.0	955.5	995.8	1040.0	1175.8	1087.5	**2009**

FOREIGN EXCHANGE

US DOLLAR vs CDN DOLLAR
MONTHLY AVG. VALUES*

	JAN		FEB		MAR		APR		MAY		JUN	
	US/ CDN	CDN /US	US/ CDN	CDN /US	US/ CDN	CDN /US	US/ CDN	CDN /US	US/ CDN	CDN /US	US/ CDN	CDN /US
1971	1.01	0.99	1.01	0.99	1.01	0.99	1.01	0.99	1.01	0.99	1.02	0.98
1972	1.01	0.99	1.00	1.00	1.00	1.00	0.99	1.01	0.98	1.02	0.99	1.01
1973	1.00	1.00	0.99	1.01	1.00	1.00	1.00	1.00	1.00	1.00	1.00	1.00
1974	0.99	1.01	0.97	1.03	0.97	1.03	0.96	1.04	0.96	1.04	0.97	1.03
1975	1.00	1.00	1.00	1.00	1.00	1.00	1.02	0.98	1.02	0.98	1.03	0.97
1976	1.00	1.00	0.98	1.02	0.98	1.02	0.98	1.02	0.98	1.02	0.97	1.03
1977	1.02	0.98	1.05	0.96	1.06	0.95	1.05	0.95	1.05	0.95	1.06	0.94
1978	1.11	0.90	1.12	0.90	1.13	0.88	1.13	0.88	1.12	0.89	1.12	0.89
1979	1.20	0.83	1.19	0.84	1.16	0.86	1.14	0.88	1.16	0.86	1.17	0.86
1980	1.16	0.86	1.15	0.87	1.19	0.84	1.19	0.84	1.16	0.86	1.15	0.87
1981	1.19	0.84	1.20	0.83	1.19	0.84	1.20	0.84	1.20	0.83	1.20	0.83
1982	1.20	0.84	1.23	0.81	1.23	0.81	1.22	0.82	1.24	0.80	1.29	0.77
1983	1.24	0.81	1.23	0.81	1.23	0.81	1.23	0.82	1.23	0.81	1.23	0.81
1984	1.25	0.80	1.25	0.80	1.28	0.78	1.28	0.78	1.29	0.77	1.32	0.76
1985	1.33	0.75	1.38	0.72	1.37	0.73	1.37	0.73	1.37	0.73	1.36	0.74
1986	1.42	0.70	1.42	0.70	1.40	0.72	1.37	0.73	1.38	0.72	1.39	0.72
1987	1.34	0.75	1.33	0.75	1.31	0.77	1.34	0.75	1.34	0.75	1.33	0.75
1988	1.28	0.78	1.26	0.79	1.23	0.81	1.23	0.81	1.23	0.81	1.21	0.82
1989	1.18	0.84	1.20	0.83	1.19	0.84	1.19	0.84	1.21	0.83	1.20	0.83
1990	1.19	0.84	1.19	0.84	1.17	0.85	1.17	0.86	1.17	0.85	1.17	0.86
1991	1.16	0.86	1.15	0.87	1.16	0.86	1.15	0.87	1.15	0.87	1.14	0.88
1992	1.18	0.85	1.18	0.85	1.19	0.84	1.20	0.84	1.20	0.83	1.20	0.84
1993	1.27	0.79	1.25	0.80	1.26	0.79	1.27	0.79	1.27	0.79	1.28	0.78
1994	1.33	0.75	1.35	0.74	1.38	0.72	1.38	0.72	1.38	0.72	1.38	0.72
1995	1.42	0.70	1.39	0.72	1.40	0.71	1.36	0.74	1.37	0.73	1.37	0.73
1996	1.38	0.72	1.37	0.73	1.36	0.73	1.36	0.73	1.37	0.73	1.37	0.73
1997	1.35	0.74	1.37	0.73	1.38	0.72	1.40	0.72	1.38	0.72	1.38	0.73
1998	1.46	0.68	1.42	0.70	1.42	0.70	1.43	0.70	1.45	0.69	1.47	0.68
1999	1.51	0.66	1.51	0.66	1.51	0.66	1.46	0.68	1.47	0.68	1.48	0.68
2000	1.45	0.69	1.45	0.69	1.45	0.69	1.47	0.68	1.50	0.67	1.48	0.67
2001	1.50	0.67	1.53	0.65	1.57	0.64	1.54	0.65	1.55	0.65	1.52	0.66
2002	1.59	0.63	1.60	0.62	1.59	0.63	1.57	0.64	1.53	0.65	1.51	0.66
2003	1.53	0.65	1.49	0.67	1.47	0.68	1.44	0.69	1.37	0.73	1.35	0.74
2004	1.33	0.75	1.35	0.74	1.31	0.77	1.37	0.73	1.36	0.73	1.35	0.74
2005	1.24	0.80	1.23	0.81	1.21	0.83	1.25	0.80	1.26	0.79	1.23	0.81
2006	1.15	0.87	1.14	0.88	1.16	0.86	1.12	0.89	1.09	0.91	1.11	0.90
2007	1.18	0.85	1.17	0.86	1.15	0.87	1.12	0.90	1.07	0.93	1.05	0.95
2008	1.00	1.00	0.98	1.02	1.02	0.98	1.01	0.99	0.99	1.01	1.01	0.99
2009	1.23	0.81	1.28	0.78	1.25	0.80	1.19	0.84	1.10	0.91	1.15	0.87

Source: Federal Reserve: Avg of daily rates, noon buying rates in New York City for cable transfers payable in foreign currencies

US DOLLAR vs CDN DOLLAR
MONTHLY AVG. VALUES

JUL US/CDN	JUL CDN/US	AUG US/CDN	AUG CDN/US	SEP US/CDN	SEP CDN/US	OCT US/CDN	OCT CDN/US	NOV US/CDN	NOV CDN/US	DEC US/CDN	DEC CDN/US	Year
1.02	0.98	1.01	0.99	1.01	0.99	1.00	1.00	1.00	1.00	1.00	1.00	1971
0.98	1.02	0.98	1.02	0.98	1.02	0.98	1.02	0.99	1.01	1.00	1.00	1972
1.00	1.00	1.01	0.99	1.01	0.99	1.00	1.00	1.00	1.00	1.00	1.00	1973
0.98	1.02	0.99	1.01	0.99	1.01	0.98	1.02	0.99	1.01	0.99	1.01	1974
1.03	0.97	1.03	0.97	1.03	0.98	1.02	0.98	1.01	0.99	1.02	0.98	1975
0.98	1.03	0.98	1.02	0.97	1.03	0.97	1.03	1.00	1.00	1.01	0.99	1976
1.07	0.94	1.07	0.93	1.07	0.93	1.11	0.90	1.11	0.90	1.09	0.91	1977
1.13	0.88	1.15	0.87	1.18	0.84	1.17	0.86	1.17	0.85	1.19	0.84	1978
1.17	0.85	1.17	0.86	1.16	0.86	1.18	0.84	1.17	0.85	1.17	0.86	1979
1.16	0.86	1.16	0.86	1.17	0.85	1.18	0.85	1.19	0.84	1.19	0.84	1980
1.23	0.81	1.20	0.83	1.21	0.83	1.20	0.83	1.18	0.85	1.19	0.84	1981
1.26	0.80	1.24	0.81	1.24	0.81	1.23	0.82	1.24	0.81	1.23	0.81	1982
1.23	0.81	1.23	0.81	1.23	0.81	1.23	0.81	1.24	0.81	1.24	0.80	1983
1.31	0.76	1.30	0.77	1.32	0.76	1.32	0.76	1.32	0.76	1.32	0.76	1984
1.35	0.74	1.37	0.73	1.37	0.73	1.37	0.73	1.38	0.72	1.40	0.72	1985
1.38	0.72	1.39	0.72	1.39	0.72	1.39	0.72	1.38	0.72	1.38	0.72	1986
1.33	0.75	1.32	0.76	1.31	0.76	1.32	0.76	1.31	0.76	1.30	0.77	1987
1.21	0.83	1.24	0.81	1.22	0.82	1.22	0.82	1.19	0.84	1.19	0.84	1988
1.18	0.85	1.18	0.85	1.18	0.85	1.17	0.85	1.16	0.86	1.16	0.86	1989
1.15	0.87	1.15	0.87	1.16	0.86	1.17	0.86	1.17	0.86	1.16	0.86	1990
1.15	0.87	1.14	0.88	1.13	0.88	1.12	0.89	1.14	0.88	1.16	0.87	1991
1.18	0.84	1.19	0.84	1.25	0.80	1.24	0.81	1.29	0.78	1.27	0.79	1992
1.29	0.78	1.32	0.76	1.33	0.75	1.32	0.76	1.34	0.75	1.33	0.75	1993
1.39	0.72	1.37	0.73	1.34	0.74	1.35	0.74	1.38	0.73	1.40	0.71	1994
1.37	0.73	1.34	0.75	1.34	0.75	1.34	0.75	1.36	0.74	1.36	0.73	1995
1.38	0.73	1.37	0.73	1.36	0.73	1.34	0.75	1.35	0.74	1.37	0.73	1996
1.38	0.72	1.39	0.72	1.38	0.72	1.41	0.71	1.43	0.70	1.43	0.70	1997
1.50	0.67	1.55	0.64	1.52	0.66	1.55	0.65	1.54	0.65	1.55	0.65	1998
1.50	0.66	1.49	0.67	1.47	0.68	1.47	0.68	1.47	0.68	1.45	0.69	1999
1.48	0.67	1.47	0.68	1.50	0.67	1.53	0.65	1.54	0.65	1.50	0.67	2000
1.53	0.65	1.54	0.65	1.58	0.63	1.58	0.63	1.58	0.63	1.59	0.63	2001
1.58	0.63	1.56	0.64	1.58	0.63	1.57	0.64	1.57	0.64	1.58	0.63	2002
1.41	0.71	1.40	0.72	1.35	0.74	1.32	0.76	1.30	0.77	1.29	0.77	2003
1.32	0.76	1.32	0.76	1.27	0.79	1.22	0.82	1.19	0.84	1.21	0.83	2004
1.23	0.81	1.19	0.84	1.17	0.86	1.17	0.85	1.17	0.86	1.16	0.86	2005
1.12	0.89	1.11	0.90	1.11	0.90	1.13	0.89	1.14	0.88	1.16	0.86	2006
1.06	0.94	1.05	0.95	1.00	1.00	0.95	1.05	0.99	1.01	0.98	1.02	2007
1.03	.97	1.06	0.94	1.06	0.94	1.22	0.82	1.24	0.81	1.22	0.82	2008
1.08	0.93	1.10	0.91	1.07	0.93	1.08	0.92	1.06	0.95	1.05	0.95	2009

U.S. DOLLAR vs EURO
MONTHLY AVG. VALUES

	JAN EUR /US	JAN US/ EUR	FEB EUR /US	FEB US/ EUR	MAR EUR /US	MAR US/ EUR	APR EUR /US	APR US/ EUR	MAY EUR /US	MAY US/ EUR	JUN EUR /US	JUN US/ EUR
1999	1.14	0.88	1.10	0.91	1.07	0.93	1.06	0.94	1.05	0.96	1.03	0.97
2000	0.98	1.02	0.97	1.03	0.95	1.05	0.91	1.10	0.93	1.07	0.96	1.04
2001	0.93	1.07	0.92	1.09	0.88	1.13	0.89	1.13	0.85	1.18	0.85	1.18
2002	0.86	1.16	0.87	1.16	0.87	1.15	0.90	1.11	0.94	1.07	1.00	1.00
2003	1.08	0.92	1.08	0.93	1.09	0.92	1.11	0.90	1.18	0.85	1.14	0.88
2004	1.24	0.81	1.24	0.81	1.22	0.82	1.20	0.84	1.22	0.82	1.22	0.82
2005	1.30	0.77	1.33	0.75	1.30	0.77	1.30	0.77	1.23	0.81	1.21	0.83
2006	1.21	0.83	1.19	0.84	1.21	0.83	1.26	0.80	1.29	0.78	1.27	0.79
2007	1.29	0.77	1.32	0.76	1.33	0.75	1.36	0.73	1.34	0.74	1.35	0.74
2008	1.49	0.67	1.52	0.66	1.58	0.63	1.55	0.64	1.55	0.64	1.58	0.63
2009	1.28	0.78	1.27	0.79	1.33	0.75	1.33	0.75	1.41	0.71	1.41	0.71

Source: Federal Reserve: Avg of daily rates, noon buying rates in New York City for cable transfers payable in foreign currencies